ABITUR 2015

Prüfungsaufgaben
mit Lösungen

Englisch

Grund- und Leistungskurs
Gymnasium • Gesamtschule
Hessen

2011–2014

D1728895

ISBN 978-3-8490-1136-9

© 2014 by Stark Verlagsgesellschaft mbH & Co. KG
10. neu bearbeitete und ergänzte Auflage
www.stark-verlag.de

Inhalt

Abituraufgaben 2014 Leistungskurs

Jeweils im Herbst erscheinen die neuen Ausgaben
der Abiturprüfungsaufgaben mit Lösungen.

Autoren

Berger-Hönge, Silvia	Lösungen GK 2011 – A, LK 2011 – A, GK 2012 – C, GK 2014 – A
Cleary, Liam	*Glossary of literary terms*
Jacob, Rainer	Hinweise zur Bearbeitung eines Diagramms; Kurzinterpretationen
Kahl, Elke	Lösungen LK 2011 – B/C
Klewitz, Dr. Bernd	Hinweise zur Bearbeitung eines Cartoons, Lösungen LK 2012, GK 2013, LK 2013 – B, GK 2014 – B, LK 2014
Moritz, Hans Otto	Hinweise und Tipps zum Landesabitur
Schuller, Hans	Lösungen GK 2011 – B/C, GK 2012 – A/B, LK 2013 – A/C, GK 2014 – C

Vorwort

Liebe Schülerinnen und Schüler,

bald werden Sie Ihre Abiturklausur im Fach Englisch ablegen. Dieser Band unterstützt Sie bei der **Vorbereitung auf die schriftliche Abiturprüfung** im Fach Englisch. Sowohl im Grund- wie im Leistungskurs werden die Aufgaben vom hessischen Kultusministerium vorgegeben. Ihnen stehen in der Regel 45 Minuten zur Verfügung, um aus drei Vorschlägen einen auszuwählen. Danach haben Sie vier Stunden (Leistungskurs) bzw. drei Stunden (Grundkurs) Zeit zur Bearbeitung.

Teilen Sie sich die Zeit gut ein, damit auch die letzte Aufgabe und das Korrekturlesen erfolgreich abgeschlossen werden können. Das Zählen der Wörter erfolgt erst nach Ablauf der Bearbeitungszeit. Als Hilfsmittel stehen Ihnen ein einsprachiges und ein zweisprachiges Wörterbuch sowie eine Liste der fachspezifischen Operatoren zur Verfügung. **Ausführliche Hinweise** zu den **Anforderungen im Abitur** sowie Hilfestellungen zur Lösung von Abiturprüfungsaufgaben finden Sie am Anfang des Buches.

Üben Sie die Prüfungssituation mit den **offiziellen Abitur-Prüfungsaufgaben, die in den Jahren 2011 bis 2014 vom hessischen Kultusministerium gestellt wurden.** Zur besseren Nachvollziehbarkeit wurden jeder Aufgabe **Bearbeitungshinweise** hinzugefügt. Die methodischen Schritte können Sie auf die Bearbeitung anderer Texte und Aufgaben übertragen. Zudem stehen Ihnen **vollständige englische Lösungen** zur Verfügung, die von unseren Autoren erstellt wurden. Dieser Band umfasst zudem **Kurzinterpretationen**, die Ihnen bei der Wiederholung und Vertiefung der **Pflichtlektüren für den Leistungskurs** nützlich sein werden.

Sollten nach Erscheinen dieses Bandes noch **wichtige Änderungen** in der Abitur-Prüfung 2015 vom Kultusministerium bekannt gegeben werden, finden Sie aktuelle Informationen dazu im Internet unter:
www.stark-verlag.de/pruefung-aktuell

Wir wünschen Ihnen viel Erfolg bei der Abiturprüfung!

Stichwortverzeichnis

Huxley, Aldous *Brave New World*
GK 11-17 f.; GK 12-15; GK 13-6;
GK 14-15 f.
Kirn, Walter *Up in the Air* LK 13-15 f.,
18 ff.
Kureishi, Hanif *My Son the Fanatic*
GK 12-11 f.; *The Black Album*
LK 12-19 ff.; *Something to Tell You*
GK 13-7 ff.
Levy, Andrea *Small Island* LK 11-8 ff.;
LK 12-6 f.
Lewycka, Marina *A Short History of
Tractors in Ukrainian* LK 14-15 f.
Manning, Kate *Whitegirl* LK 14-1 f.
Miller, Arthur *Death of a Salesman*
LK 13-19 f.
Morrison, Toni *Beloved* and *A Mercy*
LK 12-23 ff.
Nair, Preethi *One Hundred Shades of
White* GK 11-7 ff.

Orwell, George *1984* GK 11-5 f.;
GK 13-6
Palahniuk, Chuck *Fight Club*
LK 12-11 ff.
Pilkington, Doris/Garimara, Nugi
Rabbit-Proof Fence LK 11-17 ff.
Rai, Bali *(Un)arranged Marriage*
LK 12-23 ff.
Shahraz, Qaisra *A Pair of Jeans*
GK 12-13
Shakespeare, William *Othello* I 7 ff.;
LK 14-4 f.
Shearer, Alex *The Hunted* GK 12-4 f.
Smith, Zadie *White Teeth* LK 11-14 f.;
NW GK 14-9
Spark, Muriel *The Black Madonna*
GK 12-11 f.
Vassanji, Moyez G. *No New Land*
GK 12-15 ff.
Vonnegut, Kurt *Slaughterhouse-Five*
I 12 ff.

Stylistic Devices and Composition

analysis LK 12-3; LK 13-3, 17
cartoon LK 14-9
comment LK 11-2; LK 12-3, 13, 21;
GK 14-13; LK 14-3, 9, 16
comparison GK 11-2, 8, 15; LK 11-18;
GK 12-2, 8, 16; LK 12-3, 13, 21;
GK 13-2, 8, 14; LK 13-9, 17;
GK 14-2, 7; LK 14-3, 9
essay GK 11-2, 8, 15; LK 11-10, 18;
GK 12-2, 8, 16; GK 13-2, 8; LK 13-3;
GK 14-7

letter writing GK 13-14; LK 13-9;
GK 14-2
Sprachmittlung GK 11-13 f.; LK 11-16
f.; GK 12-14 f.; LK 12-18 f.;
GK 13-12 f.; LK 13-14 f.;
GK 14-11 f.; LK 14-14
summary LK 11-2, 18; GK 12-2, 8;
LK 12-3; GK 13-2, 14; LK 13-9;
GK 14-13

Hinweise und Tipps zum Landesabitur

Die Anforderungen im Abitur

1 Lehrplan, Einführungserlasse und Abiturverordnung

Für die Vorbereitung auf das Abitur im Fach Englisch ist die Kenntnis der Grundlagen von Textauswahl und Aufgabenstellung erforderlich. Sie sind im Lehrplan für die Qualifikationsphase und in der „Verordnung über die Bildungsgänge und die Abiturprüfung in der gymnasialen Oberstufe" festgeschrieben. Die Vorgaben des Lehrplans werden durch die Einführungserlasse („Hinweise zur Vorbereitung auf die schriftlichen Abiturprüfungen im Landesabitur") spezifiziert.[1] Diese geben eine verbindliche Auswahl an thematischen Schwerpunkten in Form von prüfungsrelevanten Stichworten vor. Nur für den Leistungskurs gibt es für das Abitur 2015 drei Pflichtlektüren (eine pro Kurshalbjahr). Mindestens eine Prüfungsaufgabe wird sich auf eines der folgenden Werke beziehen:

Q 1: Thomas C. Boyle: *The Tortilla Curtain*
Q 2: William Shakespeare: *Othello*
Q 3: Kurt Vonnegut: *Slaughterhouse-Five*

Der folgende Überblick ist für Sie wichtig, weil im Abitur immer die Inhaltselemente von zwei der drei prüfungsrelevanten Halbjahre miteinander verknüpft werden.

1.1 Lehrplaninhalte im Einführungserlass für 2015

Kurshalbjahr	Verbindliche Unterrichtsinhalte	Stichworte
Q 1	**The Challenge of Individualism**	
	GK + LK: USA	• the American Dream • living together *(ethnic groups: Hispanics)*
	GK: Science and Technology	• electronic media • biotechnology
	LK: Them and Us	• the one-track mind (prejudice, intolerance, ideologies)

---

[1] www.kultusministerium.hessen.de

I

Q 2	**Tradition and Change**	
	GK + LK: The United Kingdom	• social structures, social change
		• Great Britain and the world (the British Empire, the Commonwealth)
	GK: Work and Industrialization	• business, industry and the environment
		• trade and competition
	LK: Extreme Situations	• love and happiness
		• initiation
		• the troubled mind
Q 3	**The Dynamics of Change**	
	GK + LK: Promised Lands: Dreams and Realities	• political issues
		• social issues
		country of reference: South Africa
	GK: Order, Vision, Change	• models of the future (utopias, dystopias, 'progress' in the natural sciences)
	LK: Ideals and Reality	• structural problems (violence, (in-)equality)

1.2 Aufgabenarten und Bewertung

Die Abituraufgabe muss zwei der drei prüfungsrelevanten Halbjahre inhaltlich miteinander verbinden. Es gibt zwei Aufgabenarten: die Textaufgabe und die kombinierte Aufgabe:

- Die **Textaufgabe** umfasst einen oder mehrere Texte mit drei bis vier Arbeitsanweisungen. Es kommen literarische Texte und Sachtexte infrage sowie Bilder und Grafiken.
  Der im Leistungsfach vorgelegte Text umfasst zwischen 700 und 900 Wörter, der im Grundkursfach zwischen 500 und 700 Wörter. Werden mehrere Texte vorgelegt, gilt die Wortzahl für alle Texte zusammen.

- Die **kombinierte Aufgabe** besteht aus zwei Teilen: aus einer verkürzten Textaufgabe und aus einer Sprachmittlungsaufgabe. Der Umfang der Textaufgabe beträgt im Leistungskurs 400 bis 650 Wörter, im Grundkurs 400 bis 500. In der kombinierten Aufgabe werden die Textaufgabe und die sprachpraktische Aufgabe im Verhältnis 3:1 gewertet.

Bei allen Aufgabenarten wird zur Bewertung zwischen **inhaltlicher** und **sprachlicher Leistung** (Ausdrucksvermögen/Stil sowie Sprachrichtigkeit/Fehler) unterschieden. Bei der Festlegung der Gesamtnote kommt der sprachlichen Leistung im Vergleich zur inhaltlichen die größere Bedeutung zu. Sie wird im Verhältnis 2:1 gewertet. Eine mit 0 Punkten bewertete inhaltliche oder sprachliche Leistung schließt eine Gesamtnote von mehr als drei Punkten einfacher Wertung aus. In der Beurteilung der kombinierten Aufgabe wird diese Regelung für beide Teile getrennt angewendet.

Kriterien für die Bewertung der inhaltlichen Leistung sind:
– Textverständnis,
– Entfaltung des Themas,
– Folgerichtigkeit der Darstellung,
– Anwendung fachspezifischer Kenntnisse und Methoden,
– Fähigkeit zur Argumentation und Stellungnahme und
– v. a. im Leistungskurs: Erkennen der Wirkung sprachlicher und formaler Textmerkmale.

Bewertung der sprachlichen Leistung:
Die sprachliche Leistung umfasst die Bereiche Sprachrichtigkeit und Ausdrucksvermögen zu gleichen Teilen.

Sprachrichtigkeit
Der Ihre Arbeit beurteilende Lehrer ist bei der sprachlichen Korrektur Ihres Textes an Regeln hinsichtlich der Fehlergewichtung gebunden und muss sich in der Notengebung an den landesweit gültigen Fehlerindex halten.

Zur Fehlergewichtung:
– halber Fehler:
  • orthografische Fehler ohne Bedeutungsveränderung (auch Bindestrich-Fehler)
  • Präpositionsfehler, wenn kein konkreter Bedeutungswandel eintritt
  • Interpunktion in eindeutigen Fällen
  • Apostroph bei Genitiv
– ganzer Fehler: alle Wortfehler, Satzfehler und praktisch alle Grammatikfehler
– anderthalb Fehler: bei sinnentstellenden Verstößen gegen elementare Regeln
– Wiederholungsfehler bei demselben Wort bzw. in einem identischen Kontext werden nicht erneut gewertet
– Flüchtigkeitsfehler werden nicht gewertet

Der Fehlerindex errechnet sich nach der Formel: $\dfrac{\text{Fehlerzahl x 100}}{\text{Zahl der Wörter}}$

Tabelle für Fehlerindices im Fach Englisch:

Notenpunkte	15	14	13	12	11	10	9	8
Fehlerindex Grundkurs	bis 0,9	bis 1,3	bis 1,7	bis 2,1	bis 2,5	bis 2,9	bis 3,3	bis 3,7
Fehlerindex Leistungskurs	bis 0,8	bis 1,1	bis 1,4	bis 1,7	bis 2,0	bis 2,3	bis 2,6	bis 2,9
Notenpunkte	7	6	5	4	3	2	1	0
Fehlerindex Grundkurs	bis 4,1	bis 4,5	bis 4,9	bis 5,3	bis 5,7	bis 6,1	bis 6,5	> 6,5
Fehlerindex Leistungskurs	bis 3,2	bis 3,5	bis 3,8	bis 4,1	bis 4,4	bis 4,7	bis 5,0	> 5,0

Kriterien für die Bewertung des Ausdrucksvermögens sind:
– Reichhaltigkeit und Differenziertheit des Wortschatzes im thematischen und im aufgabenspezifischen Bereich,
– Angemessenheit des Registers, d. h. des Stilniveaus,
– Ökonomie und Treffsicherheit des Ausdrucks,
– Textkohärenz und Flüssigkeit der Darstellung,

- Variation des Satzbaus und
- sprachliche Prägnanz der Gesamtleistung.

Im Folgenden finden Sie die allgemeinen Kriterien für eine „ausreichende" bzw. „gute" Leistung:

Eine „ausreichende" Prüfungsleistung (5 Punkte) liegt vor, wenn

a) im sprachlichen Bereich
- der Wortschatz ausreicht, um Sachverhalte und Meinungen im Rahmen der Aufgabenstellung weitgehend verständlich auszudrücken,
- elementare Verknüpfungen zwischen Satzteilen, Sätzen und Satzgruppen in einer der Aufgabenstellung angemessenen Weise eingesetzt werden,
- formalsprachliche Verstöße die Verständlichkeit nicht erheblich beeinträchtigen und
- eine Vertrautheit mit elementaren sprachlichen Gesetzmäßigkeiten erkennbar ist.

b) im inhaltlichen Bereich
- dem bereitgestellten Material die für die Ausführung der Arbeitsanweisungen notwendigen Informationen in Grundzügen entnommen werden,
- alle gestellten Aufgaben im Ansatz gelöst werden bzw. auf den größeren Teil mehr als nur im Ansatz eingegangen wird und dabei Kenntnisse im Großen und Ganzen geordnet zueinander und zur Textvorlage in Beziehung gesetzt werden,
- die für die Bearbeitung der Aufgaben erforderlichen Grundkenntnisse und Methoden nachgewiesen werden und
- die Gedankenführung nachvollziehbar ist.

Eine „gute" Prüfungsleistung (11 Punkte) liegt vor, wenn

a) im sprachlichen Bereich
- durch einen differenzierten und weitgehend idiomatisch geprägten Wortschatz auch komplexe Sachverhalte und Meinungen dargestellt werden,
- Satzteile, Sätze und Satzgruppen differenziert und nuanciert verknüpft werden,
- formalsprachliche Verstöße die Verständlichkeit nicht beeinträchtigen,
- eine Vertrautheit mit relevanten sprachlichen Gesetzmäßigkeiten erkennbar ist.

b) im inhaltlichen Bereich
- dem bereitgestellten Material die für die Ausführung der Arbeitsanweisungen notwendigen Informationen auch im Detail entnommen werden,
- auf alle Teile der gestellten Aufgabe(n) eingegangen wird und diese analytisch-interpretierend bzw. handlungsorientiert selbstständig bearbeitet werden,
- die für das Bearbeiten der Aufgaben erforderlichen Kenntnisse und Methodenkompetenzen nachgewiesen werden,
- die Ausführungen aufgabenbezogen, schlüssig und in ihrer Wertungsgrundlage reflektiert sind.

2   Anforderungsbereiche und Aufgabenstellungen

In der Regel werden Ihnen zum Abiturtext wie bei Ihren bisherigen Klausuren drei bis vier Aufgaben gestellt, die sich im Grundsatz an der Abfolge Zusammenfassung, Analyse und Stellungnahme/Kommentar/kreatives Schreiben orientieren. Diese Abfolge ergibt sich grob aus den drei Anforderungsbereichen, die vom Lehrplan und den Abiturrichtlinien als Leitgrößen vorgegeben sind:

– Anforderungsbereich I: Textverstehen
– Anforderungsbereich II: Textanalyse
– Anforderungsbereich III: Werten und Gestalten

Abituraufgaben werden so konzipiert, dass der Schwerpunkt der geforderten Leistungen auf dem Anforderungsbereich II liegt. Grund- und Leistungskurs unterscheiden sich prinzipiell darin, dass im Grundkurs die Anforderungen aus den Bereichen I und II stärker akzentuiert sind, im Leistungskurs die Anforderungen aus den Bereichen II und III.

Die **erste Aufgabe** bezieht sich in der Regel weitgehend auf den **Anforderungsbereich I**: Textverstehen. Sie sollen unter Beweis stellen, dass Sie die Textvorlage verstanden haben und in der Lage sind, den Text zusammenzufassen oder einen Teilaspekt darzustellen.

Die **zweite Aufgabe** bezieht sich in der Regel schwerpunktmäßig auf den **Anforderungsbereich II**: Textanalyse. Die Analyse kann sich sowohl auf die Untersuchung der Gestaltungsmerkmale des Textes beziehen wie auch den Problemgehalt des angesprochenen Themas ausloten; u. a. können Sie aufgefordert werden, den Bezug zu einem im Unterricht bearbeiteten thematischen Kernbereich herzustellen. Oft werden zu beiden Teilbereichen Fragen gestellt.

Gleichwertig als Leistungen im Bereich des **Anforderungsbereichs III** werden die Stellungnahme/der Kommentar und das kreative Schreiben (z. B. aus einer anderen Perspektive) in einer vorgegebenen Textsorte angesehen. In der Regel wird nur eine der beiden Aufgaben gestellt.

3   „Operatoren"

Um unmissverständliche Aufgabenstellungen zu ermöglichen, werden sogenannte Operatoren verwendet. Das sind als Schlüsselwörter fungierende Aufforderungsverben, die auf die erwartete Leistung (und bestimmte Anforderungsbereiche) abzielen. In der Regel werden nur die in der vom Hessischen Kultusministerium veröffentlichten Operatorenliste festgelegten, definierten und mit Beispielen versehenen Verben benutzt.[2] Sie sollten Ihnen aus dem Unterricht bereits hinlänglich vertraut sein.

Trotz der Zuordnung der Operatoren zu den jeweiligen Anforderungsebenen ist eine klare Trennung nicht immer möglich. Für den Bereich kreativer Schreibaufträge werden hier keine Operatoren aufgeführt.

---

2 www.kultusministerium.hessen.de

Operator	Definition	Beispiel	AFB
Anforderungsbereich I			
delineate	present the central elements of a line of action or line of argument	Delineate the concept of …	I–II
describe	give a detailed account of sth.	Describe the living conditions of …	I–II
outline	give the main features, structure or general principles of a topic omitting minor details	Outline the author's views on love, marriage and divorce.	I–II
point out	identify and explain certain aspects	Point out the author's main ideas on …	I–II
summarise	give a concise account of the main points	Summarize the text (in your words).	I–II
Anforderungsbereich II			
analyse/ examine	systematically describe and explain in detail certain aspects and/or features of the text	Examine the author's use of language. Analyse the rhetorical means used. Analyse the relationship between X and Y.	II–III
charac- terise	describe and analyse the character(s)	Write a characterization of the heroine.	II
compare	point out and analyse similarities and differences	Compare X and Y's views on education. Compare the living conditions described in the text with the idea of the "melting pot".	II–III
contrast/ juxtapose	describe and analyse the differences between two or more things	Contrast the author's concept of multiculturalism with concepts you have encountered in class.	II–III
explain	describe and define in detail	Explain the protagonist's obsession with money.	II
illustrate/ show	use examples to explain or make clear	Illustrate the character's narrow-mindedness.	II–I

put into the context of	an incident, statement or argument is linked to relevant historical or topical knowledge (on the basis of knowledge gained in class)	Put this speech into the context of the Hispanic experience in the US.	II
relate	take an aspect (aspects) of the text at hand and establish a meaningful connection to an aspect (aspects) of the text of reference	Relate the protagonist's principles to a text read in class.	II–III

Anforderungsbereich III – Bereich Interpretation/Bewertung

comment	state clearly your opinions on the topic in question and give reasons or examples	Comment on the thesis … expressed in the text, line …	III
discuss	analyse, give reasons for and against and come to a justified conclusion	Discuss the influence of terrorism on civil liberties in the United States.	III
evaluate / assess	form an opinion after carefully considering and presenting advantages and disadvantages	Evaluate the chances of the protagonist's plan to succeed in life. Assess the importance of ethics in scientific research.	III
interpret	analyse the text and put its meaning in a wider context	Interpret the message the author wishes to convey.	III–II

Anforderungsbereich III – Bereich Textproduktion/Gestaltung

write + *text type*	creative text production on a topic within the context of a specific text type	Write (e. g.) a letter to the editor / a personal letter / a dialogue / a speech …	III

Hinweise zur Lösung von Abituraufgabenstellungen

1 Textzusammenfassung/gelenkte Textzusammenfassung

Die erste Aufgabe der Abiturprüfung zielt in der Regel auf das Textverstehen, d. h., sie beinhaltet in gelenkter oder allgemeiner Form die Erstellung einer Zusammenfassung, deren Länge in aller Regel zwischen 25 und 30 % des Ausgangstextes beträgt.

Warum wird eine Zusammenfassung geschrieben?

Die Zusammenfassung hat eine Schlüsselfunktion in der Vorbereitung der Textanalyse und der Interpretation. Zunächst muss man sicher sein, dass auch wirklich erfasst worden ist, worum es in dem Text geht. Erst dann ist es möglich, den Text auf Aufbau, Argumentationsweise, Sprache und Stilmittel, d. h. in Bezug auf seine Gestaltungsmittel zu untersuchen. Erst wenn die Textaussage und die Textgestaltung klar erfasst sind, kann man sich der Textauslegung, der Interpretation und der Analyse der Bedeutung des Textes zuwenden, erst dann kann der Text auch in einem größeren inhaltlichen oder stilistischen Zusammenhang betrachtet werden.

Wie wird eine Zusammenfassung vorbereitet?

Jede inhaltliche Zusammenfassung beginnt mit einem *umbrella sentence*, der (soweit bekannt) Angaben zum Autor, zur Textsorte, zum Zeitpunkt des Entstehens und zum thematischen Schwerpunkt des Textes enthält.

Die Gliederung des Textes entwickelt sich bei Sachtexten aus folgenden Leitfragen:
– Um welches Thema / Problem geht es?
– Was will der Autor aussagen?
– Wie baut er seine Argumentation auf?
– Welche weiter gehende Stellungnahme wird in den Folgeaufgaben verlangt?

Bei literarischen Texten als Klausurvorlage steht nicht der argumentative Charakter im Vordergrund. Es handelt sich in aller Regel um Momentaufnahmen aus einem größeren Zusammenhang, welcher in dieser Situation unbekannt bleibt. Die Gliederung des Textes ergibt sich aus Leitfragen wie z. B.:
– Welche Situation treffen wir an?
– Wer sind die Protagonisten und wie verhalten sie sich?
– Welche Grundstimmung finden wir vor?
– Um welches Thema / Problem geht es?
– Wie ist der Text strukturiert?
– Für welche weiter gehende Fragestellung wird Information benötigt?

In jedem Falle ist bei diesen Leitfragen immer wieder zu entscheiden:
– Was ist zentral wichtig?
– Was ist rein ornamental, also ausschmückendes Beiwerk?
– Was könnte man erwähnen, muss es aber nicht?

Bei der Entscheidung, was man weglassen kann, helfen Überlegungen wie: „Könnte ich den Text verstehen, wenn mir diese Information nicht zur Verfügung gestellt würde?" D. h., es gilt z. B. zu fragen:
– Was ist ein ausschmückender oder illustrierender oder konkretisierender Zusatz?
– Was wird wiederholt bzw. ist redundant?

Was ist beim Schreiben zu beachten?

Aus der Beantwortung der Leitfragen ergeben sich Grundbausteine und eine Rohstruktur der Zusammenfassung. Im Einzelfall kann eine detailliertere Gliederung unerlässlich sein.

Grundsätzlich sind nur Äußerungen niederzuschreiben, die sich an der Textvorlage auch tatsächlich überprüfen lassen. Die Argumentationslogik sollte klar, unverschnörkelt und nachvollziehbar sein. Sie wird in den meisten Fällen nicht der Reihenfolge der Argumente im Text folgen. Im Gegenteil: Sehr oft wird eine am Schluss der Textvorlage zu findende These / Schlussfolgerung oder überraschende Handlungsvariante den Ausgangspunkt der Zusammenfassung bilden.

Wie wird die Zusammenfassung formal und sprachlich gestaltet?

- **Textlänge:** Der Umfang der Zusammenfassung liegt meist zwischen einem Viertel und einem Drittel der Länge der Textvorlage.
- **Tempus:** Eine Zusammenfassung wird im Präsens verfasst. Im Text vorkommende Vor- bzw. Nachzeitigkeit bleibt erhalten.
- **Bezüge:** Personen-, Zeit- und Ortsbezüge werden wie in der indirekten Rede umgeformt, also wird z. B. *I* zu *he* oder *she*; *yesterday* wird zu *the day before*; *here* wird zu *there*.
- **Tabus:** Die Zusammenfassung enthält weder direkte Rede oder Zitate noch eine wertende persönliche Stellungnahme.

Sprachlich tendiert die Zusammenfassung zu einem leicht gehobenen Niveau und Abstraktionsgrad. Sie ist eher konzeptuell als berichtend oder ausschmückend; dies und die Textlänge unterscheiden sie von der Nacherzählung. Ein höherer Abstraktionsgrad verlangt die Verwendung von Kürzungsmitteln:

- **Allgemeinbegriffe** (wie z. B. *fruit* anstelle von *„strawberries, gooseberries and bananas"*),
- **übergreifend einschätzende Verben** (wie z. B. *to focus on, to claim, to maintain, to criticize, to report, to illustrate, ...*),
- **generalisierende Adjektive** (wie z. B. *to be worried about, to be reluctant, to be concerned with, ...*) und
- **Konjunktionen:** temporale *(before, when)*, kausale *(because, as, so)*, konditionale *(if, unless)*, konzessive *(though, although)*, kontrastive *(but, instead of)* und konsekutive *(so that, thus)* Bindewörter.

2 Analyse

Prinzipiell können sich Aufgaben zur Analyse zum einen auf die Textanalyse im engeren Sinne beziehen, zum anderen auf zusätzliches Material oder auf im Unterricht Erarbeitetes.

- Bei der **Analyse im engeren Sinne** geht es um Facetten der Textstrukturierung/Textgestaltung, die aufzuzeigen sind; es kann zusätzlich gefordert sein, das Verhältnis zwischen den Gestaltungsmitteln und dem Inhalt, der Atmosphäre oder der Textaussage auszuloten, d. h. die Funktion der Gestaltungsmittel zu bestimmen – als Teil der Interpretation (siehe a).
- Eine weitere Variante der Textanalyse besteht in der **Verknüpfung** der Textvorlage **mit einem zusätzlich in der Aufgabe zur Verfügung gestellten Material** (z. B. ein Cartoon oder eine Statistik/ein Diagramm; siehe b).
- Ebenso können Sie aufgefordert werden, die Informationen des vorliegenden neuen Textes zu **im Unterricht Gelesenem und Diskutiertem** in Bezug zu setzen (siehe c).

a) Auf der Basis der Zusammenfassung und dem so gewährleisteten Textüberblick wird das erworbene Wissen um die Textkonstitution systematisch auf den Text angewendet. Wenn in der Aufgabenstellung keine die Arbeit lenkenden Hinweise gegeben werden, so ist der Text daraufhin zu *scannen,* welche Gestaltungsmittel besonders in den Vordergrund treten. Das *Scannen* kann sich beziehen auf:
 – die Wortwahl (Register, Häufigkeiten),
 – den Satzbau (komplex/einfach),
 – Stilmittel (z. B. Kontrast, Parallelität, Repetitio) und
 – Sprachfiguren (z. B. Vergleich, Metapher)[3].

Mit dem Aufzeigen von Textgestaltungsmerkmalen kann die Aufgabenstellung erfüllt sein, in vielen Fällen allerdings ist es das Fundament für eine weiterführende Betrachtung, die über die formale Analyse hinausgeht. Hier stellt sich die Frage nach dem Zusammenwirken von Form und Inhalt, d. h., die Gestaltungsmittel werden auf ihre Funktion oder Wirkung hin überprüft. Inwiefern unterstützen sie die Textaussage oder unterlaufen sie diese, z. B. in der Satire oder der Parodie?

b) Bei der Verbindung von neuem Text mit einem zusätzlichen Material (z. B. einem Cartoon oder einer Statistik) enthält die Aufgabenstellung mit großer Wahrscheinlichkeit einen Hinweis auf gewünschte Anknüpfungspunkte zwischen den beiden Materialien (siehe LK 2014-9). Dennoch ist es wesentlich, sich mit dem Inhalt des zusätzlichen Materials auseinanderzusetzen, bevor auf mögliche Vergleichsmerkmale mit dem Text Bezug genommen wird:
 – Handelt es sich bei dem zusätzlichen Material um eine Statistik, sollten Sie sich zunächst über die Art des vorliegenden Diagramms klar werden und dieses dann genauer beschreiben. (Hilfreiche Formulierungen hierfür finden Sie auf den Seiten XVI–XVIII.)
 – Handelt es sich um einen Cartoon, ist es Ihre Aufgabe, die in Bild und Schrift dargestellte Botschaft des Zeichners zu dekodieren und in einen logischen Kontext zu stellen. Dies sollte in den folgenden Schritten erfolgen:
  • Beschreibung der im Cartoon dargestellten Personen, der Situation oder Aktion sowie der Textanteile (z. B. Sprechblasen, Bildunterschriften) im Präsens *(simple present, present progressive),*
  • Erkennen des im Cartoon angesprochenen Problems, Bezug der dargestellten Szene auf die (momentane) politische oder gesellschaftliche Situation (wichtige Informationen hierfür können in Bildunterschrift oder Sprechblasen enthalten sein),
  • Entschlüsseln der verwendeten Symbole (z. B. Taube für den Frieden etc.),
  • Interpretation der Botschaft des Cartoons, gestützt auf die gesammelten Erkenntnisse und Informationen.

Erst nach der Analyse und Interpretation des Cartoons können Sie diesen fundiert in Bezug zur Textvorlage setzen. Dabei sollten Sie sich u. a. die Frage stellen, ob ein und dasselbe Thema aus verschiedenen Blickwinkeln oder derselben Perspektive dargestellt wird oder ob es inhaltliche Anhaltspunkte in

---

3 vgl. *Glossary of literary terms* (S. XVIII ff.)

einen Vergleich der beiden Materialien gibt. (Hilfreiche Formulierungen für die Analyse eines Cartoons finden Sie auf Seite XVIII.)

c) Auch wenn ein Bezug von bereits Gelerntem zum neuen Text gewünscht ist, wird in der Regel die Aufgabenstellung die weitere Herangehensweise steuern. Sollte die Aufgabenstellung sehr allgemein sein, so müssen mögliche Anknüpfungspunkte kurz durchdacht werden. In einem weiteren Schritt ist dann z. B. zu klären, ob und, wenn ja, inwiefern sich Gelerntes und Neues widersprechen oder ergänzen.

3   Persönliche Stellungnahme/Kommentar und Diskussion

Traditionellerweise erfordert die Lösung der letzten Aufgabe eine persönliche Stellungnahme, einen kritischen Kommentar oder eine analytisch orientierte Diskussion. Zuweilen tritt an die Stelle dieser Anforderung die sogenannte kreative, gestalterische Aufgabe, die im Rahmen einer Textsortenbindung bei der inhaltlichen Ausgestaltung einen größeren Spielraum für das Einbringen eigener Ideen bietet.

In einer **persönlichen Stellungnahme** oder **einem Kommentar** wird von Ihnen erwartet, dass Sie Ihre eigene Meinung zu dem gegebenen Problem äußern. Damit steht es Ihnen frei, das Problem u. U. auch sehr emotional und unter Bezug auf Ihre eigenen Erfahrungen und Wertvorstellungen sowie auf Ihre ganz persönlichen Wertsetzungen zu beleuchten.

Es wird von Ihnen erwartet, dass Sie einen oder mehrere Hauptaspekte auswählen und diese Auswahl kurz reflektieren und begründen. Diese Aspekte werden systematisch bearbeitet und Thesen dazu aufgestellt. Über eine eng gefasste persönliche Stellungnahme hinaus sollte eine Einbettung der Problemstellung und der Hauptaspekte in einen größeren Kontext vorgenommen werden.

Im Rahmen einer **Diskussion** sollten Sie möglichst viele Facetten eines Problems entfalten, analytisch durchdringen und eine Bewertung vornehmen. Die Grundlagen dieser Bewertung müssen offengelegt und reflektiert werden.

Die Diskussion ist mehr der analytischen Schärfe verpflichtet und weniger den Bedürfnissen und Emotionen des Einzelnen. Sie können also bei der Diskussion eines Problems zu anderen Ergebnissen kommen als bei einer persönlichen Stellungnahme zu demselben Problem.

Methodisch empfiehlt es sich, vor dem Schreiben eine Stichwortsammlung zu erstellen, zusammengehörige Stichworte zu bündeln und in eine sinnvolle und für den Leser nachvollziehbare Anordnung zu bringen. Immer mit Blick auf den Adressaten ist beim Schreiben zu entscheiden, an welchen Stellen Beispiele/illustrierende Passagen eingefügt werden.

4 Sprachmittlungsaufgabe[4]

Kombinierte Aufgaben mit einem Sprachmittlungsteil werden meist für anspruchs-voll gehalten, da sie neben einer verkürzten Textaufgabe, auch noch die Bearbeitung des sprachpraktischen Teils erfordern, nämlich die sinngemäße, schriftliche Zusammenfassung des wesentlichen Gehaltes eines deutschen Ausgangstextes in der Fremdsprache. Der vom Schüler zu verfassende (englische) Text sollte dabei in der Regel ein Drittel der Länge des deutschen Ausgangstextes umfassen und sich auf einen aus dem Unterricht vertrauten Themenbereich beziehen. Er muss aber inhaltlich nicht mit der sich anschließenden Textaufgabe verknüpft sein. Infrage kommen vor allem anwendungsbezogene Texte, die sich z. B. auf naturwissenschaftliche, technische oder wirtschaftliche Sachverhalte aktueller oder zeitloser Art (in Deutschland) beziehen. Die der Mittlung vorangestellte Aufgabe versucht typischerweise, einen praktischen Kontext herzustellen und z. B. einen Adressaten anzugeben, der beim Schreiben berücksichtigt werden muss. Das könnten die Webseite einer Schule im englischsprachigen Ausland oder ein englischsprachiges Projekt sein, an dem mehrere Schulen in der EU arbeiten.

Obwohl damit zu rechnen ist, dass ungewöhnliches Fachvokabular angegeben wird, eignen sich diese Aufgaben besonders, wenn Sie ohnehin über einen breiten Wortschatz verfügen, schnell und flüssig Englisch schreiben und Ihre Zeit gut einteilen, d. h. im Grundkurs circa 45 Minuten und im Leistungskurs circa 60 Minuten für diesen Aufgabenteil einrechnen.

Sprachmittlung bedeutet nicht, dass Sie in der Abiturprüfung eine Übersetzung vornehmen sollen, sondern dass Sie die Kernaussagen des deutschen Ausgangstextes in der englischen Sprache wiedergeben. Somit lohnt es sich, zur Vorbereitung auf diese Aufgabe auch das Kapitel über die Textzusammenfassung (vgl. S. VIII f.) noch einmal durchzuarbeiten. Wesentlich ist folgende Vorgehensweise:

Schritt 1
Suchen Sie nach der zentralen Aussage des Textes.

Schritt 2
Integrieren Sie diese zentrale Aussage in Ihren *umbrella sentence*. Der *umbrella sentence* steht am Anfang Ihres Textes und informiert den Leser nicht nur über den argumentativen Kern des Ausgangstextes, sondern auch über den situativen Rahmen – inklusive Quellenangabe.

Schritt 3
Arrangieren Sie die wichtigsten Argumente um die in Schritt 1 bestimmte Kernaussage herum.

Schritt 4
Lassen Sie Details und rein illustrative Passagen aus. Wichtig sind die Aussage des Textes und seine innere Logik. Denken Sie daran, dass logische und zeitliche Bezüge

---

4 vgl. Theis/Werkmann: Sprachmittlung. Stark Verlag (Best.-Nr. 94469)

durch die geschickte Verwendung von Konjunktionen (z. B. *although, as, but, however, if, unless, when*) hergestellt werden.

5 Ausdrucksvermögen

Die Ausdrucksweise jedes Menschen ist sehr individuell, daher sind allgemeine Aussagen zur Stilverbesserung schwierig. Allerdings haben Sie bereits gelesen, welche Kriterien der Bewertung des Ausdrucksvermögens zugrunde liegen. Bei der Vorbereitung Ihrer Prüfung ist also die Aneignung bzw. Wiederholung des themen- und aufgabenspezifischen Fachvokabulars wichtig. Grundlage sollten Ihre im Unterricht erworbenen Kenntnisse sein. Es gibt auch zahlreiche Veröffentlichungen, in denen der Oberstufenwortschatz thematisch gegliedert dargeboten wird (z. B. Kompakt-Wissen Englisch Wortschatz Oberstufe, Best.-Nr. 90462, oder Abitur-Training Englisch Themenwortschatz, Best.-Nr. 82451D).
Im Zusammenhang mit der geforderten Variation des Satzbaus und dem Einsatz von Verknüpfungen zwischen Satzteilen, Sätzen und Satzgruppen lohnt sich die bewusste, aber nicht übertriebene Verwendung von Konnektoren, die auch als *connectives* oder *linkers* bezeichnet werden. Sie sind besonders für die elegante Formulierung von Kommentaren notwendig. Die themen- und meinungsunabhängigen Konnektoren werden aber zum Teil auch bei Zusammenfassungen und Analyseaufgaben immer wieder gebraucht. In einsprachigen Wörterbüchern findet man solche hilfreichen Ausdrücke des Öfteren im Anhang oder in der Mitte.
Hier eine kleine Auswahl zum Wiederholen und Üben:

1. **Einleitung**
   - it is undeniably true that ... (*es steht außer Zweifel, dass ...*)
   - for the great majority of people (*für die meisten Leute*)
   - it is sometimes forgotten that ... (*es gerät manchmal in Vergessenheit, dass ...*)
   - a problem that is often debated nowadays is that of ... (*heutzutage wird viel über ... diskutiert*)

2. **Fortführung**
   - a number of key issues arise from ... (*aus ... ergeben sich einige grundsätzliche Fragen*)
   - what it boils down to is: ... (*letztlich läuft es auf Folgendes hinaus: ...*)

3. **Bestätigung**
   - it should be stressed that ... (*man sollte betonen, dass ...*)
   - it would be ridiculous to assert that ... (*es wäre geradezu lächerlich zu behaupten, dass ...*)
   - it is undoubtedly true that ... (*zweifellos ...*)

4. **Zweifel**

- it is questionable whether ... *(es ist fraglich, ob ...)*
- it remains to be seen whether ... *(es wird sich zeigen, ob ...)*
- it may well be that ... *(es kann sehr wohl sein, dass ...)*
- it is certainly true that ... but I wonder whether ... *(es ist sicher richtig, dass ..., aber ich frage mich, ob ...)*

5. **Missbilligung**

- it is hard to agree with ... *(es fällt schwer, mit ... übereinzustimmen)*
- ... offers no solution to ... *(... bietet keinerlei Lösungsansatz für ...)*
- ... should not go unchallenged *(... sollte nicht unwidersprochen hingenommen werden)*
- I find it impossible to accept ... *(ich kann ... einfach nicht akzeptieren)*

6. **Betonung einzelner Gesichtspunkte**

- it should never be forgotten that ... *(man sollte nie vergessen, dass ...)*
- especially in view of ... *(besonders im Hinblick auf ...)*
- next I wish to focus our attention on ... *(als Nächstes möchte ich unser Augenmerk auf ... lenken)*
- what is more, ... *(hinzu kommt noch, dass ...)*
- the chief feature of ... *(das Hauptmerkmal ...)*

7. **Vergleich, Hinzufügung, Verbindung**

- as for ... *(was ... betrifft)*
- first of all ..., next ..., finally ... *(zunächst ..., dann ..., schließlich ...)*
- as far as ... is concerned ... *(was ... betrifft ...)*
- there is a fundamental difference between ... *(es besteht ein grundlegender Unterschied zwischen ...)*
- as regards ... *(was ... angeht)*

8. **Persönliche Sichtweise**

- in my opinion ... *(meiner Meinung nach ...)*
- my own view of this is that ... *(meiner Meinung nach ...)*
- it seems to me that ... *(mir scheint ...)*
- but I feel strongly that ... *(ich bin der Überzeugung, dass ...)*

9. **Andere Sichtweise**

- this line of thinking leads to ... *(dieser Gedankengang führt zu ...)*
- ..., which brings us to another side of the question *(..., was eine andere Frage aufwirft)*
- ... draws our attention to the fact that ... *(... macht uns darauf aufmerksam, dass ...)*

10. Zitate, Beispiele

- take the case of ... *(wenn man zum Beispiel ... nimmt)*
- to illustrate the truth of this *(um das zu veranschaulichen)*
- a single, but striking example of ... *(ein gutes Beispiel für ...)*
- according to ... *(laut ...)*
- this passage serves to illustrate ... *(dieser Absatz veranschaulicht ...)*

11. These

- the first thing that needs to be said is ... *(zunächst einmal sollte man darauf hinweisen, dass ...)*
- we must distinguish carefully between ... *(man muss sorgfältig zwischen ... unterscheiden)*
- this brings us to the question of whether ... *(daraus ergibt sich die Frage, ob ...)*
- it is worth stating at this point that ... *(an dieser Stelle sollte man darauf hinweisen, dass ...)*

12. Antithese

- another way of looking at this question is to consider ... *(man kann das Problem aber auch aus anderer Sicht betrachten)*
- ... is, however, a totally unjustified assumption *(... ist jedoch eine völlig unberechtigte Annahme)*
- it would be more accurate to say that ... *(es wäre richtiger zu sagen, dass ...)*

13. Synthese

- how can we reconcile these contradictory viewpoints? *(wie lassen sich diese widersprüchlichen Standpunkte vereinbaren?)*
- it is easy to believe that ... but the truth is that ... *(man könnte annehmen, dass ..., aber in Wahrheit ...)*

14. Schluss

- what conclusion can be drawn from all this? *(welche Schlussfolgerungen lassen sich aus all dem ziehen?)*
- ultimately, then, ... *(letzten Endes)*
- nevertheless, at the end of the day it is safe to assume that ... *(dennoch kann man letzten Endes davon ausgehen, dass ...)*
- all in all *(zusammenfassend)*
- I therefore reject / support ... *(daher unterstütze ich .../lehne ich ... ab)*
- in a nutshell ... *(kurzum)*

Will man sich den bewussten Gebrauch dieser Stilmittel angewöhnen, sollte man die Musterlösungen in diesem Band nicht nur nach auf die Aufgabenstellung bezogenen inhaltlichen Kriterien, sondern auf jeden Fall auch mit Blick auf die Art der sprachlichen Gestaltung durcharbeiten.

6 Beschreibung eines Diagramms

Diagrammarten

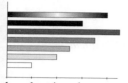

bar chart/graph
(Balken-, Säulendiagramm)

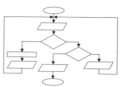

flow chart
(Flussdiagramm)

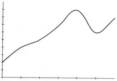

line graph
(Kurvendiagramm)

pie chart
(Kreisdiagramm, Kuchendiagramm)

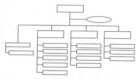

organization(al) chart
(Organigramm)

Question	Answer
a) What are the conditions that would bring about multiculturalism in a positive sense according to the author?	• individual rights should be guaranteed to everyone (cf. l. 29) • different groups should respect each other (cf. ll. 30 /31)
b) Which group makes it the most difficult to create a feeling of national identity?	white British people (cf. ll. 41/42)

table
(Tabelle)

Beschreibung des Diagramms

- **Zustand**
  to stand at ...
  to remain/stay at ...

  to amount to ...

  In December, sales stood at $ 22 million.
  Losses stayed at $ 2 million per month between January and March.
  sich belaufen auf, betragen

- **Zunahme**
  to rise/go up/increase by ... to ...
  to rise/go up/increase from ... to ...
  an increase/a rise of
  an increase/a growth in
  to rocket
  to surge

  Costs rose by 5 % to 25 %.
  Profits went up from 20 % to 25 %.

  There was an increase/a rise of 5 %.
  There was an increase in sales.
  in die Höhe schießen
  dramatisch zunehmen

to double/treble/quadruple	*sich verdoppeln/verdreifachen/vervierfachen*
to increase five-fold, six-fold	*fünffach, sechsfach zunehmen*
to jump to	*in die Höhe schnellen*

- **Abnahme**

to drop/go down/decrease/fall by ... to ...	Expenses dropped by $ 55,000 to $ 320,000.
to drop/go down/decrease/fall from ... to ...	Interest rates decreased from 18 % to 16 %.
a drop/decrease/fall of	There was a drop/decrease/fall of 2 %.
a drop/decrease/fall in	Companies experienced a drop/decrease/fall in sales.
to plummet	*stark zurückgehen*
to slump	*zurückgehen*
to fall to a trough	*auf einen Tiefstand fallen*

- **Höhepunkt**

to peak at ...	*einen Höchststand erreichen bei*
	Sales peaked at 5,000 units in December.
to reach a peak of ...	Sales reached a peak of 5,000 units in December.

- **Gleichstand**

to level off/out at ...	*sich einpendeln bei*
	Sales levelled out at 4,000 units.
figures do not change	The figures have not changed for years.

- **Tiefpunkt**

to bottom out at ...	*einen Tiefstand erreichen bei*
	Our market share bottomed out later that year at around 25 %.
to reach their/its lowest at ...	Profits reached their lowest at 8 %.

- **Adjektive**

lightly/steadly/dramatically/ sharply	Sales figures have fallen slightly.
continually *(stetig)* / gradually *(allmählich)*	Profits have gone up continually.
significantly *(deutlich)* / insignificantly *(unbedeutend)* / negligibly *(geringfügig)*	Growth is expected to rise insignificantly.

Formulierungen

The pie chart shows ...
This is an organization chart of ...
The bar graph demonstrates ...
This table gives information about ...

The pie chart compares ...
As you can see from the pie chart ...
Its most significant feature is ...
The horizontal axis represents ...
The dotted line on the graph represents ...
The figures in the table show that ...
The figures prove that ...
The statistics suggest that ...
The diagram makes it clear that ...
This implies that ...
There is evidence that ...

7 Beschreibung eines Cartoons

Formulierungen

In the upper left-hand corner / in the lower right-hand corner ...
In the foreground / in the background ...
On the right-hand side / on the left-hand side ...
At first sight, one believes ...
The cartoon displays / shows ...
The title of the cartoon refers to ...
In the speech bubbles *(Sprechblasen)*, the cartoonist indicates ...
The caption *(Bildunterschrift)* alludes to / implies ...
The message is clear to see ...
There is evidence that ...
The cartoonist makes fun of ...
From the cartoonist's point of view ...
The cartoon displays the same topic as the text at hand, but shows another perspective on the issue ...
The cartoon is more convincing than the arguments given in the text ...

8 Glossary of literary terms

1. **Allegory:** a poem, play or story in which the characters and events are used to symbolize a **deeper moral or spiritual meaning**.

   Example: Typical allegories would be Bunyan's *Pilgrim's Progress* or George Orwell's *Animal Farm*. In *Animal Farm* the pigs represent a totalitarian regime.

2. **Alliteration:** sometimes referred to as **head rhyme** or **initial rhyme**, alliteration is a term we use to describe the **repetition of the initial sounds**, usually consonants, in a line of poetry or in closely adjacent lines. A good poet uses alliteration not just because it sounds nice but because it reinforces the meaning and purpose of the lines in question. Alliteration therefore is used **to create**

melody, **establish mood, or call attention to important words**. It also highlights similarities or contrasts.

Example: "Scooping spilt, soft, broken oil with a silver spoon from a flagstone floor. ..."
(*"M-M-Memory" from* The Other Country *by Carol Ann Duffy*)

3. **Allusion:** when a writer alludes to something in the course of writing a poem, he refers to **information assumed to be known** by the reader. This can be a reference to a person or a well-known occurrence such as a battle or war, a TV character or a well-known literary character.

    Example: "'An old woman who looked like one of the witches from Macbeth' he said. This allusion was lost on Sally. Seeing her puzzlement he went on, 'wrinkled, don't you know, and hideous and so forth' ..."
    (The Ruby in the Smoke *by Philip Pullman*)

4. **Ambiguity:** the state of being **doubtful, unclear or indistinct**. It is a characteristic of writing which makes something capable of being understood in more than one way. A poet will often do this deliberately.

    Example: A simple example of ambiguity is to be found in the sentence "They found me a good worker." This is ambiguous in that it has two meanings, i. e. *They found me to be a good worker* or *They found a good worker for me*. The context is necessary for it to be properly understood. A writer making effective use of ambiguity will use language and context to leave something unclear or open to more than one interpretation.

5. **Analogy: agreement or similarity** in some things which are otherwise quite different from one another.

    Example: Sleep and death are not really similar but would be analogous in that both normally involve no movement and often happen when a person is lying down.

6. **Anaphora:** the **repetition** of a word or phrase at the start of a succession of phrases in order to achieve **rhetorical effect**. This is most commonly used in plays or famous speeches.

    Example: "*We shall fight* in France, *we shall fight* on the seas and oceans, *we shall fight* with growing confidence and growing strength in the air, *we shall* defend our island, whatever the cost may be, *we shall fight* on the beaches, *we shall fight* on the landing grounds, *we shall fight* in the fields and in the streets, *we shall fight* in the hills. *We shall* never surrender."
    (*Winston Churchill*)

7. **Antithesis:** this term refers to the exact **opposite** of something being **highlighted in parallel words or** in the **juxtaposition** of contrasting ideas or phrases.

    Example: BRUTUS "Not that I loved Caesar less, but that I loved Rome more."
    (Julius Caesar *by William Shakespeare*)

8. **Antonym:** a word which is the **opposite** of something else.
   Example: good – bad / easy – difficult.

9. **Aside: a statement uttered** in the course of a play which is intended for the ears of the audience only and is **not heard by the other characters** on stage at the time.
   Example: MACBETH "Thanks for that.
   (Aside) There the grown serpent lies, the worm that's fled."
   (Macbeth *by William Shakespeare*)

10. **Assonance:** the use of the **same vowel sound with different consonants** in successive words or stressed syllables.
    Example: "time and light"

11. **Blank Verse:** verse which does not rhyme but has a set metrical pattern, mostly of **iambic pentameters** (i. e. an unstressed syllable followed by a stressed syllable in each poetic foot). It is used extensively in **dramatic or narrative verse**.
    Example: "The qua / lity / of mer / cy is / not strain'd /
    It drop / peth as / the gen / tle rain / from heaven / "
    (The Merchant of Venice *by William Shakespeare*)

12. **Characterisation:** the method an author uses to present his characters to the reader. This may involve **physical description**, an account of **speech and behaviour**, a character's **opinions and reactions**, or finally, what a character **feels or thinks** about something.
    Example: "Frances Lennox was a minor, steady, reliable actress, and had never been asked for anything more. This part was in a brilliant new play, a two-hander, and the male part would be taken by Tony Wilde who until now had seemed so far above her she would never have had the ambition to think of her name and his side by side on a poster ..." (The Sweetest Dream *by Doris Lessing*)

13. **Cliché:** words or phrases that have been used so often that they are more or less meaningless.
    Example: "As dead as a doornail." *or* "As cool as a cucumber."

14. **Climax:** a group of sentences or clauses which starts with the weakest and then **builds to a high point** in order to achieve effect. The term can also refer to the high point of a story or play.
    Example: "It is an outrage to bind a Roman citizen; to scourge him is an atrocious crime; to put him to death is almost a parricide; but to crucify him, what shall I call it?"
    (Cicero)

15. **Conflict:** this term is used when talking about a **problem or struggle between two opposing forces** in a story. The main types of conflicts are: person against person, person against self, person against society and person against nature.

    Example: One of the central themes of *How to be Good* by Nick Hornby is the struggle the main character experiences between the person she is and the person she wants to be. This conflict is the main driving force behind her story.

16. **Consonance: repetition of specific consonant sounds** after different vowel sounds.

    Example: Consonance is the similarity between consonants, but not between vowels, as between the *s* and *t* sounds in "sweet silent thought."

17. **Elements of fiction:** certain aspects of a literary work. A criticism or analysis of a book or story might concentrate on any of the following elements: the **action**, the **antagonist** (i. e. the person or force that works against the **protagonist** or hero of the story), the **characters**, the **climax**, the **conflict**, the **dialogue**, the **exposition**, (i. e. the part of the story in which the characters first appear, the background is explained and the setting is described), the **falling action** (i. e. the action and dialogue following the climax that lead the reader into the story's end), the **mood**, the **moral**, the **narrator**, the **plot**, the **resolution**, (i. e. how everything turns out), the **rising action** (i. e. the central part of the story during which various problems arise after a conflict is introduced), the **setting**, the **style** and the **theme**.

    Example: The theme of the short story collection *Dubliners* by James Joyce is essentially one of life and human nature in Dublin as seen through the eyes of the characters involved.

18. **Ellipsis:** a stylistic device used to achieve poetic effect by **omitting a word or phrase** which is easily known to the reader.

    Example: "And he to England shall along with you." (The word "go" has been omitted between "shall" and "along.")
    (Hamlet *by William Shakespeare*)

19. **Epigram:** a **witty paradoxical remark**.

    Example: "A poet can survive everything but a misprint." *or* "I can resist everything except temptation."
    (Oscar Wilde)

20. **Euphemism:** a **polite phrase or word** which is used to say something that is considered unpleasant or hurtful in a nice and acceptable manner.

    Example: "China is a country where you often get different accounts of the same thing" *(... where many lies are told)* or "He passed away" *(He died)*.

21. **Figurative language** takes in such devices as **simile, hyperbole, personification** and **metaphor**.

    Example: "He clasps the crag with crooked hands
    Close to the sun in lonely lands
    Ringed with the azure world, he stands."
    ("The Eagle" by Lord Tennyson)

22. **Foreshadowing** happens when the author gives **hints** about things which will later come to pass in the course of a story.

    Example: In *Julius Caesar* by William Shakespeare, Caesar's wife has nightmares in which she foresees his death (Act II, Scene II):
    Thunder and lightning. Enter CAESAR, in his night-gown
    "Nor heaven nor earth have been at peace to-night:
    Thrice hath Calphurnia in her sleep cried out,
    'Help, ho! they murder Caesar!' Who's within?"

23. **Flashback:** the opposite of foreshadowing. An interruption in the action of a story or work of non-fiction **to show an episode that happened at an earlier time**. A flashback is usually used to provide background information.

    Example: In *The Snows of Kilimanjaro*, Harry Street, who is dying, becomes preoccupied with incidents in his past. In a flashback Street remembers one of his wartime comrades dying painfully on barbed wire on a battlefield in Spain.

24. **Hyperbole: exaggerated form** of language used to increase effect.

    Example: "I could eat a horse" *or* "All the perfume of Arabia could not sweeten this little hand."
    (Macbeth *by William Shakespeare*)

25. **Imagery:** those elements in a poem which evoke **mental pictures**; not just visual ones but emotional ones also. Many images are conveyed by figurative language such as **similes, metaphors and personification**.

    Example: "When the evening is spread out against the sky
    Like a patient etherized upon a table."
    ("The Love Song of J. Alfred Prufrock" – T. S. Eliot)

26. **Irony:** a humorous use of words **to imply the opposite** of what they actually mean. There is a contrast between what seems to be and what actually is. We speak of verbal irony, dramatic irony, irony of situation and irony of tone.

    Example: "Moments after Eileen shot herself, having earlier been told that John, her husband, had been killed in the war, he came walking up the drive with his rucksack over his shoulder."

27. **Literary forms:** various **types of writing**. These include such well-known types as comedy, drama, essay, historical fiction, novel, poetry, science fiction and the short story. Other literary forms include myth, folktale, autobiography, biography, realistic fiction and prose.

    Example: The novel *The Time Machine* by H. G. Wells is a good example of early science fiction writing.

28. **Metaphor:** a figure of speech that **implies comparison** without using "like" or "as". A resemblance is indicated but not expressed directly.

    Example: "All the world's a stage." (Not: … is *like* a stage)
    (As You Like It *by William Shakespeare*)

29. **Mood:** the overall **emotional effect** created by a piece of literature.

    Example: The mood created in the poem "Originally" (Carol Ann Duffy) is a reflective one, one full of memories and uncertainty. The poet is considering a time when she lived in a different country and is wondering where she actually comes from. The conclusion of the poem reads "And I hesitate", a finish which contributes to, and is typical of, the overall mood of the poem.

30. **Paradox:** a seemingly **absurd or self-contradictory statement** that is or may be true.

    Example: "What a pity that youth must be wasted on the young."
    (George Bernard Shaw)

31. **Personification:** the **attribution of human qualities** to something which is not human.

    Example: "As the wind undressed the trees, fear grabbed at his throat …"
    or "The plane began to creak and protest as it fought its way through the storm."

32. **Plot: pattern of action** in a short story, novel or play. In a book with a good plot all the details are important and are arranged so that the outcome depends on each one and the interaction of all the details with one another. The plot may have **a protagonist** who is opposed by an **antagonist**, creating what is known as **conflict**. A plot may include flashback or it may include a subplot which is a mirror image of the main plot.

    Example: In Shakespeare's *King Lear,* the relationship between the Earl of Gloucester and his sons mirrors the relationship between Lear and his daughters.

33. **Point of view:** the writer's **choice of narrator** for his story. A writer has three basic choices when it comes to deciding on what point of view will be used in a novel.

    Example: Personal or first-person: the narrator "I" is a character in the story who can reveal only his own thoughts and what he sees and is told. *Robinson Crusoe* is told from a first-person point of view.

Third person objective is where the narrator is an outsider who can report only what he sees and hears. An example would be *Hard Times* by Charles Dickens. An omniscient point of view is where the narrator knows everything and can enter the minds of his characters. He may enter the minds of all the characters or the mind of just one if he wishes to focus on one character. Joyce's *Ulysses* is told in this manner.

34. **Pun: play on words** in which words are used to exploit ambiguities in meaning, usually for humorous effect.

    Example: Ben Battle was a soldier bold and used to *war's* alarms
    But a cannonball took off his *legs* so he laid down his *arms*.

35. **Repetition:** one of the most frequently used stylistic devices. It simply involves the **frequent use of the same word or phrase** in a piece of writing.

    Example: "You cannot sir, take from me anything that I would more willingly part withal, except my life, except my life, except my life."
    (Hamlet *by William Shakespeare*)

36. **Rhetoric:** the effective use of language, particularly in a **speech**, when one is trying to persuade someone or convert them to one's opinion.

    Example: "Friends, Romans, countrymen
    Lend me your ears
    I come ..."
    (Julius Caesar *by William Shakespeare*)

37. **Rhetorical question:** a question to which **no answer is required** because the answer is obvious.

    Example: "Who knows?" (The answer "nobody knows" is clear from the question itself.)

38. **Rhyme:** a term we use to describe the **repetition of syllable sounds**. We speak of **end rhyme** and **internal rhyme**. The pattern created by rhyme in a poem is referred to as the rhyming scheme.

    Example: "I'm a lean dog, a keen dog, a wild dog and lone;
    I'm a rough dog, a tough dog, hunting on my own."
    (Irene Rutherford McLeod)

39. **Sarcasm:** particular **type of irony**. Sarcasm is usually intended to be aggressive and is often insulting and aimed at a person.

    Example: "You are a wonderful goalkeeper." (To someone who has just conceded nine goals in a match ...)

40. **Satire:** a literary work which exposes and ridicules human folly and uses **sarcasm, wit** and **irony** to do so. It is usually directed against the injustice of social wrongs e. g. poverty, corruption.

Example: Famous satirists would include Dryden, Swift, Pope and Orwell. *Animal Farm* (Orwell) and *Gulliver's Travels* (Swift) are among the most famous works of satire ever written.

41. **Setting:** the **time and place** in which the events of a story or novel take place.
    Example: The book *Ulysses*, by Irish writer James Joyce, has perhaps the most well-known setting of any modern novel. It is set in Dublin on one particular day in 1904, a day that has since become known as Bloomsday in honour of a character, Leopold Bloom, who appears in the book.

42. **Simile:** a **comparison** of two completely different objects using "**like**" or "**as**". It is not generally considered as powerful as a metaphor since it does not defy logic.
    Example: "Errors, like straws, upon the surface flow …" *(Nesfield)*

43. **Soliloquy:** a **speech** which is spoken by a character in a play at a time when he or she is unaccompanied on the stage.
    Example: The best-known soliloquy in the English language is Hamlet's speech in which he utters his famous "to be or not to be" statement.

44. **Sonnet: fixed poetic form of fourteen lines in iambic pentameter**. In the Elizabethan or Shakespearean sonnet the lines are divided into three quatrains and a couplet (abab, cdcd, efef, gg). The original Italian form is divided into an octave of two rhyme-sounds following an abba abba pattern and a sestet of two additional rhyme patterns cdc, dcd or cde, cde. Eventually, the ability to write a sonnet became part of a wealthy man's education.
    Example: Shakespeare's "Shall I compare thee to a summer's day?" is one of the most famous sonnets.

45. **Stream of consciousness: narrative technique** developed towards the end of the 19th century used to portray and evoke the psychic life of a character and depict subjective as well as objective reality. Stream of consciousness refers to the **presentation of a character's thoughts, feelings, actions** and so on.
    Example: In his work *The Butcher Boy* the Irish author Patrick McCabe uses the first person stream of consciousness to show his main character's descent into madness.

46. **Symbol:** a word which stands for or is somehow connected to an idea and is therefore a **sign** of something.
    Example: The Union Jack stands for Britain. In Robert Frost's poem "Acquainted with the Night" both the night and darkness are symbols for death or depression.

47. **Tautology:** the **repetition of an idea in different words**, phrases or in a sentence.

Example: With malice toward none, with charity for all.
("Second Inaugural Address" – A. Lincoln)

48. **Theme: unifying motif** in, or the **main meaning** of, a work; often a general truth about life. A theme can be stated directly or implied.

Example: One of the main themes of Edna O'Brien's collection of short stories *Lantern Slides* is the confinement provincial life in Ireland places upon those who live there.

49. **Tone:** when a reader refers to the tone of a poem, he or she is usually speaking about **the writer's attitude** to the subject he is writing about. More specifically it can refer to **the moral outlook** of a piece. Tone is sometimes used to describe the overall feeling of a poem and thus is quite related to the mood.

Example: The tone of the book *Cannery Row* by John Steinbeck is objective, neutral and non-judgemental. The writer does not express disapproval of the actions of Mack and his band.

50. **Tragedy:** a word used primarily at a literary level to refer to **a medieval narrative poem** or **a Renaissance drama** in which the downfall of a great person – be it a king, an emperor or a good person – is the main theme of the work.

Example: *Julius Caesar* and *King Lear* by William Shakespeare both describe the downfall of great individuals and are among the greatest tragedies ever written.

51. **Understatement:** a **comment made in a restrained and somehow less important way** to achieve heightened effect and increase the actual importance of what is being said. This is often done in an ironic way.

Example: After Macbeth murders his friend Banquo, he goes on to play down the deed by referring to the number of people who have been murdered since the beginning of time, saying, "Blood hath been shed ere now."

Kurzinterpretationen zu den Pflichtlektüren

T. C. Boyle, *The Tortilla Curtain* (1995)

Author

The novelist and short story writer Thomas John Boyle was born in Peekskill, New York, in 1948. When he was 17 he replaced John by Coraghessan in memory of his Irish ancestors. He graduated from universities in New York (1968) and Iowa (1974 and 1977) and is a Distinguished Professor Emeritus of English at the University of Southern California. Since the mid-1970s T. C. Boyle has published fourteen novels (among them *World's End*, 1987; *The Road to Wellville*, 1993; *Drop City*, 2003; *San Miguel*, 2012) and a large number of short story collections. For his most famous novel, *The Tortilla Curtain* (1995), Boyle was awarded the French *Prix Médicis étranger*.

Contents

Boyle's *Tortilla Curtain* comprises three parts, with eight chapters each. The novel is set northwest of Los Angeles in the 1990s and tells the events in the lives of two different couples: the white American Mossbacher family (Delaney, his wife Kyra and stepson Jordan) and the Rincóns (Cándido and América), illegal immigrants from Mexico.

Part One: Arroyo Blanco (= the title of the chapter refers to the estate where two of the main characters, Delaney and Kyra Mossbacher, live). The novel opens with a road accident in which the two main characters of the book are involved. Driving along in his car on the road in Topanga Canyon, near his home, Delaney Mossbacher, a member of the middle-class, hits and badly injures Cándido Rincón, an illegal Mexican immigrant. As the Mexican does not want to see a doctor and refuses any help, Delaney gives him $ 20. Whereas Delaney is deeply shaken by the incident, his wife Kyra is more worried about possible financial claims brought forward by personal-injury lawyers.

Cándido is severely injured, but makes it back into the canyon where he is hiding from La Migra, the US immigration police, together with América, his pregnant girlfriend. Both have left their poor Mexican village in search of a better future across the border in California, but the difficulty of finding work makes life extremely hard for them. As Cándido is too weak to look for work, América decides to try to earn some money in spite of Cándido's vehement opposition: He is worried about her as he feels that América is too vulnerable for the hostile environment.

gefährdet | Umgebung

       lebens-   I 1

         feindlich

One morning, a coyote jumps over the fence into the Mossbachers' garden, killing one of Kyra's two pet dogs, a Dandie Dinmont terrier. Kyra is shocked and sad, but carries on with her job as an estate agent, while Delaney writes his regular column for the nature magazine *Wide Open Spaces* under his pseudonym "Pilgrim". At the same day, the Arroyo Blanco community meets at the Community Centre. It is decided to erect a gate at the main entrance that is guarded 24 hours a day to keep unwanted trespassers with possibly criminal intents outside. Delaney tries to make his neighbours realise that leaving waste outside might attract coyotes to the estate, but he is not taken seriously and leaves. Outside, he is questioned by the son of Jack Jardine, the president of the Arroyo Blanco community, about where exactly he had hit the illegal immigrant.

Meanwhile, América has tried in vain to find work for several days. While waiting to be picked up by some employer she is hassled by a sleazy white Mexican, who calls himself José Navidad. América eventually manages to be given a job by Jim Smiley, who also lives in Arroyo Blanco. She has to scrub Buddha sculptures. Working conditions are awful as América is exposed to poisonous substances. When white youths discover Cándido's and América's hiding place and paint a threatening message on a rock ("Beaners die", p. 62[1]), Cándido decides to move their hideout further up the canyon to a more secluded and safer place.

In the local store Delaney has a conversation with Jack Jardine, whose negative views on immigrants Delaney calls racist. The next day, Delaney finds it hard to concentrate on his writing, so he decides to explore a new part of the canyon instead. He parks his car by the road and hikes down into the wilderness, which to his disgust is littered with refuse. There he stumbles across two strangers, one of them being José Navidad. When he eventually returns to the place where he has parked his car, he finds that the vehicle has been stolen.

Cándido's wounds are slowly healing, but he cannot find work. América is still scrubbing Buddhas. One night on her way back from work down into the canyon she is mugged and raped by José Navidad.

Part Two: El Tenksgeevee (= Spanish pronunciation of North America's annual national holiday Thanksgiving, on the fourth Thursday in November): Delaney buys himself a new car. The dealer Kenny Grissom blames the increasing number of criminal immigrants for the car theft. Delaney feels victimized and gets further frustrated and enraged when Kyra is insulted by a stranger because she had reprimanded him for leaving a dog locked in his car in the extreme heat. On her tour round the Da Ros property, which she tries to sell, Kyra observes two suspicious characters in the park, one of which is José Navidad, who frightens her.

In the meantime Cándido has found work with Al Lopez, a Mexican building constructor with an American passport. América tells Cándido that she has been robbed, but keeps the rape secret, although Cándido suspects that something else might have happened to her.

Kyra uses her influence to have the "labour exchange" – the street corner where immigrants gather to look for a day's work – closed. Although Delaney basically believes that

---

1 Page numbers refer to: T. C. Boyle, *The Tortilla Curtain.* Bloomsbury: London 1997.

illegal immigrants have the right to gather freely wherever they want, he finally agrees with Kyra's intervention. Again, a coyote jumps into the Mossbachers' garden, snatches and kills the family's second pet dog.

Five long days Cándido clears brush land for an employer, who in the end does not turn up to pay him for the last day's work. Cándido has been cheated, and now that the labour exchange is gone, finding work is nearly impossible. Although he has the chance to steal Kyra's handbag, Cándido just cannot do it. Warned about a raid by La Migra, he leaves the canyon together with América and heads off for Canoga Park, a part of the city where many Mexicans live. América is excited about all the shops there and the prospect of eventually renting an apartment from the money they have saved. However, a con man tricks Cándido, and after losing all their savings they are forced to return to the canyon despite América's angry protests. She is utterly disappointed and blames Cándido for taking her away from a secure home into a life of uncertainty and misery. Her depression and aversion against him increases when Cándido offers her left-overs he has recovered from a restaurant's refuse bin.

In a new column for *Wide Open Spaces* Delaney writes about the perfect adaptability of coyotes. Kyra finds an obscene and threatening inscription ("fucking whore", p. 223) painted on the Da Ros house and Delaney has an encounter with a Mexican whom he suspects of stealing. The man is José Navidad, who delivers flyers (he calls them "flies", p. 229) for Jack Jardine, inviting Arroyo Blanco residents to an important meeting. There, the majority of residents decides to have a wall built to protect their houses and property. Preparations for Thanksgiving are in full swing and for the first time Cándido has a bit of luck. In the supermarket two customers present him with a turkey they were given as a bonus for their purchases. Cándido is delighted, and América's mood improves. However, the fire which he starts to roast the bird gets out of control and starts raging through the entire canyon.

Part Three: Socorro (= Spanish for "help", the name of Cándido's and América's new-born baby daughter). The Thanksgiving party in Dominick Flood's spacious villa in Arroyo Blanco comes to an abrupt end when someone discovers fire in the canyon. As a matter of precaution, the residents have to leave the estate. Cándido and América manage to escape from the fire and eventually find shelter in a shed by the wall of the deserted Arroyo Blanco estate. Standing on top of the canyon, Delaney sees two men, one of them is José Navidad, climbing up out of the canyon. He is convinced that they are the arsonists and has them arrested. When José is led away to the police car, he spits in Delaney's face and Delaney attacks him. The wind turns, the fire threat is over and the residents can return to their homes. Delaney feels extreme shame and regrets having lost control of himself because of the Mexican. The Mossbachers' house is untouched by the fire, but their cat, Dame Edith, has disappeared. So has Dominick Flood, a shady character, who has been confined to a three years' house arrest due to dubious investments. Obviously, Flood took advantage of the general turmoil during the evacuation.

In the shed, América gives birth to a baby daughter, whom she names Socorro. In search for a safer hiding place the couple climb further up the hill. Although he does not want to steal, Cándido climbs over the wall around Arroyo Blanco several times to "borrow" tools, pallets and slats to build a shack as a protection against wind and rain.

13

Kyra is devastated when she finds out that the fire destroyed the magnificent Da Ros villa. Delaney learns that the wall around Arroyo Blanco has been spray-painted and decides to set up a few trip-wire cameras in order to catch the culprits red-handed. One night a camera wire is tripped, and the photo print shows the face of Cándido, whom Delaney remembers as the man he hit with his car.

América urges Cándido to return to Mexico because she does not want to raise her child like a wild animal in these terrible conditions. She also needs a doctor now to examine the baby because she fears Socorro might be blind. Cándido is desperate and feels guilty for having brought all this misery on his young partner and child. He tries to recover the money they had buried in the canyon in a jar under a stone, but the raging flames have baked all of it together into a worthless nugget. He is desperate enough to forget about the risk of being picked up by the officers of La Migra and goes to the post office to find a job. It is there that Delaney spots him.

As soon as Delaney sees Cándido standing by the roadside he stops his car and wants to get him arrested by the police because in his eyes, the Mexican is responsible for the vandalism, the thefts, and even the fire. In the pouring rain Cándido manages to escape, but Delaney follows his footprints which take him all the way to the Arroyo Blanco gate. He notices that the trip-wire cameras have taken more photos, but to his surprise they do not show Cándido's face as Delaney expected, but that of Jack Jardine Jr. and an accomplice. However, Delaney is now on the hunt and arms himself with a gun. He is determined to track the Mexican down and follows Cándido's footprints leading up the hill to the couple's makeshift hut. In the meantime, Cándido has made it back to the shack, where América tells him that Socorro is blind and that she was raped in the canyon. The enraged Delaney finds the hut and is about to burst in on the Mexican couple, when an enormous torrent of water and mud hurtles them away. In the raging river, América and Cándido hold on to each other, but cannot avoid losing their baby. They are saved when they manage to grasp the tile roof of the US Post Office. All of a sudden Cándido sees Delaney's white face surge up out of the current. He reaches down to save Delaney from drowning.

Characters

The Mossbachers: 39-year-old **Delaney Mossbacher**, divorced and now married to his second wife Kyra, lives comfortably in the fashionable residential estate of Arroyo Blanco. He is a **naturalist and nature lover** writing articles about his excursions and observations in the Topanga Canyon for a magazine called *Wide Open Spaces*. In the course of the novel Delaney comes to realise that the "open spaces" are disappearing. **His initially liberal and humanist ideals are shaken.** The quiet and reserved Delaney, who considers everyone his equal, irrespective of ethnicity or nationality, gradually **turns into a racist himself.** Although he himself is a descendent of immigrants from Ireland and Germany, he develops a deep hatred, in particular against illegals from across the southern US border (such as José Navidad or Cándido Rincón). In Delaney's eyes, they are a threat not only to the environment as they occupy and litter the wilderness, but also to his comfortable lifestyle. It is a bitter irony that of all people Cándido Rincón, the man who Delaney is determined to hunt down and exterminate, becomes his lifesaver.

I 4

Delaney's wife **Kyra Menaker-Mossbacher** is the **typical American businesswoman**, who **values luxury and property** more than personal relations. She works long hours as an estate agent, and is so involved in her job that meeting potential customers becomes more important to her than spending time with her family. Her **materialistic attitude** is bound to fail as not only her much-loved property, the Da Ros villa, is destroyed, but also her married life is endangered.

The Rincóns: 33-year-old **Cándido Rincón**, an illegal immigrant, has had a hard life since his childhood in Mexico. His wife, Resurrección, betrayed him and so he eloped with her younger sister América to the US in the hope of **making a new start**. However, when the novel opens, Cándido is run over by Delaney in his car, an incident which is the first in a long row of misfortunes. He **is cheated at** several times, **exploited, humiliated and persecuted**. Despite his hard work he does not get the reward he is looking for, which is merely to be able to feed his family and lead a decent life from the work of his own hands.

Cándido's partner is 17-year-old **América**, four months pregnant. The barefoot country girl is completely **naïve and inexperienced** and at first believes the promises Cándido makes. Eventually, she **emancipates herself** in as much as she protests and is no longer willing to endure the hardships in a hostile and life-threatening environment. After the birth of her daughter she makes it clear to Cándido that she is **determined to** put an end to illusions and dreams of a better future in the US and **return to the simple life in Mexico**.

The Residents in Arroyo Blanco: The people who live in the gated community of Arroyo Blanco are well-to-do Caucasians, **whites of European origin**. The tolerant Delaney Mossbacher and Todd Sweet, who shares Delaney's liberal convictions, do not stand a chance against the **racist opinion leaders** Jack Jardine, Jim Shirley and Dominick Flood, who strongly advocate the erection of a gate at the entrance to the estate and the building of a wall around it to keep out "gangbangers and taggers and carjackers" (p. 39). They strongly **oppose the influx of illegal immigrants** from Mexico and Central America. Ironically enough, Flood is no less of a criminal than some of the illegal immigrants. Nevertheless, people rather seem willing to trust in a shady businessman, who has to serve three years of house arrest due to his failed investments, just because he is white like them. Boyle's portrayal of the residents as an **egoistic and bigoted community** was in some reviews criticized as too negative and one-sided.

Themes and Interpretation

shady businessperson
unserios

The American Dream and Immigration: The US is a **nation of immigrants** and the driving force behind the influx of people from all over the world has been the American Dream. The original concept of the American Dream, which was developed in the 19th century, is the **ideal of individual independence in an open society which offers opportunities for all**. Every person, regardless of his origins, can succeed in life through his own abilities and hard work. The myth "from rags to riches" lured millions to the New World in the 19th century. They were all welcome because farmers, craftsmen and labourers of all kind were desperately needed during the times of the US industrialisation. At the turn of the century, however, many thought that "the boat was full" and legislation to limit immigration with the help of quotas was introduced (1917, 1921). Since then the debate about the advantages or disadvantages of immigration has been on the political agenda. In *The Tortilla Curtain* the diverging views on this topic are presented by Delaney Mossbacher, who believes that "immigrants are the lifeblood of this country" (p. 101), and Jack Jardine, who sees the newcomers as a burden on "welfare, emergency care, schooling and the like" (p. 102). The US administration is still undecided how to cope with the about 11 million illegal immigrants currently living in the country. Many of the undocumented come from Mexico, trying to cross the heavily guarded border along the Rio Grande River ("wetbacks").

For Cándido and América Rincón, **the American Dream turns into a nightmare**. From the very start they do not meet with an open society, but a community which takes every effort to exclude any newcomer, e. g. by erecting a guarded gate and a wall around Arroyo Blanco. **Despite the hard work and stamina they invest** into making their dream come true, **the Rincóns cannot make any progress**. On the contrary, they are thrown back into a life worse than the one they had left behind. Wherever they go and whatever they do, they become **victims of discrimination, hostility, exploitation and violence**.

T. C. Boyle is a great admirer of the works of American novelist John Steinbeck (1902–1968). In particular, Steinbeck's novel *The Grapes of Wrath* about the Dust Bowl migrant workers (the so-called "Okies", referring to Oklahoma, the US state they came from) during the Great Depression impressed him. Boyle quotes a passage from Steinbeck's book as a preface to *The Tortilla Curtain* to illustrate that Mexican immigrants today face challenges similar to the ones the poor and exploited farmers of the 1930s had to cope with. By comparing the endless suffering of Okies and wetbacks, Boyle shows that the same injustice still exists and that the world has not changed much in 60 to 70 years.

"Gated communities": To keep aliens out the residents of Arroyo Blanco turn their estate into a so-called gated community, a housing estate with strictly controlled entrances and a wall enclosing the community. They regard these fortifications as **a necessity to protect their houses and property**. Ironically enough, the invaders and perpetrators do not always come from outside, some are already within the boundary – as the example of Jack Jardine Jr. illustrates. The wall is no safe barrier; it can be climbed (cf. the coyote, Cándido and Jack Jr.) and consequently, does not provide the absolute security people have hoped for. Boyle wants to get the message across that **setting one's hopes on exclusiveness, on closing the doors and fortifying borders to keep one's own privileged standard of living, is an illusion** and the wrong approach in dealing with immigrants. The Mexicans in Boyle's novel provide just one example of the plight of immigrants in many parts the world: Refugees and migrants try to escape from oppression or poverty in their home nations to seek shelter or work in richer countries. The so-called **boat people** venture across dangerous seas in overcrowded vessels (e. g. from Cuba to the USA, Africa to Italy or Indonesia to Australia) and risk their lives for a better future. **The problem of how to provide for a more equal distribution of wealth remains unsolved**. Closing one's eyes to the issue and locking the doors is not only impossible and unfair, it can also be detrimental. In *The Tortilla Curtain*, Delaney Mossbacher owes his life to the unfortunate Cándido Rincón in the end.

The Tortilla Curtain: In comparison to the Iron Curtain that separated the former Soviet Union from Western Europe, the border between Mexico and the US states Arizona, California, New Mexico and Texas is called "tortilla curtain". It is the purpose of the heavily guarded border to keep the Mexicans, who are believed to mainly live off tortillas, out of North America if they are not in possession of a valid work permit. Like many other illegal immigrants, Cándido and América try to cross the border with the help of a *coyote*, a smuggler who illegally organises their entry to the US and deserts them as things get too dangerous (cf. pp. 59/60). Still, the couple manage to settle in the south of California only to discover that the curtain was the least difficult obstacle to overcome.

Man's interference with nature: Another theme T. C. Boyle touches upon is man's dealings with nature – and how nature hits back. The company behind the Arroyo Blanco Estate built the spacious community "comprising a golf course, ten tennis courts [...] and some two hundred and fifty homes" (p. 30) in an area which used to be wilderness, home of coyotes, gophers and rattlesnakes. Delaney is aware that we are "encroaching on the coyote's territory with our relentless and suburban development" (p. 212), and should therefore not be surprised when nature retaliates. **Man is the invader and treats his newly conquered environment carelessly.** Delaney's warning goes unheard. On his explorations into the canyon he notices that people litter the landscape, throw away food, which, in turn, attracts wild animals. **The attacks of the coyote are the first signs that nature will hit back and the apocalyptic landslide marks the final revenge** which forcefully wipes away manmade alterations to natural surroundings.

The coyote: The coyote is mentioned on several occasions in the book and Delaney shows a lot of admiration for this **clever, sly and adaptable creature**. Trying to trap and eradicate the coyote, a measure taken by the Los Angeles County Animal Control Department, does not work, nor does the installation of fences. The coyote is a survivor, and Cándido, América and other illegal immigrants show similar qualities. They also **manage to survive in a hostile environment** and cannot be fenced out – just like the coyote. The word *coyote* is also used for cunning smugglers who help people across a border (see "The Tortilla Curtain").

William Shakespeare, *Othello* (approx. 1603)

Author

William Shakespeare was baptised on April 26, 1564, in Stratford-upon-Avon, where his father was a wealthy glove-maker and town councillor, and his mother a farmer's daughter. He went to the local grammar school and probably became a teacher himself. In 1582 he married Anne Hathaway (1556–1623), and about three years later the couple moved to London. There he worked as both an actor and a playwright. His first plays, probably the comedies *Love's Labour's Lost* and the *Comedy of Errors*, were produced about 1590. There is no certainty about the dates of any of his plays, but for the next 20 years they appeared in a steady stream, 37 in all. In the middle of his career, Shakespeare wrote the tragedies for which he is perhaps most famous, among them *Hamlet*, *Macbeth*, and *King Lear*. He also wrote poems, including a collection of over 100 sonnets. His last production was *The Tempest*, staged in 1611. He died in Stratford in 1616.

Contents

Shakespeare's play *Othello* was probably written around 1603 and first performed at the Globe Theatre in 1604. The first printed version was published in 1622. The plot is based on a story of the Italian novelist and poet Giovanni Battista Giraldi (nicknamed Cinthio), which Shakespeare could have read in Italian or French. The drama comprises five acts. Act I is set in Venice, Acts II to V on Cyprus. The time is the Renaissance (about 1570).

Act I: The play opens with Iago, Othello's Ancient (= *Fähnrich*), and Roderigo, a rich Venetian gentleman meeting in a street in Venice. Roderigo has given Iago money and jewels to win Desdemona, the daughter of Venetian senator Brabantio, over for him. Iago complains that Othello has not promoted him, but chosen a less qualified man, Michael Cassio, as his lieutenant. Although Iago feels offended, he has decided to stay in Othello's service, but only to finally get what he wants. Iago and Roderigo wake Brabantio to tell him that his daughter Desdemona has secretly left the house and married Othello. Iago leaves. Brabantio calls on Roderigo to help him find and confront Othello.
Messengers led by Michael Cassio meanwhile inform Othello that he is wanted by the Duke of Venice because of an imminent Turkish invasion of Cyprus. Roderigo, Brabantio and his men appear on the scene. Brabantio is furious and accuses Othello of having used magic to steal his daughter. When Othello informs him that he has been called to meet the Duke on state matters, Brabantio joins him to put his wrong before the Duke.
In the Council Chamber various messages warn of a Turkish fleet heading towards Cyprus. Othello and Brabantio arrive, the latter repeats his accusations against the Moor. Othello, however, claims that he won Desdemona's love not by magic, but by telling her the story of his life. Desdemona confirms this and professes her love and allegiance to her husband. The Duke sees the case settled and sends Othello on a military mission to defend Cyprus. Desdemona asks permission to accompany her husband.
Roderigo is dejected about the outcome and wants to drown himself. Iago consoles him, saying that he would undermine the couple's loving relationship by convincing Othello that Desdemona betrays him with Cassio. ✳ *etw . untergraben*

Act II: A terrible storm rages, delaying the arrival of the Venetians on Cyprus. Othello eventually makes it to the island with news that the Turkish fleet has been wrecked in the wild sea. Iago tells Roderigo that Desdemona will soon become tired of Othello and is already showing an interest in Cassio. He wants Roderigo to provoke Cassio into a fight, which will disgrace and eventually eliminate the newly appointed lieutenant.
To celebrate the destruction of the Turkish fleet in the storm, the Venetians gather in a hall in the castle. Iago gets Cassio drunk, who, under the influence of alcohol, insults Roderigo and injures Montano, Othello's predecessor in the government of Cyprus. The brawl arouses Othello, who is disgusted by Cassio's behaviour and removes him from his posi-

tion: "Cassio, I love thee, but never more be officer of mine." (II, 3)[2]. Iago advises the desperate Cassio to ask Desdemona for help to regain Othello's favour. Iago's plan is to use Desdemona's pleading for Cassio to make Othello jealous.

Act III: With the help of Iago's wife Emilia, Cassio gets access to Desdemona. Iago makes sure Othello is away inspecting the fortifications of the city so that Cassio can talk to Desdemona, who promises him to speak with her husband on his behalf. Cassio leaves quickly when Othello returns because he does not want to meet the general right now. Desdemona speaks to Othello asking him to take Cassio back, but Othello hesitates. Iago uses Cassio's hasty exit and Desdemona's pleading for Cassio to rouse Othello's suspicion, insinuating that Desdemona is having an affair with the deposed lieutenant. Othello begins to doubt his wife's loyalty, but keeps it secret from her and develops a headache.

Trying to sooth Othello's pain, Desdemona accidentally drops a handkerchief she has received as a gift from her husband. Iago gets hold of it through his wife Emilia, and puts it in Cassio's room. He kindles Othello's jealousy by telling him that he heard Cassio fantasise in his dream about his love for Desdemona and that he has seen Cassio in possession of Desdemona's handkerchief. Othello vows revenge and makes Iago his lieutenant. When Othello asks Desdemona for her handkerchief, she is unable to present it. He is upset and becomes angry and unkind. Jealousy has taken hold of him.

In the meantime, Cassio asks his mistress Bianca to copy the embroidery on the handkerchief he found in his chamber. He does not know that it is Desdemona's.

Act IV: Othello suspects that Desdemona gave the missing handkerchief to her new lover. Iago torments Othello further. When he tells Othello that Cassio said he spent a night with Desdemona, Othello briefly loses consciousness. Cassio enters and Iago asks him to come back later for a conversation. When Othello recovers, Iago instructs him to hide nearby and listen to Cassio's report about his affair with Desdemona. Cassio describes his relationship with the prostitute Bianca in a light-hearted and joking manner. Othello, believing he is talking about Desdemona, is totally enraged: "How shall I murder him, Iago?" (IV, 1). Bianca, who enters to give Cassio the handkerchief back whose embroidery he had asked her to copy, only gives Othello further proof for his wife's infidelity. Iago offers the furious Othello to kill Cassio for him and suggests that he should strangle his wife in the bed where she allegedly committed adultery with Cassio. Desdemona enters with Lodovico, a messenger from Venice, who announces that Othello is commanded home and Cassio should take his place on Cyprus. As Desdemona expresses her joy about this development, assuming that it will end the hostility between her husband and Cassio, Othello strikes her in front of everyone.

Later when the couple are alone, Othello, convinced of his wife's disloyalty, calls Desdemona "whore", "public commoner" and "strumpet" (IV, 2). He tells his wife to wait for him in bed and send Emilia away. In the meantime, Iago has persuaded Roderigo that he has to kill Cassio, if he still wants to have a chance of winning Desdemona over as only Cassio's death will prevent Othello's and Desdemona's departure from the island.

---

2 Die römischen Zahlen beziehen sich auf den Akt, die arabischen Ziffern auf die Szene, auf die hier verwiesen wird.

I 9

Act V: Iago instructs Roderigo to ambush Cassio. As Cassio is seriously injured, Iago pretends to take revenge for him and stabs Roderigo, because the Venetian's death will hide the fact that Iago has kept the gold and the jewels Roderigo had given him for Desdemona.

Othello has decided to kill Desdemona to bring about justice. Although Desdemona professes her innocence, asserting she only loved Othello and did not give her handkerchief to Cassio, Othello stifles her. Emilia comes in to report on Roderigo's death and discovers the dying Desdemona. Othello claims he killed Desdemona because he had proof of her infidelity from Iago, Emilia's husband. Emilia tells him Desdemona never loved anybody else but Othello, who did not deserve her love, and raises alarm. When Emilia discloses that her husband was behind this evil plot, Iago kills her. Othello, overcome with grief, tries to kill Iago, who manages to escape, but is recaptured. The wounded Cassio is carried on the scene and explains how the handkerchief came into his possession. Othello realises his terrible mistake and, kissing the dead Desdemona, stabs himself. Iago is to be tried and executed.

Characters

Othello: The Christian Moor Othello is the protagonist and hero of the play. He is **gentle, eloquent and physically powerful**. Because of his noble qualities he won the love of Desdemona, the daughter of a Venetian senator. Like Shylock in Shakespeare's *The Merchant of Venice*, Othello is a **stranger in the Italian town**. However, in contrast to the Jew Shylock, he is highly respected and honoured by the Duke, his officers and the people of Venice, because he is a brave and reliable general. **In his military function he is urgently needed** for the defence of Cyprus, but, having **darker skin**, he is **not socially accepted** as a person. Othello is aware of this and has therefore kept his courtship and marriage secret. The fact that he is an outsider certainly contributes to his becoming easy prey to Iago.

Iago: Othello's standard bearer Iago is the **villain of the play**. For Shakespeare's contemporaries he was the **personification of evil**. A ruthless cynic, he has a low opinion of human nature and **uses the weaknesses of the people around him** (e. g. Roderigo's lust for Desdemona, Cassio's concerns about his reputation, Othello's jealousy) **to deceive and manipulate them**. Iago hates Othello because he promoted Cassio over Iago's head. He takes his revenge by contriving a plan to alienate Othello and Desdemona. With his lies and insinuations he **turns Othello's love for his wife into blind jealousy**, thus stripping the Moor of his gentle and noble nature and destroying his integrity.

Desdemona: Othello's wife is the daughter of the Venetian senator Brabantio. She knows that her marriage will not meet with the approval of her father and the Venetian aristocratic society. Therefore she agrees to be secretly married. In a confrontation with her father she defends her choice and **stands firm in her allegiance to Othello**. For Desdemona, adultery is unimaginable, and she is completely taken by surprise at Othello's suspicions and his violent behaviour. Up to the very last moment she **professes her innocence**, but falls victim to Othello, who is eaten up by jealousy. For most critics, gentle **Desdemona is the most innocent of all of Shakespeare's heroines**.

Michael Cassio: He is a **highly educated** young man from Florence, whom Othello has promoted to his lieutenant. In Iago's view Cassio is a bookkeeper well-versed in statistics, but **inexperienced in combat**. Iago is furious that Othello preferred Cassio to himself. Thus the Florentine becomes the **object of Iago's contrivances**, when Iago spreads the word that Cassio has an affair with Desdemona. He destroys Cassio's reputation by involving him in a drunken brawl and thus causing his dismissal as lieutenant.

Emilia: Emilia is Iago's wife and Desdemona's **loyal** lady-in-waiting. She knows about her husband's malign nature, but **without realising she assists Iago in contriving his plot**. When she discovers that her mistress has been murdered, she reveals Iago's deceitful manoeuver and **boldly confronts her husband**: "Thou hast not half the power to do me harm […] I care not for thy sword, I'll make thee known" (V, 2).

Themes and Interpretation

Character tragedy: In Shakespeare's early tragedies the catastrophe which destroys the protagonist results from an inescapable and unavoidable fate. For example, the young lovers Romeo and Juliet are doomed, because the stars are in an unfavourable position. In the prologue of the drama the chorus calls them "star-crossed lovers". A coincidence, which cannot be controlled by the two young people, is ultimately responsible for their deaths. In Shakespeare's later plays, the tragedy is not brought about by some higher force or destiny, **the downfall of the protagonist is due to a fault, a flaw, in his character**. These plays, amongst them *Othello*, are referred to as character tragedies. Shakespeare explains the Elizabethan view of the self-inflicted downfall of the hero in his play *Julius Caesar*, in which Cassius states, "The fault, dear Brutus, is not in our stars,/but in ourselves" (I, 2).

Jealousy: The character faults which ultimately cause the tragic development and outcome vary in Shakespeare' plays. In *Macbeth* it is the protagonist's ruthless ambition, in *Hamlet* the hero's insecurity and indecisiveness and in *Othello*, the Moor's gullibility and excessive jealousy. **Othello is a tragic character**, because he is basically a gentle and noble man, but **he fails to see through Iago's intricate net of lies**. He is naïve and therefore susceptible to Iago's ploys. He is convinced that Iago is an honest man, and **his trust in Iago increases in the course of the play**, whereas, on the other hand, **the trust in his devoted wife decreases**. Overwhelmed by suspicion, Othello does not listen to Desdemona's protestations of innocence. Instead, jealousy, the "green-ey'd monster" (III, 3), which Iago has brought to life, leads him astray. In the end **Othello** is completely convinced of his wife's guilt and **believes that it is his duty to kill Desdemona in order to bring about justice and restore order**: "Yet she must die, else she'll betray more men." (V, 2). When it is too late, he realises that he has been manipulated ("not easily jealous, but being wrought"; V, 2) and is completely heart-broken. He feels deep pain and recognises himself as "one that love'd not wisely, but too well" (V, 2). The tragic outcome rouses pity of the audience not only for Desdemona, but also for Othello.

Racial prejudice: The Venetians appreciate and respect Othello as a competent military leader. They rely on his expertise and call for his help when they need him as a soldier and general. However, racial prejudice is very much alive in the Venetian establishment. **Othello's background and the colour of his skin make him an outsider.** Roderigo and Iago **refer to him disparagingly** as "Barbary horse" (I, 1) and "thicklips" (I, 1). In their eyes, and in the view of Desdemona's father, **the match of the Venetian noble girl to the "lascivious Moor"** (I, 1) **is a disgrace**, a "treason of the blood" (I, 1) and thus totally unacceptable. The only person who is free of prejudice and accepts Othello as equal is Desdemona. She trusts him and loves him deeply. She is so devoted to her husband that she places him first, even before her parents.

Honour and reputation: For various characters in the play honour and reputation play an essential part. Iago begins his intrigue when he feels discriminated and insufficiently honoured. Talking to Othello he asserts that a person's good name, his reputation, is more valuable than any worldly possessions: "Good name in man and woman's dear, my lord;/Is the immediate jewel of their souls" (III, 3). Here he appeals to Othello not to let his honour be tarnished by Cassio's affair with Desdemona.

For Cassio, honour and reputation are of overall importance. After his involvement in the nightly brawl, while he was drunk, he feels ashamed and humiliated and implores Iago to help him restore his reputation. To him **reputation** is "the immortal part" (II, 3) which **distinguishes man from animal** and, consequently, **a life without reputation is not worth living**. From a modern point of view, Othello's, Iago's and Cassio's actions are hard to understand, but in the light of the ancient concept of honour and reputation, their train of thought might be easier to reconstruct.

Kurt Vonnegut, *Slaughterhouse-Five* (1969)

Author

Kurt Vonnegut was born in Indianapolis in 1922 into a well-to-do family with German ancestors. Vonnegut calls himself a "fourth-generation German-American". In 1940 he studied biochemistry at Cornell University in Ithaca, New York, and enlisted in the US Army in 1943. During World War II (1939–1945) he was captured prisoner by the Germans and witnessed the firebombing of Dresden by Allied forces in February 1945. After the war Vonnegut took up his studies again, worked as a police reporter and eventually took to full-time writing in 1950. His first novel *Player Piano* (1952) attracted little attention. Through the numerous short stories he wrote for the "slicks", magazines like *Saturday Evening Post*, *McCall's* und *Cosmopolitan*, he became known to a larger readership. Many of his stories and novels contain science-fiction elements, which led critics to class Vonnegut as science-fiction writer – a classification which he rejected. His works include *Cat's Cradle* (1963), *God Bless You, Mr. Rosewater* (1965), *Slapstick* (1976), *Bluebeard* (1987) and *A Man Without a Country* (2005). Vonnegut's most famous work is *Slaughterhouse-Five or The Children's Crusade* (1969) which is based on his disturbing war experiences. The book was well received by critics and readership, and became extremely popular among students. It helped improve Vonnegut's reputation as a "serious author" and was filmed in 1972. Vonnegut died in 2007.

I 12

Contents

Kurt Vonnegut's *Slaughterhouse-Five* comprises ten chapters and is usually considered a "postmodern" novel, which means the plot is not developed chronologically or in a linear order. Instead the narrator jumps back and forth in time and place. The first and last chapters are autobiographical and provide the frame for the main part of the novel which is the biography, the experiences, thoughts and preoccupations of a character called Billy Pilgrim. Billy's life story contains many elements of Vonnegut's own biography, in particular the events during World War II and the bombing of Dresden. In the opening chapter, Vonnegut tells the reader about his difficulties in writing a book about Dresden and explains why he cannot present the horrendous events in the traditional narrative form. With his "war buddy" Bernard V. O'Hare he returns to Dresden in 1967 and meets a taxi driver by the name of Gerhard Müller. Mary, O'Hare's wife, warns Vonnegut not to write a memoir glorifying the war because she thinks that wars are partly encouraged by books and movies. Feeling indebted to these two characters he dedicates his work to Mary O'Hare and Gerhard Müller. Vonnegut also introduces the catchphrase about life and death – "so it goes" – which is often repeated throughout the novel. It expresses both inevitability and predestination, the idea that one cannot escape one's destiny or change events.

In Chapter 2 Vonnegut begins the life story of the main character of the novel, Billy Pilgrim. Many of the events have parallels with Vonnegut's own experiences. The biography is not related in a straightforward manner, but is interspersed with jumps in time, backwards and forwards, from the present of narration (1960s) to the past (Billy's childhood, before his birth and events which occurred in 1945, 1965, 1958, 1961 etc.): "Billy is spastic in time, has no control over where he is going next"(p. 23).[3]

The life of Billy Pilgrim (in chronological order): Billy Pilgrim is born in Ilium, New York, in 1922. Aged 21, he is an inexperienced "college kid" (p. 42) and becomes a chaplain's assistant in the US Army. After training in military manoeuvers in South Carolina, he is transferred to the headquarters of an infant regiment in Luxembourg. During the Battle of the Bulge (= *Ardennenoffensive* in 1944), Billy's regiment is decimated by the Germans and he and three other soldiers (called "The Three Musketeers" by Roland Weary, one of the soldiers), become stranded behind enemy lines. Together with Weary, who saves Billy's life in the hope of being awarded a medal afterwards, he is captured and taken to a collecting point for prisoners of war (POWs). The prisoners are all locked up in boxcars and slowly transported to East Germany. On the train journey, which lasts ten days, Roland Weary hallucinates about "The Three Musketeers". In his delirium, he blames Billy for his plight, which makes his mate Paul Lazzaro swear to avenge him as Roland Weary dies of gangrene (= *Wundbrand*) on the ninth day. Having arrived at the camp, the prisoners are given used overcoats, which are completely frozen and have to be hacked out of an icy pile and – in Billy's case – are full of bullet holes. Billy gets familiar with one of the prisoners, Edgar Derby, a former high school teacher. Billy suffers a nervous breakdown, is taken to hospital and sedated. When he wakes up, Paul Lazzaro tells him that he will be killed after the war. The POWs are then transported to Dresden by

---

3 Page numbers refer to: Kurt Vonnegut, *Slaughterhouse-Five*. Dell Publishing: New York 1991.

I 13

train to work as contract labourers. On their arrival the American prisoners are impressed by the beautiful city. As Dresden does not contain any war industry or troop concentrations, it is untouched by the war and people go about their business as usual. The captured Americans are housed in a "one-story cement-block cube [which] had been built as a shelter for pigs about to be butchered" (p. 152): Slaughterhouse-Five. An American Nazi, Howard W. Campbell Jr., visits the POWs and wants them to join a new German military group to fight against the Russian army. On February 13, 1945, Dresden is destroyed by Allied bombers. Billy survives, but Edgar Derby is shot for stealing a teapot. After the war Billy is honourably discharged from the army. He returns to his hometown and resumes his studies at the School of Optometry. After suffering another nervous breakdown, he commits himself into a veterans' hospital ward for non-violent mental patients. In the hospital, he meets Captain Eliot Rosewater, who introduces him to the science-fiction novels of Kilgore Trout. Trout becomes Billy's favourite writer. Billy finishes his studies, marries Valencia Merble, the unattractive daughter of the owner of the Ilium School of Optometry. Having inherited the business from his father-in-law, Billy becomes a successful and rich optometrist. In 1967, Billy and his war companion Bernard V. O'Hare return to Dresden for a visit. On the night of his daughter's wedding a flying saucer from the planet Tralfamadore arrives. The aliens kidnap Billy and display him naked in a zoo, together with a beautiful movie star, Montana Wildhack. Back on earth, Billy survives a plane crash in Vermont; he was on his way to an optometrists' convention in Canada. Billy is taken to hospital for recovery where he shares a room with Harvard historian Rumfoord. On her way to her husband, Valencia is involved in a car accident and dies of carbon monoxide poisoning. After his release from hospital, Billy wants to tell the world about Tralfamadore and what he learned from its inhabitants about time and the insignificance of death. He gets on a radio talk show and writes letters to a local newspaper. His daughter Barbara believes her father is going crazy. As he had foreseen, Billy Pilgrim meets his death in a stadium in Chicago on February 13, 1976, while talking to "a large crowd on the subject of flying saucers and the true nature of time" (p. 141). He is shot either by a gunman hired by Paul Lazzaro or Lazzaro himself.

Characters

Billy Pilgrim: The main character of the novel is Billy Pilgrim, who displays two completely different personalities. On the one hand, there is the successful, rich businessman – married with two children –, who leads a comfortable life and is well-respected in society (e. g. as President of the Lions Club). On the other hand, there is the insignificant soldier Billy, who serves in World War II, a weakling who seems to have lost any trace of personality. Vonnegut explains this phenomenon: "One of the main effects of war, after all, is that people are discouraged from being characters." (p. 164). Consequently, Billy is a passive victim, constantly pushed about by others. Dressed in cheap civilian clothes or old theatre costumes he looks like a scarecrow or a clown. The most dangerous "weapon" he possesses is a two-inch pencil stub. He wanders through the war, bopping up and down because he lost a heel of his low-cut civilian shoes. Billy Pilgrim is the typical anti-hero, a fool who hardly knows what is happening to him:

I 14

The expression "Jerry", the nickname used by the Allied soldiers for the Germans, is unknown to him (cf. pp. 97/98). He cannot even say which infantry regiment he belongs to (cf. p. 66). After the firestorm in Dresden Billy thinks there are "little logs lying around" (p. 179), which in reality are the remains of people who perished in the flames. All this shows that Billy is still an innocent child taking part in a crusade which is completely beyond his grasp. This is why Vonnegut chose the subtitle *The Children's Crusade* for his book to illustrate the absurdity, cruelty and incomprehensibility of war.

Valencia: Billy marries a rich woman. His wife Valencia Merble is the daughter of the owner of the Ilium School of Optometry, who runs several shops in town. She is rather ugly and fat as she cannot stop eating, and is only interested in the simple things in life (e. g. the patterns on her crystal and silverware). Billy and Valencia enjoy a happy marriage and have two children. Billy is unfaithful only once, when he is drunk at a party.

Barbara and Robert: Billy has two children, Barbara and Robert. In high school, Robert has a lot of trouble, but then he "straightens out" (pp. 24/25), joins the Green Berets as a Marine and fights in Vietnam. Barbara marries an optometrist, whom Billy sets up in business. After Billy's plane crash and her mother's death, Barbara becomes rather worried about her father. Thinking he is senile and cannot care for himself anymore, she insists on putting him under the care of a practical nurse. She is incredibly embarrassed about his letter to the newspaper about the planet Tralfamadore.

Roland Weary: Billy's war companion, who serves as an anti-tank gunner, provides a contrast to the reserved pacifist Billy Pilgrim. He is only eighteen and, like Billy, inexperienced and new to the war. He wanders around behind the enemy lines with two scouts. He likes to refer to the three of them as "The Three Musketeers". Being fat and stupid, Roland has always been unpopular and he takes his frustration out on weaker people. He is a bully, full of aggression, loves weapons and shows a perverse interest in cruelty and torture. He threatens to shoot Billy for not being interested in saving his own life. They get separated when being transported to Germany. Before he dies, Roland Weary makes Paul Lazzaro, a former car thief, promise to have Billy killed.

Bertram Copeland Rumfoord: 70-year-old Rumfoord is a Harvard history professor and the official US Air Force historian. He is writing a book about the Air Force and wants to include a section on Dresden, but is frustrated because a lot of information about the raid is still classified. Rumfoord cannot understand why such a "howling success" (p. 191) is kept a secret. He is merely interested in glorifying the military action and brushes aside any thought on destruction or civilian deaths inflicted.

Themes and Interpretation

The atrocities of war: The major theme of Vonnegut's work is the absurdity and senseless destructiveness of war. When *Slaughterhouse-Five* was published, this subject was a most controversial issue on the political and social agenda. The opposition against the increasing involvement of the American forces in the Vietnam War (1956–1975) peaked on campuses in the USA and Europe (e. g. Germany and France). Protest marchers demanded to put an end to the killing of innocent civilians. In Vietnam, the US military

I 15

sprayed a chemical, Agent Orange, to strip the leaves from plants and forests and dropped napalm bombs to set houses and people on fire. In *Slaughterhouse-Five*, Vonnegut alludes to the Vietnam War (Billy's son joins the Green Berets) and the horrific weapons of mass destruction. Billy Pilgrim's favourite author, science-fiction writer Kilgore Trout, had written a story as early as 1932 in which he predicted the "widespread use of burning jellied gasoline on human beings" (p. 168). Vonnegut uses the bombing of Dresden, which he himself witnessed, as a symbol of the cruelty and destructiveness of any war. Most factual information on the firestorm of 1945, which Vonnegut includes in *Slaughterhouse-Five*, is drawn from a book by David Irving, *The Destruction of Dresden*, published in 1963. Parts of two forewords to the American edition by high-ranking members of the armed forces are cited in *Slaughterhouse-Five*. They show the different ways of assessing the Dresden bombings. Royal Air Force Marshal Sir Robert Saundby maintains that the bombing of the city was unnecessary from a strategic point of view, causing the death of 135,000 people (cf. pp. 187/188). Modern research and more up-to-date studies meanwhile put the death toll around 25,000 people. US General Ira C. Eaker, on the other hand, claims it should be remembered that Nazi Germany started the war, committed cruelties in the concentration camps and bombed the British city of Coventry in 1940 (cf. p. 187). Vonnegut uses *Slaughterhouse-Five* to hint at the common excuse brought forward in any war or conflict: the aggressor usually compensates the feeling of guilt with the conviction that the action, although deplorable, was necessary to avoid more evil. To illustrate this, Vonnegut quotes US President Harry S. Truman justifying the bombing of Hiroshima as a necessity for the salvation of civilians (cf. pp. 185/186). When *Slaughterhouse-Five* was published, the memories of the atomic bombings of Hiroshima and Nagasaki in 1945 (causing 150,000–246,000 casualties) were still very much alive and the fear of the total annihilation of the human race in a nuclear war was widespread. During the years of the Cold War (1949–1991) the US and the Soviet Union fought for supremacy as world leaders and there was the constant threat of an atomic war. To Vonnegut, the horrors of Dresden and Hiroshima were drastic examples of awful carnages and needless suffering that should not be forgotten. Vonnegut became a cult figure of American literature, *Slaughterhouse-Five* is known as a brilliant anti-war novel.

Predetermination versus free will: Vonnegut included science-fiction elements in *Slaughterhouse-Five* to illustrate diverging opinions about free will and predetermination. The Tralfamadorians cannot understand what "free will" is all about. They claim everything that is happening is predetermined, which means things will happen anyway and cannot be changed or prevented. This philosophy is summed up with the fatalistic and stoical formula "So it goes". The phrase recurs throughout the novel, whenever somebody dies or a catastrophe happens. The monotonous repetitions emphasise the inevitability of events and the absurdity of existence. When Billy wants to know from the Tralfamadorians how the planet can live at peace, he is told that wars will continue until finally the Earth and the universe will be wiped out due to an experiment with new fuel. Billy's original concept of "free will" is much more optimistic concerning the future: he believes that man can decide, influence and prevent events. Sadly enough, by the end of his life, Billy has completely accepted the Tralfamadorian idea of predetermination (cf. p. 142).

Scholar Says Arrest Will Lead Him To Explore Race in Criminal Justice
by Krissah Thompson, Washington Post, Wednesday, July 22, 2009

Harvard scholar Henry Louis Gates Jr. has spent much of his life studying the complex history of race and culture in America, but until last week he had never had the experience that has left so many black men questioning the criminal justice system.

Gates was arrested outside his house in Cambridge, Mass., after a neighbor reported
5 seeing two black men in the middle-class, predominantly white area pushing against the front door.

"I studied the history of racism. I know every incident in the history of racism from slavery to Jim Crow segregation," Gates told The Washington Post on Tuesday in his first interview about the episode. "I haven't even come close to being arrested. I would have
10 said it was impossible."

Instead, in a country where one in nine young black men are in prison, where racial profiling is still practiced, the arrest of a renowned scholar on a charge of disorderly conduct in front of his house last Thursday has fueled an ongoing debate about race in America in the age of its first black president. The charge against him was dropped Tuesday, but
15 Gates said he plans to use the attention and turn his intellectual heft and stature[1] to the issue of racial profiling. He now wants to create a documentary on the criminal justice system, informed by the experience of being arrested not as a famous academic but as an unrecognized black man.

Gates has come to see the incident as a modern lesson in racism and the criminal jus-
20 tice system. The police department views it as an "regrettable and unfortunate" incident that "should not be viewed as one that demeans[2] the character and reputation of Prof. Gates or the character of the Cambridge Police Department."

Here is Gates' account of what happened:

After returning from a week in China researching the genealogy[3] of cellist Yo-Yo Ma,
25 Gates found himself locked out of his house, and he and his driver began pushing against the front door. The sight of two black men forcing open a door prompted an emergency call to [the] police.

The white officer who arrived found Gates in the house (the driver was gone) and asked him to step outside. Gates refused, and the officer followed him in. Gates showed
30 him his ID, which included his address, then demanded that the officer identify himself. The officer did not comply, Gates said. He then followed the officer outside, saying repeatedly, "Is this how you treat a black man in America?" The police report said that Gates was "exhibiting loud and tumultuous behavior" and that the officer, Sgt. James Crowley, identified himself. "We stand by whatever the officer said in his report," said
35 Sgt. James DeFrancesco, a spokesman for the Cambridge Police Department. He would not comment on Gates' version of his arrest.

The department said that Crowley tried to calm Gates, but that the professor would not cooperate and said, "You don't know who you're messing with."

"These actions on behalf of Gates served no legitimate purpose and caused citizens
40 passing by this location to stop and take notice while appearing surprised and alarmed," the report said.

Gates said he does not think that anything he did justified the officer's actions. He walks with a cane and said he did not pose a threat. [...]

He has no qualms about the neighbor who called the police.
45 "I'm glad that someone would care enough about my property to report what they thought was some untoward invasion," Gates said. "If she saw someone tomorrow that looked like they were breaking in, I would want her to call 911. I would want the police to come. What I would not want is to be presumed to be guilty. That's what the deal was. It didn't matter how I was dressed. It didn't matter how I talked. It didn't matter how I com-
50 ported myself. That man was convinced that I was guilty."

[...]

(652 words)

http://www.washingtonpost.com/wp-dyn/content/article/2009/07/21/AR2009072101771_2.html?sid= ST2009072301777 [retrieved on July 13, 2010]

1   seine intellektuelle Kraft und seinen Einfluss
2   herabsetzen
3   Stammbaum

Assignments

1. Point out what seems to have happened on that summer night in Cambridge, MA. (30 BE)

2. To what extent can the way Mr. Gates is treated be seen as an act of discrimination? Explain by relating the incident to examples of racial discrimination dealt with in class. (35 BE)

3. In the text at hand the neighbor tries to be a good citizen by keeping an eye on Mr. Gates' property. It seems possible that in the future one will be able to ensure the security of each individual citizen by means of total electronic surveillance.
   Discuss the advantages and disadvantages of this development. Refer to texts read or films viewed in class. (35 BE)

Lösungsvorschläge

Teaching modules referred to:
The article at hand and questions 1 and 2 refer to the modules The Challenge of Individualism – USA *(Q1) in which the aspect of* living together *covers* ethnic groups *in general with special focus on* African Americans. *Question 3 is based on the modules* Science and Technology *(Q1) and* Order, Vision, Change *(Q3), which includes* utopian *and* dystopian *literature.*

1. *How to approach the task:*
    Step 1 *Read the text carefully and focus your attention on the events of the night in question. Underline what happened and take notes. Perhaps you will find a flow chart of the events helpful.*
    Step 2 *Make sure you do not include too much information. Gates' plans for the future, his general views on racism or the criminal justice system and what he thinks about his neighbour are not relevant in this context.*
    Step 3 *Use your own words to give a clear explanation of the incident and the people involved.*

    In the article the reader is informed that the African-American Harvard professor, Henry Louis Gates Jr., whose field of study focuses on race relations in the USA, claims that he became a victim of racist treatment by the police in July 2009. After returning home from a research trip to China he found himself locked out of his home in a mainly white middle class neighbourhood in Cambridge, Mass. Together with his driver he pushed open the front door of his house. This caused a neighbour to inform the police that two black men were intruding next door. Upon arrival a white police officer, James Crowley, ordered Gates to come out of the house. When Gates refused to do so, the policeman entered the building. Gates claims that he then identified himself and that the officer refused to show his ID. Later Gates followed the officer out of the house and complained about the unjust treatment of black men in the USA. Finally the professor was arrested for disorderly conduct.
    The white officer claims that Gates' behaviour had been disruptive, whereas he had identified himself and had tried to deescalate the conflict.   *(192 words)*

2. *How to approach the task:*
    Step 1 *There are two aspects to this question and both must be approached carefully. The first part focuses on the incident described in the text. Try to determine whether Mr. Gates was arrested as a result of racial discrimination or regular criminal investigation.*
    Step 2 *Concentrate on the material dealt with in class, whether it is literary, non-literary or film material. Towards the end relate the obvious examples of racism to what happened to Mr. Gates and come to a conclusion.*

GK 2011-3

Racial discrimination is generally defined as intentional bad treatment on the basis of race or colour of skin. In the case at hand Mr. Gates was possibly confronted with racial bias from three sides: his neighbour, the policeman who arrested him and the police department. As far as the neighbour is concerned it is difficult to assess whether she called the police because Gates and his driver were black. She might also have rung an emergency call if the intruders had been white. That is probably the reason why Gates did not feel offended by her, but praised her vigilance instead. Yet, the fact that this neighbour informed the police that the alleged intruders were black might have influenced the policeman, who was allegedly prejudiced against the professor. According to Gates, the policeman violated the rights of the suspect by intruding the house and refusing to identify himself. He possibly gave a false report on the events. Finally, he arrested Gates, although he knew that he was not a burglar.

This unlawful treatment of a suspect is more likely to happen to a black suspect than to a white one. Possibly the officer reacted that way because he was sure that he was going to encounter a black perpetrator. The many recorded cases of police violence all over the country demonstrate that many officers consider black suspects guilty upon arrival at the scene of a crime. Although the charges against Gates were dropped later, the reaction of the police department can safely be identified as an act of racial discrimination. Despite the fact that the police officer and Mr. Gates contradicted each other concerning what really happened that night, the police department backed the version of the officer in public, instead of investigating the circumstances. Obviously, the department considers white officers more credible than black suspects. Additionally, the fact that the charges were dropped indicates that the department either realized that it had made a mistake or feared further negative publicity about racial discrimination.

In general, the obvious injustices of the segregation era have been overcome since the Civil Rights Movement led by Dr. Martin Luther King Jr. It is no longer the case that African Americans are barred from white society with the help of discriminatory Jim Crow Laws or literacy tests. Neither do African Americans experience the exclusion from white society, nor are they confronted with all white courts or juries any longer. Affirmative action and fervent efforts at integration have contributed to the progress that has been achieved concerning race relations.

Nevertheless, this does not mean that discrimination and racial stereotypes have been completely eradicated. The history of police violence as it manifested itself in the Rodney King incident in the 1990s shows that there is still enough prejudice against African Americans or members of other ethnic groups. In the film *Crash* the police officer Ryan harasses a black couple and molests the woman sexually while conducting a body search for weapons. In the course of the film he is presented as an opponent of affirmative action with a special bias against African Americans, since he feels that they are competing with the common white folks on the job market. Racial profiling is another example of the police considering members of certain ethnic groups more likely to commit crimes.

Many police departments across the USA have recently become sensitive to the issue of racial prejudices within the police force itself and have implemented anti-racism programs and workshops for their officers. This was, for example, the case in New

York after nooses had been found hanging in front of lockers that belonged to black police officers. All in all, the case of Mr. Gates shows that discrimination has not stopped completely. It has become more subtle and harder to detect. *(632 words)*

3. *How to approach the task:*
   Step 1 Before you begin writing make notes on the advantages and disadvantages of total electronic surveillance. Consider its potential, as well as possible dangers. Your notes might look like this:
   Advantages
   - *efficient technology*
   - *precise face recognition*
   - *cameras have become cheaper*
   - *widespread acceptance*
   - *convey a sense of security*
   - *help to reduce crime*
   - *help prevent terrorist attacks, e. g. at airports*
   - *helpful in criminal investigations*
   Disadvantages
   - *crime is committed elsewhere*
   - *it is intrusive*
   - *privacy is infringed*
   - *private lives can be minutely reconstructed*
   - *systems can be entered and personal information can be misused*
   - *positioning technology can be used to track somebody down*
   - *racial profiling undermines basic human rights and entails inequality*
   Step 2 You are expected to discuss the question critically and to support your view on a differentiated basis. Keep in mind that your text should have a clear structure containing the advantages and disadvantages, as well as your personal opinion.
   Step 3 Consider the texts or films dealt with in class. Relevant fields of study in this context are biotechnology, electronic media and ecological developments. References to dystopian literature like e. g. George Orwell's 1984 *or Ray Bradbury's* Fahrenheit 451 *will help you to prove that you do not turn a blind eye to the possible dangers of surveillance technology.*

The increasing number of surveillance cameras and other technological devices in so many public places like banks, parking lots, airports and even in schools and hospitals shows that this technology is rapidly spreading all over the world. One reason for the popularity of this new surveillance technology is that it has become cheaper. At the same time the quality has improved. Especially face recognition technology has become a lot more precise in recent years. Surveillance cameras are also widely approved of because people are convinced that they deter criminals from committing crimes. Especially since the terrorist attacks of 9/11 people have longed for a greater measure of security, most of all in air traffic. This is understandable and it has been proven that crime rates have decreased in areas where cameras are installed. Yet, critics point out that crimes are committed elsewhere and that suicide bombers do not mind being filmed before an attack. There is no doubt, though, that modern technology supports effective investigations once a crime has been committed. Camera footage helps police officials and private security to identify criminals. Supporters believe that total electronic surveillance will be able to guarantee the security of each individual in the near future.

Nevertheless, there are always two sides to a coin. Is it really true that the measure of security will be increased? In his novel *1984* George Orwell emphasizes the dangers of being observed day and night and of not even knowing when one was under scrutiny. The message the novel conveys is that surveillance technology can curtail individual liberty and freedom when it is used in the name of a totalitarian system. In *1984* the constant supervision and control of the Inner Party members with the help of spies, helicopters, Thought Police, as well as telescreens in public places and private homes are a means of exerting power. Orwell depicts a terrible scenario of a totalitarian state that monitors its elite for signs of Thoughtcrime. Suspects and even their names disappear. Everyone is pressed into Party-related activities which further eradicate individuality, the ultimate threat to the Party.

To prevent modern technology from becoming a means of social control it is essential to weigh anti-terrorism concerns against privacy and individual liberties. The American Civil Liberties Union and other privacy groups have been demanding limitations and strict control of collected data, so that they do not end up in the wrong hands. They point out that the majority of the millions of closed circuit cameras in the USA or Great Britain are operated by private companies, which might sell or unlawfully distribute the material. This can be just as dangerous as if a smart card that reveals the complete personal or medical history of an individual within seconds is misused for, e. g., pre-employment scanning to filter out ethnic groups or disabled persons.

Face recognition technology used to scan large crowds or body search scanning can be applied to certain ethnic groups for racial profiling. If modern technology is used for targeting certain individuals, we can fall victim to an Orwellian system that ensures conformity and, for example, racial homogeneity in the name of total security. Therefore, I do think that lawmakers should pay special attention to strict supervision of the lawful gathering and use of information, because there is the danger of national identity cards and racial profiling turning innocent Arab-Americans into terrorists or innocent African Americans into criminal suspects. It should definitely be ensured that modern technology is used to make all people safer without posing a threat to individual liberties and privacy.

(597 words)

Going to work

Nalini, the first-person narrator of this extract from Preethi Nair's novel "One hundred shades of white", has been abandoned by her husband. Ashamed, she tells her two children that their father died on a trip abroad. She does not ask her family in India for help. Apart from her acquaintance Maggie she does not know anybody in London.

We had to move to a place in the East End of London, an area heavily populated by immigrants. It looked poor: filthy children were playing on the streets, fighting over whatever little toys they had. […]

I looked at the shabby home she [= Maggie] was offering us and I despaired. Smelly
5 carpets, damp, peeling ceilings with a constant drip, drip, drip from the leaking roof. What kind of place was it to bring up children?

Having abundance brings many choices and when I am faced with decisions today, I relish[1] them, revelling and indulging in possibilities and consequences. Back then, there was none of this. Even contemplating momentarily how the children were feeling was an
10 extravagance. It was a fight for survival and this eliminates the luxury of emotion: if you stop and contemplate you lose the battle and so I was grateful for the fact that there was no time. We arrived on Friday evening, I spent two sleepless nights learning how to sew and on Monday, I was taken to the factory.

The factory was situated on a run-down industrial estate a twenty-minute bus ride
15 away. These twenty minutes were filled preparing myself mentally for the day ahead and then observing the actions of the workers who clambered on at the various stops. Some of them were Irish or Polish; most were Pakistani women dressed in salvar kamise[2] and shawls. A scattering[3] were Indian women in saris, socks and sandals who glared at me in my western clothes. All managed to find their respective countrywomen and huddled to-
20 gether chatting. The Irish made the most noise and livened up the dead journey with their laughter.

Maggie had taken me to see the boss, Mr Humphries, a fat, bald man who seemed happy to see her. He was about forty-five, chewed on a pencil which he kept behind his ear, and cleared his throat every five minutes. Maggie and this Humphries man had a con-
25 versation. I don't know exactly what they said but he showed me to a table with a machine.

Maggie took a piece of red material from the basket and placed it on the sewing machine. Manoeuvring it carefully, she produced the template of a skirt that I was to copy. After I had done a few, she smiled. The Humphries man came to inspect. He nodded and Maggie left.

30 It was 1978 and I was alone in a strange country at the age of twenty-six. This first place of employment, Humphries & Co, Bow, was a badly-lit factory, where I sat making shabby dreams for two small children. I would catch the bus, punch my card in at eight o'clock in the morning and sit at my machine, just sewing. The monotony of the noise would take me far away, with my children and mother, back to India, to a beautiful home

35 with a veranda surrounded by mango trees. [...] The noise would bore through the memories, but I would stitch them together with a fabric of sunshine and laughter. [...]

I would be the first person on the bus and the first person off it, running home in the dark to see my children, but by the time I arrived, they would be almost asleep and then whilst they slept, I cooked. Cooked whatever they needed for the next day, cooked just to
40 forget. Forget that somewhere I was losing them ... I had to continue. There was no choice. At night, their warm bodies would cling to me as I stroked their hair and touched their sleeping faces, tears rolling down my cheeks, whispering over and over again, "I know I am not enough for you, not at all enough." *(614 words)*

Nair, Preethi: One hundred shades of white. London, Harper Collins, 2004, pp. 89–92

1   to enjoy
2   langes Hemd und Pluderhose
3   a small number

Assignments

1. Describe the narrator's situation after her arrival in London.   (30 BE)

2. Compare Nalini's experiences either to those of immigrants to Australia
   or to the U.S.A. Include references to texts read/films viewed in class.   (40 BE)

3. *"It was a fight for survival and this eliminates the luxury of emotion:*
   If you stop and contemplate you lose the battle."
   Explain the statement and discuss its implications.   (30 BE)

Lösungsvorschläge

Teaching modules referred to:
The focus of the extract lies on the teaching module Work and industrialization *covered in (Q2), especially on* business, industry and the environment. *The context then extends to the module* Promised lands: dreams and realities, *looking at* social issues *in* Australia *(Q3), and to the concept of* the American Dream *in the* USA *(Q1).*

1. *How to approach the task:*
   Knowledge of the social, political and economic situation of Great Britain is not relevant in this first task. Instead, emphasis should be put on the emotional situation of the character and on the setting.

   The main theme of the extract taken from the novel *One hundred shades of white* by Preethi Nair is the terrible and desperate situation of Nalini, a young mother of twenty-six who has just been abandoned by her husband and struggles hard to make ends meet. In a flashback to 1987, Nalini, the first-person narrator, gives an accurate description of her emotional and material situation shortly after her husband has left her.
   Nalini finds herself in a desperate situation. She is penniless, jobless and has two little children. Her only friend Maggie helps her find a shabby flat in a rundown area of London "heavily populated by immigrants" (ll. 1/2). The setting is violent and threatening and even little children are affected by deficiencies of all kinds and are fighting for survival (ll. 2/3). Even more depressing is the flat she moves to, which is damp, smelly and dilapidated (ll. 4/5).
   Nalini immediately realizes that this new environment is hostile to the education and upbringing of her children (ll. 5/6) and is just about to despair (l. 4). But she quickly comes to the conclusion that feelings of remorse and desperation are a form of luxury she cannot afford in their "fight for survival" (l. 10). Her desperate external situation without material resources soon stands in contrast to her strong determination to overcome poverty and the stroke of fate (ll. 10–13). She is not willing to give up but accepts the challenge in an extraordinary way.
   Her friend Maggie arranges a job in a factory for Nalini (l. 22). She just has two days to learn how to sew (l. 12). She knows that she can only rely on herself and apparently isolates herself from her fellow countrymen (ll. 18–20). She starts work early in the morning and only gets back home late at night. Not willing to complain, she prefers to overcome the monotony of the tedious work by dreaming of a paradise-like home surrounded by trees and dominated by laughter and sunshine (ll. 34–36). Nevertheless, she sadly has to admit that her relationship to her children is suffering and that she is slowly losing them (ll. 40, 42). Still, knowing she has no choice, she accepts the unsatisfying situation (ll. 40–42) by trying to get some comfort at night when she is finally able to touch and stroke her children. Although she does everything in her power to be a good mother, she is still sad and haunted by strong feelings of guilt towards her children, who she is forced to neglect during the day (l. 44).

All in all, the narrator's situation seems sad and almost hopeless. She is an abandoned young mother of two children who struggles to survive in a hostile environment, but she does try to preserve their dignity and humanity. *(497 words)*

2. *How to approach the task:*
   Before you deal with this assignment make a list of texts read, films viewed and the vo-
   cabulary learned in class concerning the topic of immigration. Then ask yourself what
   connection you can see between Nalini's situation and the situation of immigrants to
   Australia or the U.S.A., focusing on similarities but also differences. Limit the number
   of examples to three to four convincing ones. Structure your analytical essay carefully
   and explore what is typical in this situation.

The extract from the novel *One hundred shades of white* by Preethi Nair deals with the desperate situation of a mother of two little children in a strange social, economic and political environment. After emigrating from India to London, she is abandoned by her husband and thus confronted with poverty, unemployment and social insecurity. Close to desperation, she develops an unusually strong feeling of determination, suppresses her feelings of self-pity and looks for a job to support her family. She is offered help by an English friend, Maggie, who procures her a job in a factory. Nalini is rewarded for her determination to learn how to sew in only two days and is hired as a seamstress. Even though she takes the job for her children's sake, she is tortured by strong feelings of guilt because she feels that she is neglecting them as she can only see them at night.

Nalini is confronted with a number of negative but also positive experiences more or less typical of people who have immigrated to industrialized and economically superior countries. They are faced with unimaginable social and economic difficulties that can only be overcome by self-confidence, determination and the ability to suppress feelings of desperation or self-pity. Nevertheless, open societies seem to offer opportunities for people who are open-minded, strong and unwilling to give up and finally reward those people for their tenacity.

Nalini's situation can be compared to the situation of American immigrants today. Generally, one can say that the U.S.A. has always attracted people from all over the world dreaming of new social, political and economic opportunities. The new country has always promised liberty, equality and the pursuit of happiness. Liberated from the oppressive conditions of their former countries, many people have dreamt of a new beginning and have hoped to become successful examples of the American Dream.

Surveys show that the American Dream is still very much alive in all people willing to take the risk of a new beginning, even though the conditions have changed and the market has become more challenging. Sometimes, the dream turns into a nightmare.

Texts like *One Mom's Pursuit of the American Dream* by Dianne Hales show that people who immigrate to the USA have a clear vision of their future. Marinela, the protagonist, arrives in the USA when she is a little girl of thirteen. She takes intensive English lessons and becomes a very good student. After two years of college she gets married and starts a family. When divorced, she goes back to college knowing that education and hard work are the key to success. Like Nalini, Marinela is very determined and hard to stop. Unimpressed by difficulties, she feels she has a responsibility towards herself and her children, who are the driving forces in her life.

At the beginning of every process of migration there is hope. Nevertheless, song writers like Bruce Springsteen seem to be more interested in exploring the dangers of the immigration process. His song *Sinaloa Cowboys* deals with illegal immigration from Mexico. The protagonists, two young brothers, are driven by great expectations. Unskilled and poorly educated, they come to California and earn much money by getting involved in illegal drug activities, risking their health and lives. When the illegal laboratory explodes, one of the brothers dies.

Bruce Springsteen prefers to show the dark side of immigration. He criticizes people who take advantage of the immigrants' hopeless and desperate situation and describes the dangers young immigrants are exposed to. They leave their families, cross the borders full of hope and, being attracted by the promise of easy made money, end up as drug dealers. Too late the surviving brother realizes that the effort committed exceeded the profits by far. Quite symbolically, he digs up the money they have saved and buries his brother in its place. The boys do not have Nalini's moral strength and resolve. Young and inexperienced, their prospect of living a self-determined life is rather limited, and their chances to change this, too.

Only recently, newspapers reported how immigrants from Mexico were exposed to the "state's crackdown" in Arizona and were forced to leave the country as the Senate Bill 1070, passed in April 2010, aimed at "turfing out" illegal immigrants. Additionally, legal immigrants were forced to always carry their ID papers with them. *World and Press*, for example, presented the story of Patricia Rosas, an undocumented worker, who had already lived and worked in Arizona for twelve years. She was suddenly forced to pack, leave her bungalow on the outskirts of Phoenix and head towards California to eventually start a new life. Fortunately, a few months later, judges decreed that the Senate Bill 1070 would no longer come into force. This example shows that deficient immigration laws can threaten everything one has worked and suffered for.

In conclusion, one can say that immigration is not free of risks – positive examples like Nalini's cannot hide this point – but offers opportunities to everybody who is self-confident, determined, open-minded and adapts successfully to the requirements of the new environment.   *(843 words)*

3. *How to approach the task:*
    Step 1 *Briefly explain the context of the statement and then look at the words and meanings in detail.*
    Step 2 *Think about a more abstract interpretation: how could Nalini's statement refer to society in general?*

Nalini, the narrator and protagonist of the novel *One hundred shades of white* by Preethi Nair, describes the desperate situation of a single parent who, confronted with poverty and unemployment, cannot afford the luxury of contemplating the injustice of the world. The dramatic choice of words "fight for survival" underlines the seriousness of her situation, a situation in which people are dehumanized and reduced to behave by instinct.

The words "fight" and "battle" reveal the protagonist's desperate situation of existential dimensions. They allude to the fact that life is a constant threat and giving up not an option. Abandoned by her husband, too proud to ask for help and as a mother of two children she has to support and take care of, Nalini realizes that she cannot reflect on the causes of her hopeless situation but must take up the "fight for survival". The animalistic connotation of the word illustrates a world that seems to be governed by natural law, too brutal for civilized behavior.

Although Nalini is aware of the fact that emotions and contemplation are part of human existence, she prefers to suppress them and considers them as a hindering form of weakness.

Despite all that, the extract reveals that her existential situation makes her even more loving and develop a profound feeling of responsibility towards her children, who she seems to love more than anything else. Neither the inhuman living conditions nor the hard and tedious work can dehumanize Nalini and transform her into a selfish person. The extract shows that an existential threat can bring to light unexpected strength and outstanding, exceptional moral behavior in man. Too engaged in hard work and in the daily fight for survival, Nalini loses sight of her moral qualities and seems to perceive herself only as a mother who is neglecting her parental duties.

However, the statement carries strong negative implications, too. On a more general level, it also implies that our society only expects and rewards winners. It underlines that life in general is perceived as a constant fight that eliminates every kind of human and moral behavior. It indirectly shows that people are addicted to competition and fully comply to this kind of social and economic "law". Under the given circumstances, it is hard to imagine human relationships like friendship or partnership. It is more likely to imagine lose relationships of short duration basically based on short term interests.

A society which considers contemplation and emotion as a form of luxury has definitely lost its human and moral standards and has declared war to humanity. It will not be able to enjoy its great cultural achievements but perceives them as temporary and defective and in need of improvement in the daily battle for survival.

It reduces the complexity of human beings and transforms them into slaves of efficiency. Since winning seems to be everything and daily life a battle, people will not be able to enjoy art and beauty or social relationships which require a higher form of contemplation. Losers in the battle will not receive any attention and the danger of racism and discrimination increases.

In conclusion, one can say that a society governed by such a radical form of existence runs a great risk. It exposes people to a permanent threat, undesirable alienation, and destroys solidarity. *(551 words)*

Teil A: Aufgabe zur Sprachmittlung

Deutschlands heimliche Boombranche

von Carsten Görig, 05. August 2007

Kleine Mädchen spielen anders. Diese Erfahrung durfte gerade der Spielehersteller Eidos machen. Während der englische Hersteller bisher hauptsächlich Actiontitel wie „Tomb Raider", „Hitman" oder „Just Cause" vertrieben hat, ist mit „Ponyfriends" gerade das erste Pferdespiel erschienen. Und damit mussten sich die Mitarbeiter der Hamburger Niederlas-
5 sung[1] ganz neuen Herausforderungen stellen. Zum Beispiel, dass bei einem Preisaus-
schreiben[2] mit Malwettbewerb Postkörbe voller Einsendungen kommen.

„Sowas habe ich hier noch nicht erlebt", staunt PR-Manager Theodossios Theodoridis und erzählt von kunstvoll gemalten Bildern und aufwändig gestalteten Bastelarbeiten[3], die eingeschickt werden.

10 Marina Selikowitsch hat das Staunen schon länger hinter sich. Sie vertritt das Hamburger Softwarehaus dtp, das mit Titeln wie „Meine Tierpension" oder „Meine Tierarzt-
praxis" Marktführer[4] im Bereich der Mädchenspiele ist. Und davon Mengen verkauft,
über die die meisten Anbieter erwachsenerer Games mehr als glücklich wären. Im niedrigen sechsstelligen Bereich liegen die Verkaufszahlen vieler der Tierspiele. Das sind
15 Zahlen, die nur wenige Actiontitel erreichen.

Mundpropaganda statt Marketing

Dazu kommt eine Verkaufskurve[5], von der die meisten Spielehersteller träumen. Denn ei-
gentlich gilt im Spielemarkt: Was sich in den ersten drei Wochen nach Veröffentlichung
nicht verkauft hat, bleibt liegen und verkauft sich erst wieder, wenn der Preis gesenkt
20 wird. Bei den Tierspielen ist es umgekehrt: Sie erreichen die besten Verkäufe erst Wochen
nach dem Erscheinen und verkaufen sich auch Monate später noch gut. Eine treue Fan-
basis macht es möglich. Empfehlungen werden auf dem Schulhof ausgetauscht. Weshalb
sich beispielsweise „Ponyfriends" erst ab der dritten Woche richtig gut verkauft hat. [...]

Bei „Meine Tierpension" geht es darum, eine ebensolche zu betreiben und auszubauen.
25 Angefangen wird mit einer Schildkrötenschlafstelle, am Ende ist es ein ganzes Tierhotel.
Managementfähigkeiten werden mit Tierliebe verknüpft, denn natürlich darf keiner der
Gäste vernachlässigt werden. Hunde brauchen Auslauf, Katzen müssen geknuddelt werden und Pferde gestriegelt. Jungs werden sich mit Grausen abwenden, die Mädchen finden es toll. [...]

30 **Zur Abwechslung haben die Deutschen die Nase vorn**
Bei vielen dieser Spiele handelt es sich um deutsche Produkte. Kleine Entwicklerstudios
aus der ganzen Republik arbeiten mit vergleichsweise niedrigen Budgets an diesen Titeln
– und liefern gute Qualität ab. Das müssen sie auch: „Es spricht sich sehr schnell rum,
wenn ein Spiel nicht gut ist", sagt Selikowitsch. Weshalb es für die Firmen auch wichtig

ist, ein offenes Ohr für Kundinnenwünsche zu haben. „Die Mädchen sind sehr mitteilsam", erzählt sie, „weshalb wir unsere Foren[6] sehr genau lesen und auch schnell reagieren, wenn Fragen aufkommen." [...]   *(387 Wörter)*

http://www.spiegel.de/netzwelt/spielzeug/0,1518,497981,00.html [retrieved on July 13, 2010]

1   branch
2   competition
3   handicrafts
4   market leader
5   sales curve
6   discussion forum

Assignment

You are doing an internship with Game Developer Cobra Mobile Ltd in Dundee.
Write a summary of the article for your boss to help him decide about investing in a new game from Germany.

Teil B: Verkürzte Textaufgabe

FTC[1] Facts for Consumers

JULY 2006 – At-Home Genetic Tests: A Healthy Dose of Skepticism May Be the Best Prescription

Could a simple medical test tell you if you are likely to get a particular disease? Could it evaluate your health risks and even suggest a specific treatment? Could you take this test in the privacy of your home, without a doctor's prescription or guidance?
   Some companies say genetic testing can do all this and more. They claim that at-home
5 genetic testing can screen for diseases and provide a basis for choosing a particular diet, dietary supplement, lifestyle change, or medication. They sell their tests in supermarkets and drugstores, and they advertise their services in print, on television, and online. [...]

Interpreting Test Results

Most genetic tests look at only a small number of the more than 20,000 genes in the hu-
10 man body. A positive result means that the testing laboratory found unusual characteristics or changes in the genes it tested. [...] A negative result means that the laboratory found no unusual characteristics or changes in the genes it tested. This could mean that a person doesn't have a particular disease, doesn't have an increased risk of developing the disease, or isn't a carrier of the disease. Or it could mean that the test missed the specific
15 genetic changes associated with a particular disease. [...]

Company Claims

Be wary of claims about the benefits these products supposedly offer. Some companies claim that at-home genetic tests can measure the risk of developing a particular disease, like heart disease, diabetes, cancer, or Alzheimer's. But the FDA[2] and CDC[3] say they

20 aren't aware of any valid studies that prove these tests give accurate results. Having a particular gene doesn't necessarily mean that a disease will develop; not having a particular gene doesn't necessarily mean that the disease will not.

Some companies also may claim that a person can protect against serious disease by choosing special foods and nutritional supplements[4]. Consequently, the results of their at-
25 home tests often include dietary advice and sales offers for "customized" dietary supplements. But the advice rarely goes beyond standard sensible dietary recommendations. The FDA and CDC say they know of no valid scientific studies showing that genetic tests can be used safely or effectively to recommend nutritional choices.

Be skeptical of claims that the tests can assess a person's ability to withstand certain
30 environmental exposures, like particular toxins or cigarette smoke. The FDA and CDC aren't aware of any valid scientific studies that show that genetic tests can be used to predict whether a person can withstand environmental exposures.

Recently, some companies have claimed their at-home tests can give information about how a person's body will respond to a certain treatment, and how well people will
35 respond to a particular drug. This claim is based on current medical research that shows differences in drug effectiveness based on genetic make-up. But, say federal experts, while these tests may provide some information your doctor needs or uses to make treatment decisions for a specific condition, they are not a substitute for a physician's judgment and clinical experience.   *(495 words)*

© *US Federal Trade Commission; http://www.ftc.gov/bcp/edu/pubs/consume/health/hea02.shtm*
[retrieved on August 20, 2010]

1   FTC – Federal Trade Commission: U.S. government agency for consumer protection
2   FDA – U.S. Food and Drug Administration: government agency for health protection
3   CDC – Center for Disease Control and Prevention: government agency for disease control
4   nutritional supplements: Nahrungsergänzungsmittel

Assignments

1. Point out what the text says about at-home genetic tests.   (30 BE)

2. Compare the attitude favoured in the text at hand to attitudes towards genetic testing and engineering in a utopia or dystopia encountered in class.   (40 BE)

3. Discuss the roles of consumers, business and government, especially considering the role you would expect the government to play in regard to profit-driven genetic testing.   (30 BE)

In die Gesamtwertung gehen die Ergebnisse der Teilaufgaben A und B im Verhältnis 3:1 ein.

Lösungsvorschläge

Teaching Modules referred to:

The mediation material refers to the teaching module Science and technology *(Q1)*, especially in respect of electronic media. *The second text is concerned with* utopias *and* progress in the natural sciences *from the module* Order, vision, change *(Q3)*. *The topic* Work and industrialization *(Q2) with its issues* business, industry and the environment *is also an important point of reference.*

Teil A: Aufgabe zur Sprachmittlung

Your summary should not exceed one third of the original text, which would make up 100 to 130 words in this case. You may want to add a title to your mediation.

Girls find their way into game world

In his *Spiegel* article "Deutschlands heimliche Boombranche", published online on July 13th, 2010, Carsten Görig illustrates how gender based preferences influence the game industry.

Manufacturers so far specialized in action and war games are highly surprised by the success of games like "Ponyfriends" and the active fan base formed by girls, a new target group. Some companies now offer games strictly for girls, exceeding the sales figures of games for boys by far. The increasing demand and the ascending sales curves of games for girls indicate that this new branch is influenced by word of mouth instead of price. Animal games – strongly rejected by boys – are particularly successful.

Many of these new games are developed by German low budget manufacturers sensitive to girls' expectations and providing good quality.

(135 words)

Teil B: Verkürzte Textaufgabe

1. *How to approach the task:*

   Before you deal with the assignment read the text carefully, underline the key facts and plan carefully. Since the text opposes two very antagonistic points of view, information can be collected in two columns and then brought together in one text.

The text "At-Home Genetic Tests: A Healthy Dose of Skepticism May Be the Best Prescription" by the FTC from July 2006, contrasts the views of companies that claim the success of genetic home-tests with the warnings of government agencies for consumer and health protection that question the seriousness and validity of these tests.

The text illustrates how companies claim that they are able to evaluate health risks and recommend a specific treatment or diet, although they test and verify only a small amount of the existing genetic material. Not only can they predict the risks of contracting certain diseases or illnesses but in their view they can also calculate the risk of getting a disease, offer strategies for protection and even predict how people will respond to a certain form of treatment. Subsequently, they offer food and nutritional supplements to avoid a particular disease like cancer or diabetes. In contrast to these companies, U.S. government agencies for consumer and health protection warn of the companies' claims and their very optimistic way of interpreting test results, which do not seem to be representative and have not been scientifically verified. Moreover, they suspect the companies of manipulating the consumer with their optimistic health forecast.

Although government agencies admit that such tests may have a certain explanatory power, they suggest to also consult specialized personnel like physicians with clinical experience and double-check the validity of the at-home test. *(235 words)*

2. *How to approach the task:*
   Step 1 The question implies that there are at least two different opinions on the matter of genetic testing, and one of them is preferred in the text at hand. Therefore, illustrate the contrasting opinions briefly and point out which one is favoured and why.
   Step 2 Think of novels read in class which are concerned with the same issues emphasised in the text. In the context of utopia and dystopia, the influence of big companies on the behaviour of people who are exposed to constant and subtle forms of manipulation iseespecially relevant. Make a list of arguments and find criteria to establish connections.
   Step 3 Structure your arguments logically and start writing. You should contrast the pros and cons based on convincing examples and use suitable linking words (conjunctions) to mark logical transitions.

The given article contrasts two different views on genetic tests. On the one hand, some companies specialized in genetic testing understandably argue that their tests can help anticipate a certain disease (ll. 16–19), protect people from getting a disease (ll. 23–26), and even predict whether a person can resist environmental influences (l. 32). On the other hand, governmental agencies for consumer and health protection warn consumers not to believe in the optimistic pledge of these companies. They argue that the tests have only very limited explanatory power (l. 9) and have not been scientifically confirmed (ll. 20, 27).

Although the article offers two different views, it is not necessarily neutral. The attitude favored is that of skepticism and concern. The text intends to warn the reader and probable consumer of risks and too high expectations regarding genetic test results. Its critical attitude is revealed when the text questions the explanatory power of the tests (ll. 11–15). Its warning attitude is also reflected in the syntactic construction with imperatives like "be wary of claims" (l. 17), "be skeptical of claims" (l. 29) and the normative references underlining the lack of valid scientific studies (l. 20). The tests' supposedly predictive force is a rather limited view on the matter ("look at only a small number", l. 9; "some information", l. 37). Finally, government agencies express their warnings openly and directly when questioning or denying the scientific seriousness of the tests (ll. 20, 27–28). That commercial interests dominate over health concerns is illustrated by the fact that the companies mentioned offer these tests in supermarkets supported by extensive advertising (ll. 6/7).

In the dystopian novel *Brave New World* by Aldous Huxley this critical attitude of concern has been replaced by a form of authoritarian belief in the scientific possibilities of genetic engineering used by the government for social, economic and political reasons. The action of the novel is set in a technologically advanced society, ruled by an authoritarian government and based on a restrictive ideology. In contrast to the article, which refers to the state of our world at present, the balance between political and economic powers has been abolished in favor of the political ruling class in *Brave New World*. Science, mainly genetic engineering, is abused by the political rulers to exclude individuality, to create subordination and to make people love their servitude. The government takes massive advantage of the scientific progress to secure their power and create a uniform society in a highly controlled standardized production process.

The warnings of political organizations illustrated in the text at hand can be perceived as a contribution to self-determination and thus a lively, democratic society, whereas in *Brave New World* individuality as a vivid example of self-determination has been completely abolished and replaced by uniform human beings, conditioned to accept their destiny, unable to experience the burden or blessing of the free will that is alluded to in the text above. Mustapha Mond, the World Controller justifies his oppressive ideology of genetically engineering, conditioning and manipulating people as a way to maintain social stability.

The warnings of the governmental organizations can also be seen as an attempt to undermine the subtle form of manipulation by commercial companies who try to influence the habitual buying behavior of the consumer prone to suggestions. The government seems to have an interest in a consumer who is mentally and physically healthy, knowing that any form of manipulation is a step towards alienation and a social danger.

All in all, the novel shows how people have created a highly sterile world under the influence of science, and genetic engineering has become a powerful instrument of manipulation and adaptation. It stands in contrast to the content of the article above which – with all its frightening tendencies – creates an image of stable political circumstances.

(639 words)

3. *How to approach the task:*

   The assignment expects you to come up with ideas which should reflect the role of the basic market players: consumer, business, government in a difficult, highly sensitive market situation. The first part of the assignment has a more descriptive orientation, so start from a wide, general point of view and include positive and negative aspects of genetic testing. Then you can become more specific and critical by including economic, religious and moral aspects as well as thoughts regarding health. Contrast the different issues and offer your view on the government's role in all this.

Genetic testing has become one of the most controversially discussed topics in public life all over the world. It is a highly sensitive issue since it touches and is able to considerably shake moral and religious beliefs. The advocates of genetic testing argue that it is an outstanding scientific achievement because it can predict and even "measure the risk of developing a particular disease" (l. 18). The opposition not only questions such claims, but also warns of consequences of all kind. But what role should each and every market participant play in regard to profit-driven genetic testing?

The companies involved understandably argue that genetic testing is a contribution to scientific progress which cannot be stopped. It is a result of complex team-work between different scientific branches. It has taken years of scientific work, set-backs and considerable capital investment. Although companies have invested millions in research and should have the right to recuperate their money, they claim they are most concerned in people's well-being.

The possibility to predict diseases is appreciated mostly by people who suffer from genetically conditioned diseases and are afraid that their offspring will have to suffer, too. They embrace scientific progress like pre-implantation genetic diagnosis (PGD) as a way of easing and even eliminating unnecessary suffering. From their point of view it is a basic human right to receive medical and scientific assistance and take advantage of scientific progress.

Even people addicted to drinking and smoking might have an interest in genetic testing. The knowledge that one is not able to withstand a certain form of toxin can possibly affect one's behavior in a positive way. At the same time, however, the information that one is resistant to harmful substances could encourage behavior detrimental to one's health.

Organizations for consumer protection warn of a business that could easily get out of control because the prospect of being able to predict one's future arouses an enormous interest and can be financially very stimulating. This could affect the moral standards of our society. Companies could stoke fears and could easily take advantage of anxious and hopeful people. Doctors and scientists could become neglectful and develop more economic interests. Additionally, the ability to eliminate diseases and the prospect of creating a "healthy" society in the future could create a lack of solidarity towards the less fortunate members of society.

Until recently governments have been able to cope with this delicate matter. They have given the required consideration to the problem and warned people of the risks and limited possibilities of genetic testing.

In my opinion companies should have the right to offer profit-driven genetic testing. If general consent was required for every scientific and medical intervention, progress would not be possible. Scientists and doctors do not become less caring only because they are paid for their services. Recent medical advancement makes it reasonable to allow such a market.

However, the government should strictly check the effectiveness of genetic testing and allow only highly reliable products. The government should also define the moral standards according to which genetic testing is justifiable. I would completely oppose a liberalization of the market where naïve or unsuspecting customers could become victims of economic interests. Governments should also be able to set a framework for expenditures and protect the consumer against unaffordable costs. A highly regulated market could frighten companies, though, and hinder scientific work if companies feel they are not rewarded for their endeavors.

The government should also set a legal framework for genetic testing. It should only be allowed under strict medical observation and by consent. Sales of genetic tests in supermarkets should definitely be prohibited, because not everyone has the knowledge to understand the results and the recommendations offered.

In conclusion, one can say that profit-driven genetic testing cannot be stopped. It is the result of scientific progress and a helpful instrument for improving the state of health within society. It can also be perceived as a cultural achievement and has a right to exist. Yet in spite of all the advantages it can offer, governments should still interfere actively and offer the moral and financial framework for such a delicate matter.

(690 words)

Immigrants Shunning Idea of Assimilation

By William Branigin, Washington Post Staff Writer, Monday, May 25, 1998

OMAHA – Night is falling on South Omaha, and Maria Jacinto is patting tortillas for the
evening meal in the kitchen of the small house she shares with her husband and five children. Like many others in her neighborhood, where most of the residents are Mexican immigrants, the Jacinto household mixes the old country with the new.

5   As Jacinto, who speaks only Spanish, stresses a need to maintain the family's Mexican
heritage, her eldest son, a bilingual 11-year-old who wears a San Francisco 49ers jacket
and has a paper route, comes in and joins his brothers and sisters in the living room to
watch "The Simpsons".

Jacinto became a U.S. citizen last April, but she does not feel like an American. In
10 fact, she seems resistant to the idea of assimilating into U.S. society.

"I think I'm still a Mexican," she says. "When my skin turns white and my hair turns
blonde, then I'll be an American."

In many ways, the experiences of the Jacinto family are typical of the gradual process
of assimilation that has pulled generations of immigrants into the American mainstream.
15 That process is nothing new to Omaha, which drew waves of Czech, German and Irish
immigrants early this century.

But in the current immigration wave, something markedly different is happening here
in the middle of the great American "melting pot".

Not only are the demographics of the United States changing in profound and unprec-
20 edented ways, but so too are the very notions of assimilation and the melting pot that have
been articles of faith in the American self-image for generations. *E Pluribus Unum* (From
Many, One) remains the national motto, but there no longer seems to be a consensus about
what that should mean.

There is a sense that, especially as immigrant populations reach a critical mass in
25 many communities, it is no longer the melting pot that is transforming them, but they who
are transforming American society.

American culture remains a powerful force – for better or worse – that influences people both here and around the world in countless ways. But several factors have combined
in recent years to allow immigrants to resist, if they choose, the Americanization that had
30 once been considered irresistible.

In fact, the very concept of assimilation is being called into question as never before.
Some sociologists argue that the melting pot often means little more than "Anglo conformity" and that assimilation is not always a positive experience – for either society or
the immigrants themselves. And with today's emphasis on diversity and ethnicity, it has
35 become easier than ever for immigrants to avoid the melting pot entirely. Even the metaphor itself is changing, having fallen out of fashion completely with many immigration
advocacy and ethnic groups. They prefer such terms as the "salad bowl" and the "mosa-

ic", metaphors that convey more of a sense of separateness in describing this nation of immigrants.

40   "It's difficult to adapt to the culture here," said Maria Jacinto, 32, who moved to the
United States 10 years ago with her husband, Aristeo Jacinto, 36. "In the Hispanic tradition, the family comes first, not money. It's important for our children not to be influenced too much by the *gueros*," she said, using a term that means "blondies" but that she
employs generally in reference to Americans. "I don't want my children to be influenced
45 by immoral things." […]

    Among socially conservative families such as the Jacintos, who initially moved to
California from their village in Mexico's Guanajuato state, then migrated here in 1988 to
find jobs in the meatpacking industry, bad influences are a constant concern. They see
their children assimilating, but often to the worst aspects of American culture. […]

50   Immigrants such as the Jacintos are here to stay but remain wary of their adoptive
country. According to sociologists, they are right to be concerned.

    "If assimilation is a learning process, it involves learning good things and bad things,"
said Ruben G. Rumbaut, a sociology professor at Michigan State University. "It doesn't
always lead to something better."

55   At work, not only in Omaha but in immigrant communities across the country, is a
process often referred to as "segmented" assimilation, in which immigrants follow different paths to incorporation in U.S. society. These range from the classic American ideal of
blending into the vast middle class, to a "downward assimilation" into an adversarial
underclass, to a buffered integration into "immigrant enclaves". Sometimes, members of
60 the same family end up taking sharply divergent paths, especially children and their parents.

    The ambivalence of assimilation can cut both ways. Many native-born Americans also
seem to harbor mixed feelings about the process. As a nation, the United States increasingly promotes diversity, but there are underlying concerns that the more emphasis there
65 is on the factors that set people apart, the more likely that society will end up divided.

    With Hispanics, especially Mexicans, accounting for an increasing proportion of U.S.
population growth, it is this group, more than any other, that is redefining the melting pot.

(829 words)

http://www.washingtonpost.com/wp-srv/national/longterm/meltingpot/meltingpot.htm
[retrieved on July 13, 2010]

Assignments

1. Summarize the text.   (25 BE)

2. Taking the given text as a starting point, examine central aspects of the
American Dream, including its historical roots.   (35 BE)

3. *"Immigration Without Assimilation Equals Invasion"*
(The American Daily, March 24, 2005)
Comment on this headline taking into account the situation in Great Britain.   (40 BE)

Lösungsvorschläge

Teaching modules referred to:
The topics dealt with here mainly concern the teaching module The Challenge of Individualism – USA *(Q1). The second task also requires a profound knowledge of the* American Dream *and its historical roots. The third task focuses on the assimilation of immigrants in Great Britain, which is a central issue in the module* Tradition and Change – The UK *in Q2. The themes of multiculturalism and social change are also dealt with in the module* Promised Lands *in Q3.*

1. **Step 1** *Read the text very carefully and underline the most important statements. Concentrate on these statements and on the line of argumentation because the summary must not exceed one fourth to one third of the original number of words, i. e. 210–280 words.*

   Step 2 *Start by writing an umbrella sentence that includes the author, date, source and topic of the newspaper article. Be careful to use your own words as far as possible and to make the line of argumentation clear. Your summary must neither contain quotations nor your personal opinion.*

   The article at hand by W. Branigin, which was published in the *Washington Post* on May 25, 1998, deals with the increasing reluctance of immigrants to adopt mainstream American culture.
   At first the author gives the example of a Mexican family living in an ethnic neighbourhood in Omaha. Whereas the mother, who speaks Spanish only and does not feel like an American, seems to resist integration despite being naturalized, the children grow up bilingually and live like other American youths.
   In the past immigrants from Europe gradually assimilated to mainstream American culture, yet, nowadays, with changing patterns of immigration, people no longer believe in the traditional concept of the melting pot. The large group of Hispanic immigrants even seems to be altering their host society and the melting pot.
   Although American culture has a worldwide impact, it is often rejected by immigrants. Branigin gives several reasons for this. While the melting pot concept is often equated with conformity and viewed as negative, the concepts of diversity and ethnicity, as well as the metaphors of the salad bowl or the mosaic, have gained popularity. Some immigrants fear the loss of their cultural heritage and family values and, therefore, want to protect their children from immoral influences. They are supported by sociologists who stress negative experiences in the assimilation process.
   Assimilation increasingly takes place in a segmented way, either to the middle class, to an underclass or to a parallel society. This has caused many native born Americans who fear a fragmented society to become sceptical about these developments.

   (257 words)

2. **Step 1** *Make a mind map or a list of the different tenets of the American Dream you dealt with in class. It should include the melting pot, the hopes of immigrants to obtain freedom from political or religious oppression, liberty and equal opportunity, as well as the idea of becoming successful on the basis of hard work.*

Step 2 *Add notes on the historical dimension of these central tenets of the American Dream and keep in mind that these are aspects of a dream which did not come true for everyone, although it is still widely accepted and continues to attract people who want to start anew. Add ideas which illustrate that the American Dream does not reflect reality. Remember that e. g. slaves, women and Native Americans were excluded and that many hopeful immigrants ended up in poverty. You may refer to texts and films dealt with in class.*

Step 3 *Be careful to write a coherent answer and to structure your text effectively with the help of paragraphs. You can take the article's central issue, the melting pot, as a starting point.*

The concept of the melting pot, which is currently changing due to changing patterns of assimilation, as depicted in the text, is a central element of the American Dream. The idea that immigrants from Europe were melted into a new race of Americans dates back to J. Hector St. John de Crèvecoeur, who published his notes on American society in his "Letters from an American Farmer" in 1782. Crèvecoeur defined Americans as people who had left behind their old heritage and manners when they came to America. He emphasized that individuals of all nationalities were melted into a new race of men who acted upon new principles because they were allowed to harvest the fruits of their labour without being exploited by aristocrats or the church. Crèvecoeur observed that people in the new world were happier and more self-reliant and independent than in Europe.

After the successful breakaway from England many writers documented the great optimism concerning the liberal ideas of life, liberty and happiness that Thomas Jefferson had written in the Declaration of Independence in 1776. The fact that the Founding Fathers succeeded in setting up a democracy led may people to believe that life in classless American society stood in contrast to the unjust conditions in Europe. Of course, people overlooked the fact that these rights mainly applied to white male settlers. Women, slaves in the southern states, indentured servants and Native Americans were excluded.

Yet, the conception of the new world as a model society dates back to the very first settlers, the Pilgrims, who had set out to escape from religious persecution and to build a society that would serve as a beacon light to the rest of the world. The male passengers aboard the Mayflower signed the so-called Mayflower Compact in 1620, in which they agreed to form a government and to be bound by its rules. Many central tenets of the American Dream had their origin in Puritan religion, which stressed commitment to individualism and equality, hard work and the responsibility for one's personal success or failure in life.

Throughout the 19th century many immigrants were attracted to the United States by the promise of being freed from bondage or exploitation and abuse by feudal lords. Immigration to America seemed to promise individual liberty and freedom from control and, in fact, many immigrants did find better chances to succeed than in their home countries. As the frontier was gradually pushed further west, cheap land was available. In their letters home many immigrants idealized America as a land of plenty where every individual could start anew. As a consequence, countrymen in Europe increasingly attempted to escape from famines, unsuccessful democratic revolutions and religious and political persecution. Nevertheless, life turned out to be hard and dangerous. For many it was not the land of milk and honey that was propagated in pamphlets and letters.

During the industrial revolution and after the closing of the Frontier in 1890, the careers of inventive businessmen who proceeded "from rags to riches" promoted the idea that everyone could strike it rich in America if they only worked hard enough. The belief in equal opportunity in a classless society continued to attract immigrants to the United States. By that time the structure of immigration had changed. The new immigrants increasingly came from southern and eastern Europe in great numbers. These people found it harder to fit in and to adapt to American culture. They often encountered bad working conditions in sweatshops, slaughterhouses and factories and many of them ended up living in slums. At the same time Americans became sceptical about the "huddled masses" that tried to enter the U.S. As a result, the first anti-immigration legislation was passed. Ellis Island, the "isle of tears", was set up to curb the high immigration rates. Those who were accepted found out that the chances of social mobility had decreased and that prospects had become bleak. Many experienced severe competition, tenement housing, gang wars among ethnic groups and life in poverty. Others found it hard to deal with so much freedom, individuality, and moral liberty, like the text at hand indicates for the Jacinto family (ll. 40–49). The situation today is quite similar concerning the influx of immigrants from Mexico and South America.

All in all, the American Dream has reflected the hopes and wishes of immigrants and Americans alike since the days of the first settlement. Although people tend to overlook the fact that reality can turn out to be strikingly different from ideals and that they might have to pay a high price for a new beginning, the Dream still continues to attract many immigrants to the USA. Today the wish to make a decent living, to have a house and a car of your own is especially attractive to immigrants who are trying to escape the third world conditions in their home countries.   *(814 words)*

3. **Step 1** Concentrate on the quotation from the American Daily and its meaning. It basically implies that people feel threatened if immigrants are not willing to assimilate to mainstream culture.

   Step 2 Consider the literary and non-literary texts on assimilation and integration dealt with in class. Remember that the task requires you to focus on assimilation in Great Britain.

   Step 3 Develop a structure for a convincing comment and be prepared to come to a conclusion on whether or not you agree with the headline. You should consider the following aspects:
   - the meaning of the quotation
   - definition of assimilation

- *obstacles to assimilation*
- *immigration to Great Britain before and after 1962*
- *impact on multicultural society*
- *your personal opinion*

In the given quotation immigration is equated with invasion of the host country if the immigrants fail or refuse to assimilate. It underlines that some native people obviously reject the idea of a multicultural society in which everyone may keep their cultural heritage and customs. Assimilation as it is demanded in the quotation is a rather strict concept that requires immigrants to sever their cultural ties and to fully accept the mainstream culture of their host country. At the same time it has to be considered that the speed and degree of assimilation strongly depend on the cultural background and on the amount of education or professional training a new immigrant has. Knowledge of the language also makes it easier to adapt to new surroundings. Many first generation immigrants, especially from developing countries, are confronted with a fight for survival if they have little or no education and do not speak the language. They are often discriminated against, work in badly paid jobs and remain living in their ethnic neighbourhoods, which are referred to as parallel societies. They keep their traditions and their language without leaving the neighbourhood, since they even find their native food stores there. Many older people and women do not feel the need to assimilate. Younger family members may encounter fewer problems concerning the language or establishing contacts outside of the ethnic neighbourhood, which often leads to collisions with traditional family values. In Great Britain, for example, young girls from traditional Asian families find it extremely difficult to fit in if their parents insist on traditional clothing or arranged marriages.

Conflicts like these and other social and economic problems, as well as high crime rates fuel anti-immigration sentiment and even xenophobia. This is especially the case in times of economic crisis when competition is feared on the labour market.

Great Britain developed into a multicultural society after the breakdown of the British Empire. After World War II the government encouraged immigration because of acute labour shortages. Many immigrants were attracted from the Caribbean or from the Indian subcontinent. Until 1962 people from all over the Commonwealth were free to enter Britain and to obtain British citizenship. When the economic situation changed, many British people complained about massive immigration allegedly undermining Anglo-Saxon society. As a result, the government decided to limit the influx of immigrants. In 1968 Enoch Powell, the conservative politician, summed up the fears that were spreading, especially among members of the working class. In his famous speech "I seem to see the River Tiber foaming with much blood" he depicted a scenario in which the English would soon be outnumbered by countless immigrants and their descendants, who would be competing for hospital beds or jobs. Powell warned the public of an upcoming fragmentation of society in first and second class citizens and encouraged re-emigration with the help of generous grants. The stigmatization of immigrants as mass invaders contributed to an increase in racial tensions within multicultural Britain. Since the riots in Brixton, Birmingham and Liverpool in the 1980s, mutual trust between the police and ethnic minorities has been strongly affected.

Nowadays many people feel particularly threatened by members of Muslim communities due to the attacks of 9/11 and bombings in England. The British author of Pakistani descent Hanif Kureishi points out that many younger Muslim teenagers feel exposed to mistrust and feel rejected. According to Kureishi it is the suspicion they are confronted with that makes it hard for them to assimilate. In addition, they feel underprivileged in schools and fear for their future careers. Some of these young people who were almost fully integrated in society are now looking for new traditional ethnic identities. In Kureishi's short story *My Son the Fanatic* the protagonist, Ali, the son of a taxi driver of Pakistani origin, gives up his western lifestyle, his English girlfriend and a promising career in favour of radical Muslim fundamentalism. Ali finally preaches holy war against the corrupt western culture, which he considers to be based on prostitution, materialism and drug abuse.

To come to a conclusion, I would say that it is unrealistic and somewhat intolerant to demand complete assimilation. This demand actually implies the idea that mainstream culture is superior to others. Personally, I feel that everybody should be allowed to make his or her choices as freely as possible and to keep the heritage he or she feels comfortable with, as long as others are not harmed in any way. Multicultural society creates a colourful pluralism which we all benefit from in different fields of everyday life. Notwithstanding, I am convinced that multicultural society can only work out if it is based on mutual tolerance and on the general acceptance of the laws based on human rights. Consequently, I favour concepts that integrate different cultures into society without demanding full assimilation. *(805 words)*

Uncle Sam's Guests

In the novel 'Small Island' by Andrea Levy a group of black Jamaican WW II Royal Air Force volunteers are trained in an American air force camp in Virginia.

'Okay, boys, now listen up here,' was how he began, this officer from the US military. Perched[1] informal on the edge of a desk he was relaxed, the only white man in this room full of volunteer servicemen from the Caribbean.

'Pay attention, you lot,' our British NCO[2], Corporal Baxter, had warned us while we
5 waited for this American officer. 'He's got something he has to say and you're guests here, so listen to him politely. All right.'

This American officer's head was angular – a square jaw is not unusual especially for an officer, but a square skull! Lenval whispered, 'Him mummy still cross eye from giving birth,' and my smile made this officer pin two penetrating blue eyes on me and me alone.
10 'You are now the guest of Uncle Sam.'

Resting easy – some of the boys even smoking – our bellies full, looking forward to a few days in the land of the free, some of us, as Jamaicans are prone[3] to do, concurred[4] verbally: 'Yes, sir – umm, umm.'

This momentarily took the officer by surprise, his back stiffening before carrying on.
15 'While you are here, all facilities pertinent to your rank will be open to you.' He stopped here, waiting for a reaction more animated than just the nodding and grinning he received. 'You will be able to use the movie theatre, the playing fields, all mess facilities, et cetera, et cetera.' [...]

'But ...' I was not the only one waiting for this first catch[5] '... you will be, for the du-
20 ration of your stay, confined to the camp'.

Oh there was much sucking of teeth and moaning, 'Cha ... cha ... cha ...' snapping around like firecrackers. There was no eyebrow left unknitted.

The officer had to put up his hand to settle the room. 'The reason ...'

'Cha ... cha ... cha ...'
25 'Your attention, please. The reason for this decision, which your NCOs can go into in more detail – but the reason for this is to minimise the risk of contracting disease. The British military authorities are quite clear that any serviceman contracting a disease while here will not be allowed to travel any further and will be returned to his country of origin forthwith.'
30 This did not settle us. With stomachs full, our thoughts had all returned to women. Al-though I did not want to be turned round having come so far, this war business was get-ting me down. No one knew how long we would be immured on this camp without seeing a curvaceous[6] bosom, a rounded hip, a shapely leg. How long without female company? No American girl was to see me in uniform – oh, boy, this was serious. The room
35 hummed – this officer had put his finger in and stirred up the nest.

'I know, I know, you're all disappointed. But while you are at this military establishment,' his voice was rising, 'and guests of the Government of the United States of America you will have the run of this camp. Everyone here has been ordered to see that your stay with us is the best welcome Uncle Sam could give to the negroes of an ally.'
40 He was shouting now. 'You will mix with white service personnel. Have you boys any idea how lucky you are? You will not be treated as negroes!' […]

Now, from what I could understand, this American officer with the angular head was telling us that we West Indians, being subjects of His Majesty King George VI, had, for the time being, superior black skin. We were allowed to live with white soldiers, while the
45 inferior American negro was not. I was perplexed. No, we were all perplexed. We Jamaicans, knowing our island is one of the largest in the Caribbean, think ourselves sophisticated men of the world. Better than the 'small islanders' whose universe only runs a few miles in either direction before it falls into the sea. But even the most feebleminded small islanders could detect something odd about the situation. While being shown round the
50 camp a smiling face would tell us, 'You see, your American nigger don't work. If his belly's full he won't work. When he's hungry again then he'll do just enough. Same kinda thing happens in the animal kingdom. But you boys being British are different.' While being shown to our seats in the all-white picture show, handed bars of chocolate and cigarettes to share, men would say, 'I am loyal to my flag but you would never catch no self-
55 respecting white man going into battle with a nigger.' At a dance in the mess being persuaded to boogie-woogie and jive – to let go, man, go! – into our black faces, up against our black skin they said, 'We do not mix the negro and the white races here because it lowers the efficiency of our fighting units. Your American nigger ain't really cut out to fight.'
60 Apparently our hosts had tried every solution to their nigger problem. 'Only one that works in this country, and certainly in the military, is segregation.' This was apparently how everyone liked it – black man as well as white. They had a name for it – no, not master-race theory: Jim Crow!7   (862 words)

Andrea Levy: Small Island, Headline Publications, London 2004, pp. 127–312

1 perched on – lässig sitzend
2 NCO – non-commissioned officer (Unteroffizier)
3 prone to – dazu neigen etwas zu tun
4 to concur – to agree
5 catch – der Haken (an einer Sache)
6 curvaceous – kurvenreich
7 Jim Crow laws: a system of laws and regulations in the southern states of the U.S. after the Civil War, making segregation seemingly legal

Assignments

1. Describe what the narrator learns about the way black soldiers are seen. (25 BE)

2. Explain the system of racial discrimination and segregation that developed in the U.S. in the past and that lasted well up to the time referred to in the text at hand (World War II). (35 BE)

3. *"Multiculturalism makes our country more diverse, but does it actually make it any better?"*
   (from a letter to the BBC in reaction to Prime Minister Blair's 'Multiculturalism Speech', December 8, 2006)
   Based on the comment cited above, discuss the situation of ethnic minorities in the United Kingdom. Refer to your reading/viewing experience in class. (40 BE)

---

3 – commonwealth
→ economy
- concept melting pot ↓
- keep cultures ↑
→ learn
→ intru

Teaching modules referred to:
The literary excerpt and the first two tasks deal with the module USA (Q1) and take a
closer look at the concept of the American Dream and the issue of living together (African
Americans). The third task extends the focus to The United Kingdom (Q2) and the mod-
ule social structures, social change.

1. **Step 1** *Scan the text carefully for relevant information and highlight all important*
   points that refer to the American image of the black man. Other items mentioned in
   the text are not relevant to your answer. Consider briefly who the narrator is (in this
   case, a black Jamaican soldier).
   Step 2 *Think of an introductory sentence: in many cases, it is a safe start to use the*
   wording given in the question itself. Answer the given task using the points you have
   just highlighted. Use your own words as far as it is appropriate and do not forget to
   give evidence from the text (line numbers).

When being trained in an American air force camp in Virginia during the Second
World War, the narrator, a black Jamaican Royal Air Force volunteer, learns about the
way black soldiers are seen in the United States of America.
Apparently, black men are expected to not have the same manners as whites do and
even have to be told how to behave when dealing with a white person (ll. 4–6, 10).
Consequently, the white American officer seems rather surprised when the group of
colored Caribbean servicemen answers him politely (l. 14).
Additionally, it is a big step for US military authorities to give the black Jamaican soldiers access to all military facilities, such as the movie theater, the playing fields and
much more. Therefore, the U.S. officer is quite astonished that the Jamaicans seem to
take this permission for granted and do not show the expected enthusiasm and joyous
surprise (ll. 15–18).
Despite the permissions to use all entertainment facilities they want to, the Jamaican
soldiers are disappointed because they will not be allowed to leave the camp and, thus,
have no opportunity to meet any women. The reason they are given for this prohibi-
tion is "to minimise the risk of contracting disease" (l. 26); yet, it remains uncertain if
this is the only explanation why blacks have to stay in the camp; other possible motives remain untold. The Jamaicans' negative reaction to this confinement shows that
they are probably used to different, more liberal rules in their home country (ll. 30–
35).
In general, the narrator learns that black people in the United States are considered to
be of lesser value and abilities than white people, so American authorities do not hesitate to point out that the black soldiers from Jamaica should consider themselves lucky
to be allowed to "mix with white service personnel" (l. 40) and "not be treated as negroes" (l. 41). This takes the narrator quite by surprise, because it seems totally paradoxical to him that British blacks are actually considered to be worth more than the

"American negro" and are, in turn, allowed to do more than American blacks are (ll. 42−45).

On top of that, the narrator and his fellow soldiers encounter open discrimination and intolerance in Virginia, such as racist statements from American military personnel. For instance, they are told that a white man would never go into battle with blacks, because they diminish the "efficiency of [American] fighting units" (ll. 57/58). Even though Americans tell the Jamaicans that these restrictions only apply to American blacks, who "ain't really cut out to fight" (ll. 58/59), and not to the British blacks, the narrator seems to be offended by such statements being told straight to his face (ll. 50−59).

Finally, the narrator states in a rather ironic way that American whites, in accordance with blacks, have resorted to some kind of "master-race theory" after having unsuccessfully approached the "problem" with blacks in other ways: segregation in the military, as well as in American society in general seems to be the only effective solution to the black-and-white issues (ll. 60−63).   *(528 words)*

2. *Make a short list / take some notes on a separate piece of paper listing all the important events and issues that have defined and shaped the role of black Americans in the past and up to World War II.*
   It is strongly advisable to answer the question in the chronological order of events.

Racial discrimination against African Americans began a couple of centuries ago: from the 1600s well up to the early 1800s, Africans were brought to North America and sold as slaves to work on the huge plantations in the American South. These black slaves were considered cheap farm labourers and had no rights, since most of their owners did not treat them as human beings, but as an object that could be owned; some "masters" even put collars on their "possessions", the slaves. The slaves had to work extremely hard and were often punished, whipped or even hanged straight away if they disobeyed their owners or did not do their work right. Understandably, in the 19th century more and more people – mainly in the North of the United States – felt that slavery should be abolished and wanted to ship the slaves back to Africa. These people were called "abolitionists". The primarily agricultural South protested strongly against these plans, because in contrast to the more industrialized North, its economic prosperity relied heavily on slavery, so Southerners opposed any call for change. Although slave trade was officially ended in 1808, slavery itself was not.

The different attitude towards the issue of slavery is one of the reasons why the American Civil War broke out between the North and the South in 1861. During this war, eleven slave-holding Southern states left the Union and founded the Confederate States of America, since no compromise on slavery could be found between the North and the South. President Abraham Lincoln's "Emancipation Proclamation" in 1863 promised freedom for slaves and made the abolishment of slavery an official war goal for the Union. Indeed, the Union's victory and the defeat of the Confederate South in 1865 brought the official abolition of slavery, which is written down in the 13th amendment of the US Constitution and marked the end of the American Civil War.

However, life for black people did not considerably improve after the war: although they became free men, blacks were freed into a racist society. Often working as cotton pickers on the same plantation as before, they were hardly better off. In those days, blacks had to defend themselves against white racists, who for example in 1865 had founded the Ku Klux Klan, an organization that aimed at terrorizing black people. The Ku Klux Klan has become the epitome of white racism against black people and can be held responsible for thousands of illegal whippings and lynchings.

At the end of the 19th century, it became more and more obvious that blacks were still not considered equal members of American society. For instance, special new laws, called Jim Crow laws, were created which stopped blacks from voting and, in general, supported the "separate but equal" policy, which the Supreme Court ruled on in the court case Plessy vs. Ferguson. It can be said that at this point, slavery had been replaced by segregation. This term is similar to the concept of South African apartheid and meant that black Americans had to go to other hospitals, schools and churches than white Americans; they even had to use different buses and bathrooms and were not given any access to "white" facilities at all: racism was now written down in US law.

Consequently, black people were not able to lead the same life as white people: they did not stand a chance in attending good schools or universities and were subsequently denied well-paid jobs, which again prevented them from being accepted or rising to a higher level in society. Whites did not want (former) slaves to attain the same status as they had. Giving black people access to "white" parts of society, such as politics, would have required whites to give some of that power up and hand it over to blacks – hardly any white person at the time was willing to do that. It was (and maybe still is) a long process for blacks to be seen as equals. Not until 2008 did a black man hold the highest political office of the country, the US presidency. *(678 words)*

3. **Step 1** *Make sure you understand the task including the quote given in it: what is said here? Where is the connection to the issue of multiculturalism? Is multiculturalism seen as something positive or negative?*

   Step 2 *Think of the issues that ethnic minorities in the UK have to deal with (draw up a list on a separate piece of paper). To illustrate your points, think of any book or movie you dealt with in class that might provide useful examples for your arguments. You might want to elaborate on about three to four points/arguments. Remember that you have to provide arguments for either side (pros and cons) of the issue.*

   Step 3 *Arrange a logical structure for your arguments and start writing. A good way to introduce a topic can be historical facts, surveys or quotes – maybe there is something you know of in connection with the topic? You may also want to give your comment a title.*

Multiculturalism – blessing or curse?

In the previous decades, the United Kingdom has been a country of increasing ethnic diversity: since the Second World War, large numbers of people have entered the country as immigrants or to seek asylum. Almost eight percent of the British population is non-white; fifty percent of the members of ethnic minorities were already born in Great Britain. The UK has long adopted a policy of multiculturalism in relation to immigrants, meaning that the government allows people from different cultures to live in the UK and continue to practice their own cultural traditions in addition to adapting to British ways. As a result, the country has become a vibrant mixture of cultures and a centre of financial and cultural exchange, but the question whether this diversity is a blessing or a curse for British society still remains.

On the one hand, ethnic minorities can definitely be seen as a gain for British society in general: by adding their cultural background, traditions and ways of life to the British one, they have made the country more complex and diverse. Numerous immigrants have integrated into British society quite well and have preserved aspects of their language, religion and culture at the same time. Many of them hold British citizenship; some of them have even made considerable careers as politicians, artists, athletes or in other professions. A lot of immigrant children feel British, as well as Indian, Pakistani or African, one of the issues that the movie *Bend it like Beckham* deals with. In this movie, a girl of Indian descent has adapted an English name (Jess) alongside her Indian one (Jesminder), is a soccer fan and is trying to combine British and Asian lifestyle.

On the other hand, British society is not always tolerant and understanding. Many immigrants and their descendants have also experienced prejudice, racism and xenophobia. Research has shown that members of ethnic minorities as a whole experience a greater number of social disadvantages than other groups. For example, their children are more likely to need additional help in education; also, the unemployment rate is higher among ethnic minorities than among the native population in general. Moreover, in the late 20th century, race riots have occurred in Brixton, Birmingham, Liverpool and other industrial cities. On top of that, many non-whites in Great Britain experience racial discrimination on a daily basis. This issue is dealt with in Zadie Smith's novel *White Teeth*. Alsana for example, a Bangladeshi woman, has to face the prejudices of London society many times, as do other characters. Doubtlessly, Zadie Smith, daughter of a Jamaican mother and a (white) English father, had to face similar issues herself and includes her own experiences in the novel.

From time to time, Jess in *Bend it like Beckham* is also an outsider who encounters discrimination, which she will ultimately overcome as a member of the soccer team. Such conflicts highlight the lack of trust and understanding between the white and non-white communities, including their authorities such as the police. Consequently, several anti-discrimination laws have been passed by the British government in recent years. These developments seem to argue against multiculturalism as a blessing, and rather present it as a concept that confronts the United Kingdom with many problems to be dealt with when it comes to the issue of race.

In addition to having to face discrimination from the outside world or society, many members of British racial minorities have to deal with an inner conflict of identity and belonging: they are caught between assimilating and preserving their cultures. This conflict is shown in *White Teeth* as well: although the main families attempt to create lives for themselves in Great Britain, there is still a struggle to hold on to their past. Samad, for example, feels that English life is not good for an adequate Islamic upbringing, which is why he sends his son Magid to preserve and strengthen his Muslim heritage. At the same time, Samad has accepted Britain as his home country. In the movie *Bend it like Beckham*, the same dilemma can be observed: Jess is from a traditional Pakistani family who does not approve of her Western ways of behavior and lifestyle; they even forbid her to play soccer at some point, although her biggest dream is to become a famous soccer player. Her family wants her to dress appropriately, marry within her ethnic group and behave like a good Pakistani woman.

As a conclusion, it can be said that the question "Multiculturalism makes our country more diverse, but does it actually make it any better?" cannot be answered clearly. People from all over the world with different cultures, languages and traditions enrich a nation on the one hand, but on the other definitely add to already existing problems. Nevertheless, a BBC poll from 2005 states that the majority of British people do think that multiculturalism makes their country a better place – certainly a promising basis and maybe even an offer of support for tackling the issues concerning multicultural society in the future. *(840 words)*

Teil A: Aufgabe zur Sprachmittlung

Die Jugend wird wieder politischer

Klaus Hurrelmann, Leiter der neuen Shell-Studie, spricht im Interview über die Jugend in der Krise.

ZEIT ONLINE: Was ist Ihre Prognose: Wie tickt die Jugend 2010? [...]

HURRELMANN: Heute beginnt die Jugend wesentlich früher – mit zwölf. Dann hat bereits mehr als die Hälfte eines Jahrgangs die biologische Geschlechtsreife erlangt. Generell gilt inzwischen die Definition: Man ist kein Kind mehr, wenn man selbst Kinder be-
5 kommen kann. Noch viel schwieriger ist es, das Austrittsalter aus der Jugend zu defi-
nieren: Dafür gibt es nämlich kein biologisches Kriterium. Wir setzen es, eine Hilfs-
konstruktion, bei 25 Jahren an: Dann ist die Mehrheit mit der Ausbildung fertig, ver-
dient Geld, denkt über Familiengründung nach.

ZEIT ONLINE: Jugendlich ist man heute also gut 13 Jahre lang?

10 HURRELMANN: Ja, Jugend beginnt so früh und endet so spät wie nie seit Menschengeden-
ken. Wann ist man endlich ein vollwertiger Gesellschaftsbürger? Anders als früher ga-
rantiert heute schließlich eine gute Ausbildung nicht mehr unbedingt ein hohes Gehalt
oder eine feste Anstellung. Wir konstatieren, soziologisch gesprochen, eine lang anhal-
tende, tief sitzende strukturelle Unsicherheit. Das war schon bei unserer letzten Shell-
15 Studie, 2006, ein zentrales Ergebnis.

ZEIT ONLINE: Wie geht die junge Generation damit um?

HURRELMANN: Zu unserer Überraschung: ungeheuer sachlich. „Pragmatische Generation"
haben wir sie 2006 genannt. Es gab damals eine unheimlich hohe Bereitschaft, in die eigene Bildung zu investieren. Man konnte von einer auffallend hohen Karriereorientiert-
20 heit sprechen, fast von einem Schuss Opportunismus. Nach Kritik und Unzufrieden-
heit mussten wir fast mit der Lupe suchen. Was wir allerdings festgestellt haben, war
ein ziemlich hoher Angstpegel. 50 Prozent der Jugendlichen spürten Druck im Alltag.

ZEIT ONLINE: Dabei war 2006 die Krise noch nicht einmal so allgegenwärtig wie heute ...

HURRELMANN: Eben. Eine Vermutung ist, dass der gefühlte Druck zugenommen haben
25 dürfte.

ZEIT ONLINE: Irgendwann muss sich doch der Druck entladen oder ein Ventil suchen.
Rechnen Sie mit einer Repolitisierung oder gar Radikalisierung der Jugend?

HURRELMANN: Es gibt verschiedene Ventile: Das abgespaltene untere Fünftel der Generation ist aggressiver als früher. Sie suchen Sündenböcke, verarbeiten den Druck nach
30 außen. Es ist sicher kein Zufall, dass fremdenfeindliche Gewalt zunimmt. Auch die
jüngsten linken Ausschreitungen, etwa in Berlin, weisen allgemein auf ein gestiegenes
Gewaltpotenzial bei den Jüngeren hin. Andere weichen vor dem Druck aus, nehmen
Drogen, flüchten sich in Computerspiele. Ebenfalls ansteigend und noch wenig unter-
sucht ist die Anzahl depressiver Jugendlicher.

35 ZEIT ONLINE: Aber politisch …

HURRELMANN: Politisch im klassischen Sinn ist die heutige Jugend nicht. Im Gegenteil. Das Interesse für Politik ist auf einem historischen Tiefpunkt: Heute schätzt sich nur noch ein Drittel als politisch ein, in den siebziger Jahren waren es noch zwei Drittel einer Generation. Aber, meine Hypothese ist: Das Politische wird wieder zunehmen.

40 ZEIT ONLINE: Wieso?

HURRELMANN: Es gibt neuen Zündstoff: etwa durch die doppelten Abiturjahrgänge in Folge der Gymnasial-Verkürzung auf acht Jahre, die jetzt die Schulen verlassen. Dadurch, und durch den Bologna-Hochschul-Prozess, kommt es zu einem großen Konkurrenzkampf und zu einer Verstopfung der Uni-Zugänge. Nicht einmal mehr die

45 Besten eines Jahrgangs können sich sicher sein, den bevorzugten Studienplatz zu erhalten. Das provoziert eine Gegenbewegung, wie wir in diesem Wintersemester bei den Hochschul-Streiks gesehen haben. Auch die neu aufgelebten Anti-AKW- und Friedens-Demos, an denen übrigens mehr Frauen als früher teilgenommen haben, sind mögliche erste Signale einer neuen Protestkultur. *(538 Wörter)*

ZEIT ONLINE; Michael Schlieben, 30.12.2009
http://www.zeit.de/gesellschaft/generationen/2009-12/interview-hurrelmann-shell-studie-2010
[retrieved on Jan. 16, 2010]; orthografische Fehler wurden korrigiert.

Assignment

As an exchange student in GB, you are doing comparative sociological studies on the problems of young adults in Great Britain and Germany. Summarize the given text in English for your fellow students.

Teil B: Verkürzte Textaufgabe

Rabbit-Proof Fence

In this excerpt from a novel Constable Riggs has just received the order to remove the Aboriginal girls Molly, Gracie and Daisy from their home at Jigalong to Moore River, a settlement where half-caste children are kept and trained to be domestic servants or farm labourers for the whites.

Molly and Daisy finished their breakfast and decided to take all their dirty clothes and wash them in the soak further down the river. They returned to the camp looking clean and refreshed and joined the rest of the family in the shade for lunch of tinned corned beef, damper and tea. The family had just finished eating when all the camp dogs began

5 barking, making a terrible din.

"Shut up," yelled their owners, throwing stones at them. The dogs whinged and skulked away. Then all eyes turned to the cause of the commotion. A tall, rugged white man stood on the bank above them. He could easily have been mistaken for a pastoralist or a grazier with his tanned complexion except that he was wearing khaki clothing. Fear

10 and anxiety swept over them when they realised that the fateful day they had been dreading had come at last. They always knew that it would only be a matter of time before the government would track them down. When Constable Riggs, Protector of Aborigines, fi-

nally spoke his voice was full of authority and purpose. They knew without a doubt that he was the one who took their children in broad daylight – not like the evil spirits who
15 came into their camps in the night.

"I've come to take Molly, Gracie and Daisy, the three half-caste girls, with me to go to school at the Moore River Native Settlement," he informed the family.

The old man nodded to show that he understood what Riggs was saying. The rest of the family just hung their heads refusing to face the man who was taking their daughters
20 away from them. Silent tears welled in their eyes and trickled down their cheeks.

"Come on, you girls," he ordered. "Don't worry about taking anything. We'll pick up what you need later."

When the two girls stood up, he noticed that the third girl was missing. "Where's the other one, Daisy?" he asked anxiously.
25 "She's with her mummy and daddy at Murra Munda Station," the old man informed him.

"She's not at Murra Munda or at Jimbalbar goldfields. I called into those places before I came here," said the Constable. "Hurry up then, I want to get started. We've got a long way to go yet. You girls can ride this horse back to the depot," he said, handing the reins
30 over to Molly. Riggs was annoyed that he had to go miles out of his way to find these girls.

Molly and Gracie sat silently on the horse, tears streaming down their cheeks as Constable Riggs turned the big bay stallion and led the way back to the depot. A high pitched wail broke out. The cries of agonised mothers and the women, and the deep sobs of grandfathers, uncles and cousins, filled the air. Molly and Gracie looked back just once before
35 they disappeared through the river gums[1]. Behind them, those remaining in the camp found strong sharp objects and gashed themselves and inflicted wounds to their heads and bodies as an expression of their sorrow.

The two frightened and miserable girls began to cry, silently at first, then uncontrollably; their grief made worse by the lamentations of their loved ones and the visions of
40 them sitting on the ground in their camp letting their tears mix with red blood that flowed from the cuts on their heads. This reaction to their children's abduction showed that the family were now in mourning. They were grieving for their abducted children and their relief would come only when the tears ceased to fall, and that will be a long time yet.

(625 words)

Doris Pilkington/Nugi Garimara, Rabbit-Proof Fence. Hyperion Books, NY 2002, pp. 43–45

1   river redgum, a eucalyptus tree

Assignments

1. Summarize the text. (25 BE)

2. Compare the policy behind the systematic abduction of Aboriginal children to the attitudes that minorities in the USA were and are exposed to. (40 BE)

3. Discuss the concepts of assimilation and multiculturalism including references to Australian and non-Australian contexts. (35 BE)

Lösungsvorschläge

Teaching modules referred to:
The mediation text focuses on the teaching module Ideals and reality *(Q3), in particular*
on structural problems *during times of change. The second text deals with the topic* Prom-
ised lands: dreams and realities (Q3) in relation to Australia. *The wider context is that of*
the one-track mind (prejudice, intolerance) *concerning the relations between* Them and us
(Q1).

Teil A: Aufgabe zur Sprachmittlung

Your English summary should be much shorter than the German article (between one
third and one fourth of the original, which is 135–180 words). Try to concentrate on the
information that refers to the issues concerning young adults in Germany. (Highlight them
in your copy or take notes before you start writing). Mention problems and changes that
affect these people.
Do not forget to state the topic, author, source, and date in an umbrella sentence at the
beginning and try to find an appropriate heading for your summary.

Young people's interest in politics increasing
In an interview for ZEIT ONLINE published on December 30, 2009, Klaus Hurrelmann,
director of the latest Shell Study, talks about the recent changes among young German
adults, such as their attitude towards education and politics.
For Hurrelmann, youth starts with biological maturity at 12 and ends with social maturity
at 25. Since well-paid and secure jobs have become increasingly rare, young people
nowadays invest in quality education to increase their chances and are, therefore, often
called the "pragmatic generation". Yet, they are insecure and afraid, too. To cope with the
pressure, some direct it towards other people, often foreigners, in an aggressive way or
seek comfort and distraction in drugs or computer games; the number of young people
suffering from clinical depression has increased also. This pressure does not lead to increased political commitment, however.
Nevertheless, Hurrelmann thinks that the young generation will eventually rediscover
politics as competition at universities and on the labor market will become even tougher
due to the Bologna process and higher numbers of graduates after G8.   *(178 words)*

Teil B: Verkürzte Textaufgabe

1. *Highlight or take notes of the information that is relevant and important to understand*
    the whole context. Eliminate insignificant details that do not contribute to the under-
    standing of the action.
    Create an umbrella sentence again, including the name of the author, the title and the
    publication date. In this introductory sentence you can also refer to the main charac-
    ters and the setting.

Produce a summary in complete sentences that is about one third of the total length of the text (160–215 words). Use your own words as much as possible. Remember that you are not allowed to quote in a summary.

The excerpt from the novel *Rabbit-Proof Fence*, written by Doris Pilkington and Nugi Garimara and published in 2002, describes a scene in which two Australian Aborigine girls, Molly and Gracie, are taken away from their families on the order of the Australian government to be raised in a settlement where Aborigine children are trained to be servants or farm workers for white Australians.

One day after lunch, a representative of the Australian government, Constable Riggs, shows up at the Aborigine camp where three girls, Molly, Gracie and Daisy, live, to bring them to a white institution to be raised there. Two of the three girls are at the camp when Riggs arrives, and, already having expected his visit, their families sadly give in and, in silent tears, hand over Molly and Gracie to the authorities.

When leaving their home on horseback, the two girls can hear the agonized cries of their families, who react to the abduction by inflicting wounds to themselves to express their mourning. This makes the girls cry also, since Molly and Gracie picture their loved ones in physical and mental pain out of grief for their lost children, which will not be overcome for a long time.   *(201 words)*

2. **Step 1** *Note that the question consists of two parts: you have to write about the Australian policies of systematic abduction of Aboriginal children and, as a second step, compare this policy to the issues that concern ethnic minorities in the US.*
   Step 2 *Take notes on a separate sheet of paper, structure them and arrange them in a logical order.*
   Step 3 *Answer the task in complete sentences and use appropriate language. Do not forget to structure your answer by applying paragraphs and linking words. Feel free to be critical toward the task and do not hesitate to express your personal opinion.*

When white people first arrived in Australia in the 18th century, it soon became clear that they did not consider the indigenous population, the Aborigines, as equals. The whites considered themselves superior to the indigenous population at any time, taking their land, treating them brutally and offering them badly paid jobs in dangerous and hard working conditions. The discrimination of Aborigines reached its sad peak when, from the early 1800s on, most Australian states and territories carried out a policy of forcibly removing Aboriginal children from their parents, placing them in foster families or institutions. These children became known as the "Stolen Generations" and were deliberately kept separate from their culture in the hope that they would eventually assimilate into white society and culture, losing their Aboriginality. The white government claimed rather cynically that this method, officially called the "indigenous child welfare system", was the only way of saving the indigenous race from dying out and served only for its protection. The "Stolen Generations" doubtlessly are one of the most controversial chapters in the country's history. It was not until the 1960s that Aborigines were finally recognized as Australian citizens with equal rights. Functioning well up to the 1970s, the agencies carrying out the abductions hardly kept any records of children's origins. Others were lost and destroyed, so up to today, thousands of Aborigines know little about their original tribes or families and have not overcome the emotional and psychological torments of family separation.

To add to the problem, the Australian government was rather slow when it came to apologizing to the Aborigines for what had happened; some efforts to compensate them were made, but in many cases were not sufficient to improve the situation of many Aborigines. Even if the "Stolen Generations" are an element of the past, Aborigines suffer from many social disadvantages, such as limited access to education, health and substance abuse problems, high rates of poverty and they have the highest unemployment rate among Australians.

The latter is also true for ethnic minorities in the United States: although their situation is not as extreme as that of Australian Aborigines, compared to the white population, African Americans and Hispanics in America still are at an economic, educational and social disadvantage. Issues such as crime, insufficient health care and poverty still prevail among these groups in American society. Moreover, racism and discrimination against ethnic minorities may have been officially abolished, but sadly keep persisting in the minds of many white Americans.

African Americans especially have suffered greatly during the course of American history. From 1600 to 1800, black Africans were brought to North America as slaves to work on the huge plantations in the American South. They were neither treated as human beings, nor did they have any rights: masters saw them as their "possessions", nothing more. If they did not work properly or disobeyed their owners, slaves were often punished, whipped or hanged.

This racist attitude that made white Americans assume they were superior to non-white people is quite similar to the one British settlers showed when they came to Australia. White Americans not only applied it to blacks who were brought to the country after whites had come, but also to the ones that were already there, such as the Native Americans: white settlers took away the Native American lands without hesitation or remorse as well and treated the native population as a less valuable race that had to be "civilized" by the superior white race.

Although something like the "Stolen Generations" never existed in the US, ethnic minorities, particularly blacks, had been far from equal for a long time. After abolishing slavery as a result of the Civil War (1861–1865), life for black people did not considerably improve for a long time. Even if blacks were free now, the society they lived in was racist. It was even established by law that they were not considered equal members of American society. The Jim Crow laws were created to stop them from voting, for example. A Supreme Court ruling allowed whites to force blacks to go to different schools, hospitals and churches. At this point, their legal status was defined as "separate but equal" – white people were not ready to welcome black people in society.

In the 1950s, many black people felt that it was time to take action to end the denial of civil rights and stop discrimination. In Montgomery, Alabama in 1954, a black woman called Rosa Parks refused to give up her seat in a bus for a white person – this act of defiance triggered the Civil Rights Movement, which took thousands of black people to the streets, demanding equal rights as whites and the end of discrimination. Dr. Martin Luther King Jr. was one of the most prominent figures of the Civil Rights

Movement, leading non-violent protests for civil rights in all parts of the country. Change did not come easily and racial violence took the lives of a great number of mainly black people, among them Martin Luther King himself. Nevertheless, blacks slowly but surely made their way into American society.

All in all, American minorities seem to have made greater progress towards equality than Aborigines in Australia and have significantly improved their social status and economic standing. Similar efforts have been made in Australia and civil rights groups did and do exist, yet they have never had the huge impact the Civil Rights Movement had in the United States. Still, Aborigines have achieved official equality to the rest of the Australian population and, officially at least, have the same chances and opportunities as other Australians. Sadly, this remains a theory in many cases, because many Aborigines have not overcome their dark past yet – it can only be hoped that they soon will.

(962 words)

3. **Step 1** *Make sure you understand the task: you will have to explain both the terms "assimilation" and "multiculturalism" (a dictionary might help you with a good definition), as well as clarify them with Australian and non-Australian examples. Take your notes /do your brainstorming on a separate sheet of paper.*

Step 2 *In the main part of your essay, you might want to elaborate on about three to four points/arguments. Provide arguments for either side (pros and cons) of both concepts. Take notes again.*

Step 3 *Arrange your arguments and start writing. A good way to introduce a topic can be historical facts, surveys or quotes that you can think of in connection with the topic. You may also want to give your comment a title.*

Melting Pot or Salad Bowl?

Both "melting pot" and "salad bowl" are well-known images when it comes to discussing the ways of living together in a country, especially if someone is part of an ethnic minority. Which concept is the better one: is it assimilation, through which everyone becomes a member of society by adapting to it, creating a society where everything melts together into one big pot? Or is it one big unity, a salad in a bowl, but still made from different ingredients (the vegetables) – in other words, multiculturalism, which a dictionary defines as "the practice of giving equal importance to all members of society and to include people of different languages, races and traditions in it"?

In many cases, assimilation seemed to be the right thing in the past. It used to be rather common for mostly the white race to expect or even force people from a different ethnic and cultural background to adapt to their white way of life. Along with that, whites considered themselves superior to other races. Thus, assimilation was not a voluntary act, but imposed on people. An example of this can be found in 19th and 20th century Australia, when the (white) government forcibly took children, the so-called "Stolen Generations", from their indigenous Aborigine families. The reason for this legal form of abduction was to turn these children into valuable members of society by raising them according to white tradition and lifestyle, because the Aborigine way of life was not acceptable for the white government.

Today, assimilation can be defined in a more positive way: when assimilating to a country and its society, newcomers willingly become part of it and are not excluded or seen as outsiders. Numerous immigrants from India, Africa or Pakistan have integrated into society quite well in Great Britain, for instance. Some of them have even made considerable careers as politicians, artists, athletes or in other professions.

However, a certain price has to be paid in order to fully assimilate: traditions and customs that are a vital part of one's heritage have to be suppressed or even given up completely. Many members of ethnic minorities all over the world have been struggling with assimilating to the new culture and preserving their original cultures at the same time. Therefore, they constantly have to deal with an inner conflict of identity and belonging.

This is why multiculturalism might be a better concept, because a connection to one's origin can be kept here: there are various examples of ethnic minorities that have maintained their traditions and have found their place in a society different from the one they were once born into. For instance, Asian people in the United States have a strong sense of belonging to their new home country, the US, and are equally proud of their Asian heritage and customs.

To add to that, a multicultural society can doubtlessly be seen as a gain for a country in general: with multiple cultural backgrounds, a country is more complex and diverse. The United Kingdom, for instance, has become a country of increasing ethnic diversity in the previous decades and is carrying out a policy of multiculturalism concerning immigrants, which means that people from different cultures are allowed to live in the UK without fully adapting to British ways of life or shedding all their cultural traditions. This makes Britain an alluring mixture of different cultures, which many British citizens approve of, as a survey conducted by the BBC in 2005 showed. A simple question may serve as evidence: can you imagine London without its Indian restaurants and New York without Chinatown or Little Italy? Hard to do so, isn't it?

On the contrary, some people see multiculturalism as a burden rather than a blessing and are concerned. People from all over the world with different cultures, languages and traditions enrich a nation on the one hand, but on the other definitely add to a country's already existent problems. Research has shown that members of ethnic minorities who have not adapted to their new country well experience a greater number of social disadvantages, such as the lack of education or unemployment, than those who have.

As a conclusion, a healthy mix of both assimilation and multiculturalism seems a good concept. You should voluntarily adapt to the country you live in to a certain degree; for example be able to speak its language or accept, as well as understand, the moral and cultural principles it is based on – something that fits into the concept of assimilation. Of course no one should ever be forced to do so, such as Aborigine children were in the past – this would guarantee failure, because you should not give up your heritage entirely; an idea which goes along perfectly with a multicultural approach that attempts to create unity through difference. *(805 words)*

From tips to clicks: restaurants try e-menus

by Rebecca Harrison; TEL AVIV (Reuters) – Enter the e-waiter, Monday, Feb 25, 2008

Restaurants in Europe, the United States, and Japan are testing technology to let diners order their food directly from a screen at their table instead of depending on a fellow human being to note their choice – sometimes grumpily[1] or erroneously[2].

Besides cutting costs, companies that sell the "e-menu" argue the bytes-for-bites ap-
5   proach has a novelty value that can lure younger customers and boost revenues as tantalising[3] photographs of succulent[4] steaks and gooey[5] desserts tempt diners to order more.

It also could extend the TV dinner. How about a computer-game dinner?

The idea may be only the latest gimmick[6] in a trade which is driven by consumer ap-
petites and where fads[7] help. But at least for now, it appears to be boosting business.
10   In Israel, privately owned start-up Conceptic has already installed e-menu technology in sushi bars, pubs, and family restaurants. The system is based on touch screens already used in self-service canteens or for ticketing in airports and cinemas.

"It's about impulse-buying," said Adi Chitayat, Conceptic's chief executive. "If a person starts looking at pictures of chocolate cake, the chances are he'll order it." […]
15   Frame, a trendy sushi restaurant in Tel Aviv, Israel, which has installed the system, said sales on tables with the e-menu have increased by about 11 percent. Customers often call ahead to reserve spots equipped with the screens, manager Natalie Edry told Reuters.

At one of the e-menu tables, information technology worker Gil Uriel and his young family were enthusiastic as they checked out pictures of the dishes on offer and squabbled
20   over desserts.

"It's more visual," said Uriel, as his children clicked away furiously on a games func-
tion between courses. "We can still choose, we can still argue – but it's much easier when you can all see it." […]

Microsoft says its new Microsoft Surface system, which transforms an entire table
25   into one big touch screen, is due to go live in spring 2008 in some U.S. hotels and casi-
nos, letting customers order food directly as well as play music and games.

The Seattle-based giant says on its Web site it will "transform the way people shop, dine, entertain, and live." Both Conceptic and Microsoft argue their examples of interactive and communal technology represent the future.
30   "We are living in a technology age," said Conceptic's Chitayat. "People are not afraid of screens." The company, which launched its pilot in 2006, expects to turn a profit in mid-2009, he added. […]

Chitayat said taking computers into restaurants is an obvious next step after technology revolutionized the workplace, although he noted restaurants with the e-menu – in-
35   cluding Frame – still rely on waiters to deliver the food. […]

But many diners doubt the e-menu idea will take off.

"I don't believe in screens; I believe in humans," said businessman Yoash Torkman as he lunched at Frame. "I'll wait for 15 minutes for a waitress instead of using this. It's a gimmick and gimmicks have very short lives."

40 In Europe, where dining out is a time-honored tradition as much about good conversation and etiquette as staving off[8] hunger, waiting staff were unsurprisingly circumspect[9].

"See this man here? He's been coming here for 25 years," said a waitress at Italian restaurant Rosticceria Fiorentina in Brussels, who gave her name only as Giovanna. "I know his wife; I know his daughter. Do you think it would be better if he was welcomed 45 by computer?" […]

"There are always some people who embrace a new technology but others will avoid it for as long as possible," said Jackie Fenn, emerging technology analyst at Gartner consulting group.

"Will a bunch of teenagers have a blast using it? Yes. But it will take time to move 50 from being an attraction in a small number of restaurants to something that is widespread." *(622 words)*

© *Reuters; Rebecca Harrison; Enter the E-Waiter; 25 Feb 2008*

1 grumpily – mürrisch
2 erroneously – irrtümlich
3 tantalising – extremely tempting
4 succulent – juicy
5 gooey – sweet and sticky
6 gimmick – Masche, Trick
7 fads – Modeerscheinungen
8 stave off – vermeiden von, abwehren
9 circumspect – vorsichtig/zurückhaltend

Assignments

1. Summarize the text. (Material) (30 BE)

2. Compare the influence of innovative technology on everyday life to the influence of innovative technology on life in a utopian/dystopian society dealt with in class. Take the text at hand as a starting-point. (40 BE)

3. *"But, in fact, is it true that the happiness of the individual advances as man advances? Nothing is more doubtful"* (Emile Durkheim, 1893).
   Discuss the problem raised by Durkheim, taking the text at hand as a starting point. (30 BE)

Teaching modules referred to:
The tasks you have to complete here centre on the main teaching module The Challenge
of Individualism – Science and technology *(Q1), with a focus on* electronic media. *Know-*
ledge of the teaching module The Dynamics of Change – Order, vision, change *(Q3) with*
special reference to models of the future *is also necessary.*

1. *How to approach the task:*
   Your summary should not exceed one third of the original text (between 150 and
   200 words). Use the present tense and do not quote from the text. Explore the struc-
   ture of the text first and then put your ideas in a logical order.

   The article from "Enter the e-waiter" by Rebecca Harrison, Tel Aviv (Reuters), published on February 25, 2008 and retrieved on July 13, 2010, revolves around the new
   trend of the e-menu adopted by some restaurants in Europe, Japan and the United
   States.
   Harrison portrays a restaurant in Israel that is offering e-menu technology by a company called Conceptic, which started a test project in 2006 and expects profits from
   2009. The company considers interactive technology at restaurants to be the next step
   after changing people's working environment by means of technological innovations.
   Microsoft's futuristic concept of a full-screen table combining e-menu with entertainment features, scheduled to launch in 2008, follows similar objectives.
   Advocates of the e-menu argue that ordering food from a screen on your table is not
   necessarily about cutting costs but about the novelty factor and visually tempting pictures that boost business.
   However, e-menus might remain a short-lived trend. Especially in Europe, where eating in restaurants is a social event, the technology is regarded with suspicion as it
   lacks human interaction. It might attract young people and those eager to try out new
   technological features but it will take time for e-menus to spread more widely than
   that.   *(200 words)*

2. *How to approach the task:*
   Step 1 Make a list of relevant texts you have read, films you have viewed and vo-
   cabulary you have learned in class.
   Step 2 Looking for similarities and differences, establish connections between the
   narrative situation in this material and the situation illustrated in the text at hand.
   Step 3 Structure your essay carefully and explore the influence of new technology on
   people's lives with examples from the different texts.

   The text "From tips to clicks: restaurants try e-menus" by Rebecca Harrison deals
   with people's positive and antagonistic reactions to technological progress. Depicting
   a real-life example from Israel, the author illustrates that technological advancement
   is embraced by some people as a chance to set new business standards and revolu-

tionize social life in general or family life in particular. Yet she also portrays it as a "trend" or "fashion" that does not meet the requirements of long-standing traditions. Whereas some members of society, like the chief executive of Conceptic or the information technology worker Gil Uriel, are thrilled by the prospects offered by a new technology (ll. 10–14 and 18–23), others, like a waitress from an Italian restaurant in Brussels, cannot understand their enthusiasm and refuse to accept the new invention (ll. 40–45). However, technological progress is regarded from an economic point of view in the text and is perceived – at least for now – as an opportunity offered by a free market that one can accept or refuse (ll. 16/17 and 50/51). Additionally, this example visualizes technological progress as a minor, accessory phenomenon that only slightly influences consumer behavior during leisure time, with no or hardly any grave social or political implications.

Technology's influence seems much larger, however, considering that new innovations are not only present at trendy establishments but pervade all areas of life, from our workplace to health care, home entertainment and everyday communication. Technology is omnipresent and it seems normal for it to spread everywhere, even into social life with networks like Facebook substituting digital communication for real-life interaction.

Consequently, many seem concerned with the political, social and moral implications of technological progress in everyday life. A lot of the utopian/dystopian texts dealt with in class try to increase awareness about the threats, disadvantages and dangers that arise from new technologies and offer solicitous views on such innovations.

A rather humorous approach to the topic is offered by Dave Berry in his text *Remote Control*. He portrays appliance manufacturers as narcissistic, unworldly people who create gadgets that are smarter than their owner, put him under tutelage and, in the end, create a desperate consumer who is completely overtaxed and no longer able to lead a self-determined life. A new remote control is thus able to offer access to the internet, it can turn on the dishwasher from the office, remind the owner that the refrigerator is empty, give the necessary nutritional advice and serve as a telephone, smart phone and so on – if the user manages to understand it.

Even though the new remote control is not initially designed to control people, its complexity and omnipresence threatens people's individuality, privacy and liberty.

In *The Hunted*, Alex Shearer portrays a society without a moral and social conscience. Genetic engineering and medical and pharmaceutical advancements are finally able to provide the means to stop the aging process. In an aging society, where youth has become rare and therefore a very valuable economic commodity, smart racketeers take advantage of the sparseness of "supplies". They try to become owners of children and convince them to take the medicine required in order to remain young. The high demand for young people makes their business model very profitable and children are rented out by the hour to elderly people, sold for a lot of money or used as stakes in card games.

Alex Shearer convincingly portrays negative effects of innovative technology. In his dystopian vision, children are abused by greedy, ruthless adults to satisfy their temporary interest in youth. They are considered to be economic commodities that can be disposed of at will like toys, whereas their needs, like playing with peers, are disregarded.

An even more dangerous outlook is offered by Aldous Huxley in his novel *Brave New World*. Huxley successfully explores what happens when political leaders are able to control scientific progress and innovative technologies. Genetic engineering has created the conditions for a caste system ruled by a World Controller that has eradicated unemployment and abolished families and emotional relationships. The price of social stability is high. A perfect drug keeps people happy, whereas a new religion controls their obedience and loyalty. Additionally, technological progress has created a thoughtless form of consumerism that is alluded to in Rebecca Harrison's article as well.

In conclusion, one can say that utopian/dystopian texts see innovative technology very critically, confronting the reader with complex moral, social and political implications. *(742 words)*

3. *How to approach the task:*
   Step 1 Explain the quotation in your own words.
   Step 2 Make notes on what you think of the issue. You can agree, disagree or partly agree/disagree. You must give reasons to support your opinion and find convincing examples. Remember to refer to the text at hand in some way.
   Step 3 Structure your ideas in paragraphs and start writing.

In the quotation given the French sociologist Emile Durkheim raises the question of whether happiness is a constant of progress and denies its validity. Durkheim distinguishes between mankind and the individual. Although he admits the existence of progress in general, he doubts that individuals will profit from it to the same extent. I agree with Emile Durkheim's point of view.

In my opinion happiness is not always related to progress, but progress always influences the level of happiness, which includes pleasure and satisfaction during an ongoing process, as a result of a process one is directly involved in, or gained as a spectator. In America, it was even included in the Declaration of Independence as an important political precept: "Life, Liberty and the pursuit of Happiness" are unalienable human rights. This phrase has deeply shaped not only Americans' expectations and understanding of the world.

Starting with the 18th century, progress – political, technological or moral – has always been perceived as a significant contribution to human happiness. Feudal and other forms of authoritarian systems turned into democracies, technological progress improved the poor working conditions of many people, and moral values like tolerance created the conditions for a much wider acceptance of people with special abilities or minorities. Therefore, progress was looked upon as something that changed people's lives significantly for the better and thus increased their level of happiness one way or another.

At the same time one can hardly deny that people can fall victim to progress. Technological progress leads to mechanization and rationalization, which can cause unemployment and dissatisfaction, at least temporarily. The invention of the computer comes to mind here, of course. Before that, the invention of the mechanical weaving loom at the end of the 18th century, for example, caused pain and distress that even led to riots.

More recently, the nuclear disaster at a power plant in Japan offers evidence of the downside of unquestioned progress.

In the text at hand, technological progress is dealt with from an economic point of view. Its contribution to human happiness is very short-lived, if it exists at all. From the author's point of view it is described as a "gimmick" (l. 8) or "fads" (l. 9), both words revealing the rather superficial contribution to human happiness. The alliteration "boosting business" (l. 9) points to the fact that the interest in the e-menu as an example of technological progress is purely financial without any moral significance. In addition, the position and range of application of the new invention in self-service canteens, airports or cinemas alludes to the temporary nature of its relationship with the consumer, which one could very well do without.

What is also traitorous is the fact that the new example of technological progress is only welcomed by representatives of advanced technology companies (ll. 18–34). Their enthusiasm seems prejudiced and not without strong personal and economic interests. From their point of view, progress is celebrated as a form of liberation and simplification of human life ("it's much easier when you can all see it" ll. 22/23). Global market leaders like Microsoft insist that this form of progress is the future.

The author might add a point in favor when she describes how a grumpy and erroneous waiter (l. 3) is replaced by a neutral screen, thereby satisfying the customer – making him happy. Yet the waiter is an individual human being as well and a victim of progress. Similarly, the customer might regret the loss of face-to-face interaction.

In conclusion, it is to be doubted whether this kind of progress makes the individual happier. On the contrary, it is more likely to increase people's isolation and limit their ability to interact physically and morally with other human beings. It will increase the synthetic atmosphere of our already superficial environment and will contribute to human alienation. People's happiness is rather a result of successful and meaningful human relationships. It can often be caused by small things such as a smile or the helping hand of a friend. Technological progress, on the other hand, has a destructive element.

Under these circumstances it is more than doubtful that individual happiness advances as man advances. In times of advanced environmental destruction and overpopulation, the relationship between technological progress and happiness will certainly have to be redefined.

(715 words)

Multiculturalism has been Canada's solution, not its problem

by Irene Bloemraad, *The Globe and Mail,* October 28, 2010

German Chancellor Angela Merkel recently made headlines when she pronounced multiculturalism in Germany a failure. Shortly before, a Globe and Mail editorial argued that Canadians should eradicate "multiculturalism" from their vocabulary and refocus on "citizenship". Multiculturalism isn't just out of style, these statements suggest – it's dan-
5 gerous for building unity in increasingly diverse societies.

Unfortunately, both analyses are dead wrong.

Social scientists can measure multiculturalism in a given society by examining the number and content of public policies and government pronouncements around cultural recognition and accommodation.

10 Such indices show that Germany is not, and has never been, a multicultural society. Multiculturalism can't have failed in Germany because it was never tried. Turkish guest workers and other immigrants were never welcomed as future citizens – only as temporary labour. If Germans are now concerned about the consequences, the blame certainly doesn't lie with multiculturalism.

15 These indices also group countries such as France and Norway with Germany as least multicultural, Sweden, the Netherlands and the United States as moderately multicultural, and Australia and Canada as most multicultural.

Have Canada's past practices and policies hurt attempts to forge common citizenship out of diversity?

20 Absolutely not. Consider how many immigrants become citizens. The least multicultural countries count the lowest levels of citizenship; the moderate multicultural countries have somewhat more. In comparison, an overwhelming majority of immigrants proudly take up citizenship in Canada and Australia, the two countries that went furthest in the multicultural experiment.

25 The positive link between multiculturalism and citizenship is further supported by comparing Canadian policy with that of the United States. In 1971, the Canadian government began promoting a multiculturalism-based integration policy, which was enshrined[1] in the Charter of Rights and Freedoms in 1982 and expanded in 1988, when the Multiculturalism Act[2] became federal law. Over this same period, the U.S. enacted no formal im-
30 migrant integration program or multiculturalism policy.

In 1970, in both Canada and the U.S., about 60 per cent of foreign-born residents had acquired citizenship. By 2006, the American Community Survey estimated that, of the 37.5 million foreign-born people living in the U.S., just 42 per cent were naturalized[3] citizens. By that same year, 73 per cent of immigrants to Canada had acquired citizenship,
35 one of the highest rates in the world.

There are, of course, many possible explanations for this statistical gulf, but here are some factors that did *not* play a predominant role: different immigrant streams; the large undocumented population in the U.S.; different costs and benefits of citizenship; easier or faster processing in Canada.

40 My research points to multiculturalism as a key factor driving Canada's success at citizenship integration. It legitimates diversity, provides a sense of inclusion and, through the multitude of (oft-maligned[4]) government grants given to community-based organizations – not only for multiculturalism but also for a host of integration programs – it provides the support structures to help newcomers join the country as full citizens.

45 Canadians certainly can, and should, have thoughtful debates about recognizing and accommodating diversity – just as we debate health-care policy or Stanley Cup[5] contenders.

Like health-care and hockey, multiculturalism has become a symbol of what defines Canada. In poll after poll, Canadians say multiculturalism is one of the top three defining
50 features of the country. What's more, they are proud of it.

They should be. Over four decades, incredibly rapid demographic change has transformed Canada, especially its largest cities. In Europe, similar change has resulted in riots and cultural tensions that have tarnished[6] the concept of multiculturalism there. But, in Canada, these changes, despite many challenges, happened peacefully, productively and
55 positively. Multiculturalism was part of the solution, not the problem.   *(641 words)*

© *Irene Bloemraad*

1 enshrined – niedergelegt
2 Multiculturalism Act – the act acknowledged the right of ethnic groups in Canada to preserve and share their unique cultural heritage; it also guaranteed equal opportunity for Canadians of all origins. This act has remained largely unchanged since 1988 with the exception of some minor amendments.
3 naturalized – eingebürgert
4 maligned – schlechtgemacht
5 Stanley Cup – North American hockey championship
6 tarnish – mit einem Makel versehen

Assignments

1. Summarize the article. (Material)   (30 BE)

2. Relate Canada's approach to multiculturalism to the situation in either the USA or Great Britain. Refer to material discussed in class.   (40 BE)

3. *"Is wanting to preserve your country's cultural identity a bad thing?"*
    (http://www.sherdog.net/forums/f54/wanting-preserve-you-countrys-cultural-identity-bad-thing-1173076/index3.html [retrieved: September 29, 2011])
    Discuss.   (30 BE)

Lösungsvorschläge

Teaching modules referred to:
The tasks centre on the teaching module Promised lands: dreams and realities *(Q3) with particular focus on* Canada *and* political and social issues. *Depending on your line of argument, knowledge of the module* USA *and the topic of* living together *(Q1) or* social structure *and* social change *in the* United Kingdom *(Q2) is necessary.*

1. *How to approach the task:*
   Your summary should be between 160 and 215 words (about one third of the original text). Remember to use the present tense, avoid quotations and start with an umbrella sentence. You should focus on the author's line of argument and omit unnecessary detail.

   In *The Globe and Mail* from October 28, 2010, Irene Bloemraad discusses the importance of multiculturalism in diverse societies based on the example of Canada. Contrary to recent comments by German Chancellor Angela Merkel and some Canadian journalists, the author is convinced that multiculturalism is the key to integrity and peace despite diverse influences.
   Her argument is verified by scientific indices which show that Germany, France and Norway have never been real multicultural societies, whereas Australia and Canada rank highest on the scale. These statistics are linked to the number of immigrants becoming citizens in these areas, with the latter countries featuring the most.
   According to the author, the importance of acquiring citizenship is confirmed further by Canada's active integration policies from 1971 onwards, including the Charter of Rights and Freedoms in 1982 and the Multiculturalism Act in 1988. In the United States, in contrast, where the rate of naturalizations is decreasing, there were no official attempts to integrate immigrants and encourage multiculturalism.
   Multicultural policies make immigrants feel included and welcome and offer support in the process of becoming a citizen, thus guaranteeing unison and avoiding cultural tensions like those in Europe. Canadians should indeed be proud of multiculturalism as it is the solution for peaceful unity in increasingly diverse societies.   *(211 words)*

2. *How to approach the task:*
   Step 1 Make a list of texts and films dealt with in class that focus on the situation of immigrants and their experience with diversity, multiculturalism and integration policies.
   Step 2 Decide which country you want to use for comparison with Canada, the USA or Great Britain, and find examples from the texts or films you listed.
   Step 3 Structure your essay carefully and explore what is typical in the respective country.
   The following solution will deal with the situation in Great Britain and offers two possible ways of dealing with the task: one is based on non-fictional material, and the other on fictional texts offering a more emotional view of the topic.

GK 2012-9

Canada is often proclaimed the ultimate multicultural society. It actively fosters unity in spite of diversity through legal acts, integration programs and "support structures" (l. 44), as can be seen by political measures established, for example, in the Charter of Rights and Freedoms Act (1982) or the Multiculturalism Act (1988), but also by sheer numbers: by 2006 about 73 percent of the country's immigrants received Canadian citizenship. This is one of the highest rates in the world and fully proves Canada's commitment to and approval of cultural diversity. Multiculturalism is something that Canada's citizens are proud of.

Multiculturalism in Great Britain, in contrast, is more a result of colonialism and a delayed immigration process. Although it has a history of accommodating immigrants, the numbers of immigrants in former centuries were small. Many arrived after the Second World War to counteract the labor shortage and due to Great Britain's conviction that it had a moral responsibility to host people from former colonies. Immigrants from India, Bangladesh and Pakistan mainly settled in big cities, where they found job opportunities and housing. Another wave of immigrants came from the West Indies and the Caribbean. Although they have the same colonial past, this group of people insists on their cultural difference.

Immigrants from Commonwealth countries were guaranteed citizenship until 1962, when the government decided to limit the number of immigrants. The immigration process today is controlled by a number of measures started in 1971 and completed by the Immigration Act in 1988.

However, multiculturalism is dealt with differently in works of fiction, the media and on day-to-day politics, and each decade has its own approach. In addition, immigrants perceive the topic differently from people who are not personally affected by the problem.

(290 words)

Variante 1

In the article "The New Empire within Britain", first published in 1982, the British Indian writer Salman Rushdie deals with doubtful aspects of immigration law and Great Britain's attitude towards multiculturalism in the eighties. Rushdie criticizes the discriminative practices of British authorities towards immigrants from the former colonies. According to him, white immigrants with one British-born parent are offered immediate citizenship, whereas blacks are denied this basic right.

This attitude is even more dubious against the backdrop of the Macmillan initiative, which, based on hopeful and optimistic advertising campaigns, invited these people to immigrate and apply for British citizenship in the first place. Now they are accused of abusing the welfare state and confronted with hate, threats and other forms of discrimination by parts of British society and institutions like the police. What is even more shameful is that a larger number of people prefer to ignore the situation and thus indirectly encourage racism and cultivate a very selective attitude towards a multicultural society.

This attitude seems to have changed in the nineties. In his speech "Chicken Tikka Massala", delivered on 19 April, 2001, Robin Cook, British Foreign Secretary from 1997 to 2001, points out the advantages of an immigration process that leads to a multicultural society. He claims that multiculturalism enriches British society, makes it more vivid and innovative and more tolerant. He also points out that immigration is a part of British tradition which can be traced back to the very beginning of time and has invigorated the nation.

However, Cook also points out that tolerance towards immigrants is more common among the younger generation, who accept cultural diversity and seem to understand its positive impact on the British economy. Nevertheless, he sees British society as being capable of integrating foreign cultures.

The text "Down Up North" from *The Economist*, 15 December, 2001, explores the idea of multiculturalism from an economic point of view. The author of this article observes that a multicultural society adapts more easily to the immediate needs of the modern economy and attracts a much larger number of companies because they appreciate this kind of variety. In his view, a multicultural society is more flexible, and people with a multicultural background usually speak more languages and have a deeper and more genuine understanding of foreign cultures. At the same time he warns of the negative consequences of racism. He makes clear that it is not the high number of immigrants that cause social tensions but the unemployment rate that can affect both natives and immigrants. He therefore claims that more concern should be devoted to the question of education, which can contribute substantially to the success of a multicultural society. *(446 words)*

Variante 2

Contemporary short stories by Muriel Spark, Qaisra Shahraz, Hanif Kureishi or Salman Rushdie describe a rather incomplete multicultural society and try to explore the reasons for its deficiencies.

In her short story *The Black Madonna*, Muriel Spark explores the idea of multiculturalism in a middle-class Catholic environment, where unintentional discrimination, lack of education, ignorance and hidden hypocrisy impede the success of an inclusive, diverse society.

The childless couple and firm believers Raymond and Lou Parker make the acquaintance of two Jamaicans, Henry Pierce and Oxford St. John. The couple somehow feel responsible for them and consider it their duty to help them integrate into English society.

At the same time, the Parkers are trying to have a baby and pray to the Black Madonna for help. Their prayers are answered, but the Parkers are shocked when they realize that the baby is black. Although the test clearly shows that Raymond is the father, they decide to have the baby adopted and distance themselves from their Jamaican acquaintances.

Muriel Spark draws a very hypocritical picture of English society and its attitude towards multiculturalism. People pretend to be open-minded and welcoming but in fact are prejudiced and narrow-minded. They use immigrants to display their tolerance as long as it is necessary and convenient, but show racial intolerance and lack of understanding when their moral reputation is at stake. By giving their own black baby up for adoption, they reject multiculturalism. At the same time, the author suggests that multiculturalism is a young social experiment and needs protection. Everyone is invited to "adopt" the idea and foster it.

In his short story *My Son the Fanatic*, which is set in the Pakistani community, Hanif Kureishi blames religious fundamentalism for the tensions within the community and British society.

When Parvez, a taxi driver, finds out that his son Ali has become a religious fundamentalist, rejects a modern way of life, has given up higher education, insults his female clients and is isolating himself more and more from friends and family, he is more than shocked. Emotionally devastated, he tries to understand the reasons for the change in his son. When he realizes that Ali is not open to rational arguments anymore, he kicks and beats him.

The two characters, father and son, symbolize different generations of immigrants and different attitudes towards British society. Whereas the father has successfully adopted the British way of life and internalized their moral and social values, like tolerance and a more relaxed view of religion (although he was born and grew up in Pakistan), the son seems to be looking for something else. He is not capable of adapting to the needs of modern British society and looks for comfort and orientation in religion. He rejects democracy and any form of worldly pleasure, becomes incapable of critical thinking and starts hating people who are different. He thinks his father has betrayed his culture and distances himself from him.

Kureishi alludes to the fact that a multicultural society can only be successful if it finds a healthy balance between two different cultures. Complete accommodation of British values does not seem to be the solution because it ends in assimilation. Kureishi seems to suggest that a society can profit more if people can keep their traditions and adapt to the social, economic and political requirements of a society.

In conclusion, one could say that the success of a multicultural society depends on its ability to create a social and moral climate of tolerance, understanding, acceptance and recognition – as can be seen in Canada. *(592 words)*

3. *How to approach the task:*
   Step 1 *Try to put the question in your own words.*
   Step 2 *You should find arguments for and against the preservation of one's cultural identity and then express your own opinion, so make notes on what you think about the issue. Find convincing examples and justify your views.*
   Step 3 *Structure your ideas in paragraphs and start writing. It is a highly sensitive topic and should be handled with care. Try to avoid stereotypes and prejudiced ideas.*

Traditions acquired over centuries form the basis for cultural identity. Identity confers people with unique characteristics but also promotes similarity with others: we are all the same, but different. Ideally, cultural identity gives people the chance to preserve uniqueness within sameness. A society with strong liberal traditions, for example, provides the framework for undisturbed personal development. On the other hand, people can easily lose their individuality and personal identity in a more restrictive cultural environment coined by religious fundamentalism, for example.

I therefore think that in the context of immigration and multiculturalism, preserving one's cultural identity is not a bad thing if a cultural environment with its traditions does not distort your personality and does not lead to alienation and hostile behavior towards other cultures. Thus, I think that cultural identity is a bad thing if it leads to segregation and hostility.

Cultural traditions and, accordingly, cultural identity can help people overcome the difficulties they have to face at the beginning of the immigration process when they are struggling to learn a new language or improve the skills required by the new job market. A tradition of compassion and understanding like in Canada, for example, can create a climate of hope and one can easily overcome setbacks or any form of disillusionment and disappointment.

Additionally, cultural identity can help close the gaps between cultures. If people understand that every culture is incomplete and has potential for development, they will not feel offended and be more likely to adopt new traditions that enrich their own culture. Cultural identity is therefore a visual extension of traditions and a never-ending process. Local and traditional dishes are a good example of permanent and accepted changes brought about by diverse cultures in a multicultural society.

Furthermore, the will to preserve one's cultural identity increases cultural awareness and makes people more tolerant. A new culture can be perceived as a mirror that reflects one's perception of oneself and can help assess advantages and disadvantages in a constant process of evaluation. Questions of a balanced diet, for example, or a wasteful attitude towards the environment, can lead to new and unexpected answers if discussed with people who have a different outlook on things.

On the other hand, a cultural identity that distorts your personality can have negative consequences and is therefore a bad thing. The writer Qaisra Shahraz refers to such a situation in her short story *A Pair of Jeans*, where she describes the conflict between a young Muslim girl, who has adopted the values of a modern society, and her parents and future parents-in-law, who perceive her lifestyle as a violation of their cultural identity. The pair of jeans symbolizes emancipation and a threat to cultural identity at the same time. The different cultural identities in this case lead to alienation and oppression. Their respective restrictions violate the characters' personalities, isolate them from people and society and strain family relations. Such a situation is even more dangerous if it is accompanied by the rejection of the official language.

Religious fundamentalism is another form of cultural identity that should be questioned and looked at critically. Although it promises orientation and moral guidance, it incapacitates people and reduces their ability to think and lead their own lives. It transforms the followers' perception of the world, creates feelings of hatred and fear and isolates them from society. Honor-killing, for example, is often a consequence of religious fundamentalism. It stands in contrast to civil law and is, to us, a very doubtful form of cultural identity. Additionally, followers of fundamentalist movements feel morally superior and justify their intervention in the name of a divine power or a superior culture. In the end, they perceive everybody who is different as someone inferior and themselves as superior.

Concluding, one could say that the process of preserving cultural identity can only be successful if the balance between adjustment and refusal is kept. *(650 words)*

Material A: Aufgabe zur Sprachmittlung

Öl – war da was?

Bislang haben wir bei jeder Umweltkatastrophe dazugelernt. Diesmal nicht.

von Andrea Böhm, 22. 7. 2010

Die Empörung über die Umweltkatastrophe ist grenzenlos. Protestaktionen gegen Ölfirmen im ganzen Land, in Kalifornien verbrennen Bürger ihre Kreditkarten, mit denen sie an Tankstellen Rabatt bekommen. Der Kongress handelt, der amerikanische Präsident unterzeichnet mehrere radikale Gesetze zum Umweltschutz.

5 Barack Obama im Jahr 2010? Nein, Richard Nixon[1] im Jahr 1970.

Auch damals ging es um eine Ölkatastrophe (und um verseuchte Flüsse). Das Fernsehen zeigte Bilder von toten Seevögeln, stillgelegten Fischereiflotten[2] und ölverschmierten Stränden – in diesem Fall lagen sie in Kalifornien[3]. Aber die politischen Zeiten waren offensichtlich andere. Vor vierzig Jahren zog der Schock über die ökologischen Folgen

10 des Energiehungers politisches Handeln nach sich, um ebendiese Folgen zu korrigieren. Und er beschleunigte den Aufstieg der amerikanischen Öko-Bewegung.

Erst kommt die Katastrophe, dann der Lernprozess, dann die Politik. Dieser Dreisatz prägte bislang die Geschichte des Umweltschutzes. Bislang. Angesichts des Desasters im Golf von Mexiko, verursacht durch die BP-Ölplattform *Deepwater Horizon*, zeigt sich

15 der Staat ebenso hilflos wie die Austernfischer[4] in Louisiana. Politischen Aufwind verspüren in den USA offenbar nicht die Befürworter neuer Auflagen zum Schutz von Natur und Klima, sondern deren Gegner. [...]

Mit der Verhängung eines vorläufigen Bohrstopps scheiterte Barack Obama an der amerikanischen Justiz und an der öffentlichen Meinung. Sein Appell an seine Landsleute,

20 unter dem Eindruck der Katastrophe eine neue, nachhaltige Energiepolitik zur nationalen Mission zu machen, verhallte.

Das Paradoxe dabei ist: Wir – denn es geht ja nicht nur um die Amerikaner – ertrinken bei der Berichterstattung über solche Katastrophen inzwischen in absurden wie erschreckenden Informationen über unser eigenes Zerstörungspotenzial. [...]

25 Wir wissen, dass die über 700 Millionen Liter Rohöl, die in den vergangenen Wochen in den Golf geflossen sind, etwa einem Fünftel des täglichen Verbrauchs der USA entsprechen. Wir haben außerdem gelernt, dass *oil spills* andernorts seit Jahrzehnten zur Tagesordnung gehören. [...]

Nur will der Lernprozess, also die Umsetzung dieser Informationen in politisches

30 Handeln, heute nicht mehr so recht gelingen – nicht in den USA, nicht im Rest der Welt. [...]

Womöglich folgt die heilsame Wirkung des Schocks über *Deepwater Horizon* ja noch. Womöglich wird irgendwann eine überfällige Konvention ausgehandelt, eine Diskussion über ein Moratorium für Tiefseebohrungen[5] angeschoben und die Debatte über

35 Klimaschutz aus dem Keller geholt. Aber vorerst ist keiner in Sicht, der den Anfang machen will oder kann. Barack Obama schon gar nicht. Der muss im November bei den Kongresswahlen mit einer verheerenden Niederlage rechnen. *(381 Wörter)*

Die Zeit, 22. Juli 2010, Nr. 30, S. 8, http://www.zeit.de/2010/30/Umweltkatastrophe-Oelfirmen-Klimadebatte [abgerufen: 20. 08. 2011]

1 Richard M. Nixon – 37th President of the United States, 1969–1974
2 Fischereiflotte – fishing fleet
3 This refers to a major oil spill off Santa Barbara, CA, in January 1969
4 Austernfischer – oyster farmer
5 Tiefseebohrung – deep-sea drilling

Assignment

A group of environmental activists in Louisiana is interested in international opinions on U.S. environmental policies after the oil spill disaster in the Gulf of Mexico in 2010. Summarize the excerpt for them. (Material A)

Material B: verkürzte Textaufgabe

Dashed Hopes

M. G. Vassanji's novel portrays the Lalani family, who are East-Indian immigrants to Canada, now living in the run-down apartment block 69 in Toronto's Don Mills district. The following excerpt describes a decisive moment for their daughter Fatima.

Fatima Lalani was standing squeezed into an elevator on her way up to receive the tidings[6] which she did not as yet know were bad. Her mother Zera had phoned her at the drugstore, where she worked after school, to tell her "it" had arrived, meaning the long-awaited letter from the university, and Fatima took off. In the elevator, although she
5 greeted two small boys and threw a brief but disdainful glare at some of the more ordinary-looking people returning from work bearing parcels of groceries, she was as nervous as she had ever been in her life. It seemed to her that when she opened the envelope which was waiting for her, her entire life would be decided. It did not occur to her that the decision she awaited had already been made a few days before, and she whispered a
10 prayer in much the same way her mother sometimes did; although she had never believed in, in fact had begun to scoff at[7], the efficacy[8] of this remedy, and her mother was the last role model she had in mind. [...]
  When the elevator stopped on her floor, [...] Fatima could push herself out. Then, with a swing of her shoulders and a shake of her head, as if to banish the odours of cheap
15 perfume and sweat and groceries, she strode off to her apartment. When she let herself in, her mother was waiting like an attendant, envelope in hand. Fatima grabbed it, tore it open, quickly read the gist, and slumped down on the sofa with a loud groan.
  "What's it?" asked Zera, her mother, having guessed the answer.

"Arts and Science[9]," spoke Fatima in a mixture of grief and anger tinged with[10]
20 drama.
"So? This is the end of the world then? Arts and Science – what's wrong with it?"
Fatima sulked, picking up the telephone and cradling it in her lap. During the last
year, whenever any well-wisher asked her what she wanted to "become", she had given
one unequivocal[11] reply: "Become rich." To many of the girls and boys of Sixty-nine and
25 Sixty-seven and the other high-rise apartment buildings in this part of Don Mills, this is
what growing up meant – making it. To the brighter ones, those with averages in the
eighties and nineties[12], making it meant going to university: not to study pure science or
humanities, but something more tangible[13], with "scope"[14], computer science or pharmacy for instance. For the girls, the latter of the two was preferable. It was more feminine,
30 less threatening to the boys. Among the brighter girls of Don Mills the competition for a
place to study pharmacy at the university is intense. Fatima Lalani, with an average of
eighty-six, had struck out.
To Zera Lalani, of the old school, any education was a way out, a way up, and her
daughter's disappointment carried no significance beyond her having to put up with a
35 bout of adolescent sulkiness. *(490 words)*

Moyez G. Vassanji, No New Land, Toronto 1991, pp. 3–5

6   tidings – news
7   scoff at – make fun of
8   efficacy – Wirksamkeit
9   Arts and Science – Geistes- und Sozialwissenschaften
10 tinged with – mixed with
11 unequivocal – unmissverständlich
12 averages in the eighties and nineties – *Ergebnisse gemessen im 100-Punkte-System; entspricht in
    etwa guten bis sehr guten Ergebnissen im deutschen System*
13 tangible – handfest
14 scope – Entfaltungsmöglichkeit

Assignments

1. Describe the situation. (Material B)   (30 BE)

2. Compare Fatima's attitude to that of immigrants to the United States discussed in class. Refer to material discussed in class.   (40 BE)

3. Discuss how important money is for you when choosing your job. Take
   the text at hand as your starting point.   (30 BE)

**In die Gesamtwertung gehen die Ergebnisse der Teilaufgaben A und B im
Verhältnis 1:3 ein.**

Lösungsvorschläge

Teaching modules referred to:
The mediation assignment centres upon work done in the module Science and technology *(Q1) with special emphasis on* ecology. *Part B focuses on the module* Tradition and Change – Work and industrialization *(Q2), especially on the key issues* business, industry and the environment, *and requires you to refer to texts about or by immigrants to the USA (module* United States – American Dream, *Q1).*

Teil A: Aufgabe zur Sprachmittlung

How to approach the task:
Step 1: Read the text carefully and concentrate on the main objective of the article, which already becomes visible in the title and subtitle.
Step 2: Start out with an umbrella sentence containing the source and the topic.
Step 3: Write a maximum of 100–130 words.

The article from the German newspaper *Die Zeit* (July 22, 2010) deals with the increasing indifference towards ecological catastrophes. Forty years ago media coverage of an oil spill and contaminated rivers caused an uproar among the American public and finally led to strict environmental policies. The Deepwater Horizon disaster of 2010 did not entail any consequences. Obama's attempts to put an end to deep sea drilling and to support sustainable energy were rejected by the courts and the public. Everyone – not only in the USA – has become used to hearing of the destructive impact of ecological disasters and no one is able or willing to take action – especially not Obama, since environmental protection policies might result in his defeat in the upcoming congressional elections.

(124 words)

Teil B: Verkürzte Textaufgabe

1. *How to approach the task:*
   Read the text carefully and describe the situation Fatima is in. Pay special attention to describing her feelings and the reasons for her disappointment. Consider her aims in life and what a successful career means to her.

In the extract, Fatima Lalani, the daughter of an East-Indian immigrant family in Toronto, is eager to come home after she is informed by her mother that she has received a reply to her university application. Fatima is extremely edgy since the reply will determine her future. She rushes from the elevator to her apartment, where she grabs the envelope from her mother's hands and opens it. The admission to an Arts and Science program provokes deep disappointment and anger in Fatima because it is her ultimate aim to strike it rich through a successful career. She shares this dream with other good students in the run-down high-rise buildings in her district who equate growing up with making it to the top by studying hard in subjects like computer science or pharmacy. The reader discovers that the girls prefer pharmacy because of its feminine appeal and that there is a lot of competition for a place to study it. As an above-average student Fatima is crushed because she has only been accepted for the less promising Arts and Science. Her mother, Zera Lalani, who considers any education a means of climbing the social ladder and leaving the run-down neighbourhood, cannot comprehend her daughter's disappointment. *(204 words)*

2. *How to approach the task:*
   Step 1: *Read the text carefully and underline the passages that provide an insight into Fatima's attitude to work, education and a future career.*
   Step 2: *Try to pinpoint why she is so disappointed about her admission to an arts and science program.*
   Step 3: *Portray her attitude and compare your findings with the expectations and attitudes of immigrants to America, referring to texts or films you know. Develop a clear structure and concentrate on the following aspects:*
   – *the idea of success*
   – *higher education as a means of climbing the social ladder and acquiring prestige*
   – *higher education as a means of becoming rich*
   – *subjects that guarantee a high income*
   – *subjects with a feminine aura*
   The following essay focuses on T. C. Boyle's The Tortilla Curtain. *Other possible examples would be the Lithuanian immigrants in Upton Sinclair's novel* The Jungle. *You could also refer to short stories by Asian-American authors, e. g. Amy Tan, or Hispanic writers, e. g. Sandra Cisneros. Non-fictional accounts of successful immigrants like Arnold Schwarzenegger can also be related to the text at hand.*

In the following I will compare Fatima's attitude to education and material success to that of Cándido and América in T. C. Boyle's *The Tortilla Curtain*. In the extract at hand we meet Fatima Lalani, the daughter of East-Indian immigrants to Canada, who lives with her family in a lower-class housing area in Toronto. Obviously, her parents support her in her attempt to enter upon a successful career through a university education. Although she graduated from high school with a high average, she is terribly disappointed when she is notified that she has only been accepted for an Arts and Science program. Her mother cannot understand why Fatima is so devastated.

In Boyle's novel the main characters have a completely different background. As illegal immigrants in the United States they do not even have a roof to sleep under. They live in even worse circumstances than Fatima. Cándido's and América's home is a canyon and their beds are some blankets in the sand. The canyon is full of shrubs with thorns, snakes and spiders. They drink water from a stream and have to make a fire every time they want to cook. As illegal immigrants they are forced to move about in eternal fear of being stopped by the Migra or Border Patrol and sent back to a desolate life in Mexico. Nevertheless, they still dream of having a better life in the United States.

This evidently applies to Fatima as well. She sees a university degree as a means of climbing the social ladder and leaving her run-down neighbourhood. Fatima is disappointed about only being accepted for so-called soft subjects. She would have preferred computer science or pharmacy (ll. 28/29) since such hard subjects will most probably result in higher pay. Her priority is pharmacy, as it has a more feminine appeal. It is her ultimate aim to strike it rich, as is pointed out in l. 24. In the extract it is also emphasized in ll. 24–26 that she shares this dream with many boys and girls in the apartment blocks in her district, who view material success as a way of escaping from their poor neighbourhood. They might also want to escape from their ethnic environment or their family.

In contrast to Fatima, Cándido's and América's dreams of a better future are a lot more modest. The seventeen-year-old América, who is pregnant, cherishes a simple dream of a house, a yard and maybe a car and a TV. She does not fancy the palaces of the gringos she works for. Four walls and a roof are the most she can hope for. Education is beyond her reach. Both Cándido and América take up any kind of work for little money. They work extremely hard without complaining. Without the right to stay in the United States and without medical care or a regular income, professional training or higher education remains unattainable.

To sum up, both Fatima and the illegal immigrants in Boyle's novel share a dream of a brighter future in the countries they immigrated to. Whereas Fatima aims at "making it" (l. 27) through university education and a prospective career, Cándido and América are absorbed in their fight for survival. They are willing to bear any hardship and suffering in order to stay in the USA. That is why they humbly accept the most terrible circumstances, such as working with toxic detergents or being pushed away like dogs in the parking lot of a supermarket, for example. Seen in this light, Fatima seems to be privileged and extremely ambitious in her pursuit of material success.

(601 words)

3. *How to approach the task:*
   Step 1: Start off by examining how important money is for Fatima.
   Step 2: Consider other factors that might be rewarding.
   Step 3: Come to a conclusion and give reasons.

Quite obviously, Fatima is an extremely ambitious young lady who dreams of making it to the top. She is utterly disappointed upon hearing that material success will not easily come her way since she has not been accepted for computer science or pharmacy. From the extract it is hard to tell whether she is really interested in these hard subjects or whether she has only fallen for the status they might promise in the future. The reader is not informed about what she is really good at. Fatima seems to view a successful career as a means of leaving her run-down surroundings.

On the one hand, I can understand that especially the children of immigrants view higher education as a ticket to the job market and perhaps as a way of leaving their ethnic environments. In the text at hand Fatima looks down on hard-working people carrying their grocery bags (ll. 5/6).

On the other hand, one should keep in mind that money and material success or status are not everything. There are other factors that I consider important when choosing a career.

Personally, I feel that job satisfaction is an extremely important aspect to be considered. It can only be achieved if you choose very carefully and attain a balance between your talents, motivation and your desires for the future. I reject the idea of choosing a career only because of the material benefits or the status that it is connected with. Fatima's wish to study pharmacy because it has a feminine appeal and promises money seems to be very superficial. Long working hours in a laboratory or in a pharmacy might be the wrong choice if she is not intrinsically motivated.

In my opinion it is important for every individual to choose a worthwhile and meaningful field of occupation since money alone does not necessarily entail satisfaction or happiness. The increasing number of stress-related diseases such as the burn-out syndrome clearly indicate that stressful situations might result from increasing demands and perhaps also from the wrong choices made when choosing a career. Inability to work and early retirement might result from the urge to strike it rich and make it to the top. Very often, highly paid positions, for example in the computer industry, require a fierce competitiveness that not everyone wants to develop. To me, factors like flexibility of working hours, family-friendliness or the opportunity to travel are just as important as cooperating with others.

Nevertheless, the choice of a personal career should definitely be made on the basis of a realistic assessment of whether or not you can make a living with it and support yourself and perhaps, later, your family. It is important to consider the risks that accompany unrealistic aspirations for so-called "dream jobs".   *(462 words)*

Should Huck Finn get a 21st-century revision?

by Seán O'Driscoll, The Irish Times, January 7, 2011.

The word 'nigger' has been replaced by 'slave' in one US publisher's new versions of Mark Twain's classic novels – but should texts really be sanitised?

SITTING AT his desk in Montgomery, Alabama, Prof. Alan Gribben is weathering a storm he knew was coming. "Of course there was going to be trouble," he says with a shrug. "You don't change Mark Twain and not expect the walls to come crashing down."

5 This week, an Alabama publishing company, NewSouth, announced it will be releasing Gribben's altered version of Mark Twain's classics, *The Adventures of Tom Sawyer* and *The Adventures of Huckleberry Finn*, in which the word "nigger" is replaced with "slave", while the word "injun" is replaced by "Indian".

It's the removal of the first word (used 219 times in *Huckleberry Finn*) that has cultural commentators frothing with outrage this week. Some have called the new version an 10 "abstinence-only" approach to discussing racism, while others have heralded the arrival of the politically correct apocalypse, the point of no return for liberal thought police.

"Let's get one thing straight," says Gribben, an Auburn University professor who has been vilified by both the left and right. "Mark Twain was a notoriously commercial and populist author. If he was alive today and all he had to do was change one word to get his 15 book into every schoolhouse in America, he couldn't change it fast enough." But he isn't here and he can't answer for himself. Maybe Twain would have screamed in indignation that his work was being robbed of its original meaning.

Gribben, a likeable straight talker, is adamant that he is not robbing Twain of anything, merely making a small change so that English teachers are no longer embarrassed 20 to read out loud in class.

But should literature really be changed to avoid the blushes of English teachers? For a cut-and-paste digital generation, is literature just another mash-up that can be altered to suit demand? "I sincerely hope not because it would be very, very bad for American literature," says Randall L. Kennedy, who is probably the world's greatest expert on the N 25 word (he never uses such euphemisms), having written a widely discussed social history book called *Nigger: The Strange Career of a Troublesome Word*.

Kennedy, an American law professor at Harvard University, is among a large group of black commentators who denounced Gribben this week.

"It's a profoundly bad idea," he says. "The word 'nigger' appears in the autobiogra-30 phy of Malcolm X, should that be removed as well?" But it's not the same thing, is it? Mark Twain was white, Malcolm X was not, the context is very different.

Kennedy sighs. "No, I really don't think so. If the word is hurtful and contemptuous, then it ought to be condemned no matter who is speaking."

I wonder if there isn't a certain power play going on here. A white professor wants the
35 word removed because it makes him squirm, a black professor wants it included. Isn't that
squirming a form of social control over white people? A way of keeping them forever
awkward and eager to please? "Now that's an interesting argument," says Kennedy.

"By removing the word from Mark Twain, we are losing the opportunity to discuss. If
I was an English teacher, I would relish the opportunity to talk about my own feelings and
40 open the discussion to the classroom. Now that's having a real argument, that's showing
your students respect."

I wondered what other black people thought of the N word and whether removing it
from Twain would help bury a painful past or save white America from confronting its
own history. I was pondering all on the subway on the way home when I heard two black
45 teenagers talking. "Hey nigga, what's up with you?" said one. The reply was instant "Ain't
nothin' wrong with me nigga, something wrong with you though."

Enter white Irish reporter with a copy of *Huckleberry Finn* and a massive avalanche
of awkwardness. I stutter through an explanation of my article and show them a few of
Mark Twain's offending passages.
50 The first, 17-year-old Laurence Johnson, picks up the book, studies it for a moment
and shuts it suddenly.

"So he said 'nigger'. So what? People think slave owners called us African-Americans?" he says loudly.

His friend laughs, so do some middle-aged black women sitting nearby, all of whom
55 nod in agreement. Johnson, who is in his final year of high school in Brooklyn, puts himself in the place of a slave owner counting his slaves.

"One, two, three, four … damn, we got an African-American escaped up north!"

More laughter, some of the women are clapping their hands. "It's about the timing,"
says one of them, Katicha Spencer, a 42-year-old dental nurse from Bedford Stuyvesant
60 in Brooklyn. "If some white person said that word to me, I'd be mad as hell. But if it's
from 100 years ago, and it's someone trying to get the flavour of what people are saying,
then that's what people said. You can't sugarcoat the past of this country, you can't pretend it didn't happen." Her friends nod in agreement. "Mark Twain's alright," says one.
"He's not my boss." Katicha gives her a high five and they laugh as they leave the train.
65 […]

(881 words)

http://www.irishtimes.com/newspaper/features/2011/0107/1224286958314.html
[retrieved: January 8, 2011]

Assignments

1. Summarize the article. (Material) (25 BE)

2. Analyse the attitudes towards racial discrimination in the article at hand and relate them to forms of discrimination in Great Britain or Canada as encountered in material discussed in class. (40 BE)

3. *"I've never seen a sincere white man, not when it comes to helping black people. Usually things like this are done by white people to benefit themselves. The white man's primary interest is not to elevate the thinking of black people, or to waken black people, or white people either. The white man is interested in the black man only to the extent that the black man is of use to him. The white man's interest is to make money, to exploit."* (Malcolm X)
Comment on this quotation taking the history of African Americans and their current situation into account. (35 BE)

Lösungsvorschläge

Teaching modules referred to:
The task relates to the teaching module USA *(Q1), with particular reference to the theme* living together (ethnic groups: African Americans). *Other modules are also touched on, such as* The United Kingdom (Q2), *with particular emphasis on* social structures, social change *and the theme* Promised lands (country of reference: Canada) *from Q3.*

1. *One particular point to watch out for here is the fact that the newspaper article contains different viewpoints. The author juxtaposes opposing views as to whether it is politically correct to use the word "nigger" in writing and whether this word should be replaced in literature.*

   Step 1 *Make sure you identify the different points of view correctly. You need to allocate the viewpoints to a specific person <u>and</u> their skin colour.*

   Step 2 *Without going into unnecessary detail (your summary can only be 220–300 words long), you can structure your writing according to the different points of view.*

   Step 3 *Bear in mind that there seems to be a difference as to whether the N word is used by a white or a black person and in which context, historically or in the present. This forms the second layer of the controversy.*

   Step 4 *Your umbrella sentence, apart from stating author, newspaper, headline and date of publication, should also include the cause of this debate.*

   In this newspaper article, which appeared in *The Irish Times* on January 7, 2011, Seán O'Driscoll describes a heated debate amongst American cultural commentators about the release of Mark Twain's two classical novels in an altered version.

   The editor, Prof. Alan Gribben from Alabama University, replaced the word "nigger" in *Tom Sawyer* and *Huckleberry Finn* with "slave" and used "Indian" instead of "injun". Although expecting trouble, his reason for doing so is to avoid racist references in the new version and enable teachers to use it in their classrooms without embarrassment. He maintains that Mark Twain himself would have made these small changes if his popularity or chances of being read at school had been at stake.

   The African-American Professor Randall L. Kennedy, from Harvard University, and author of a social history book about the N word, attacks his white colleague Gribben, fearing for the reputation of American literature if such changes are made to please public demand. He argues that even in the autobiography of Malcolm X this word is used, and points out that it would be a shame to forego the opportunity to discuss the use of the word "nigger" for educational purposes.

   The author of the newspaper article asks whether the uncomfortable feeling of Whites concerning the use of the N word is about social control on the part of African-Americans and conducts short interviews with random black people. Here, reactions range from those who believe that replacing the N word for historical reasons is ridiculous to those who claim you cannot make history sound better or who even make fun of the idea. Used by Whites nowadays, however, the N word is supposed to be politically incorrect.

   (282 words)

2. **Step 1** *Focus on the range of attitudes as expressed in the newspaper article. What is also important is the skin colour of the people quoted in the text and their different expectations of dealing with ethnic minorities in the USA.*

Step 2 *Draw up a list of novels, short stories, articles, films or other material you have dealt with in class that provide sufficient background for your analysis of attitudes towards discrimination.*

Step 3 *Decide whether you want to use Great Britain or Canada as a country of reference. In the following, a sample solution for both countries will be presented.*

For Great Britain, Andrea Levy's novel Small Island *is included. What is also discussed is an undercurrent of xenophobia visible in the rejection of immigrants depending on the needs of the labour market in times of economic recession. The changes in British legislation concerning Commonwealth citizens and migration within the European Union are also of importance. If you want to include inter-ethnic discrimination, you could refer to Bali Rai's novel* (Un)arranged Marriage. *For a more recent focus, the practice of sharia courts in GB could also be mentioned.*

If you would like to base your argument on the situation in Canada, you would have to concentrate on a different historical situation and differences in the make-up of ethnic minorities in this British dominion. Here, the Franco-Anglo bilingualism is of consequence as well as the situation of the First Nations and Stephen Harper's apology for their maltreatment and the disadvantages encountered. Dawn Dumont's novel Nobody Cries at Bingo *would be a good starting point as there is a similar discussion to that in the US as to whether it is politically correct to use the term "Indian" if addressing members of the First Nations. Canadian attitudes towards multiculturalism and the concept of a melting pot or salad bowl could also be compared with those in the US.*

The history of racial discrimination in the US starts with the arrival of African slaves in the 17th century. This is why the use of the word "nigger" – even in a historical context such as Mark Twain's classics – triggers such controversy in the USA when the white Professor Alan Gribben changes the word to "slaves" in two of Twain's novels. By purifying these time-honoured texts he believes he will be able to avoid racial discrimination and, above all, act in accordance with what Mark Twain himself would have done.

Gribben's attitude towards African-Americans can be seen as marked by caution and respect, taking into account difficulties high school teachers and their students may experience in a politically correct world. He does not shy away from changing even well-known classics, fully aware of the public outcry this will undoubtedly provoke. The criticism which Gribben has to face, however, is less about this caution and political correctness (although some cultural commentators are quite outraged about this "abstinence-only" approach [l. 10] and even denounce it as a "point of no return for liberal thought police" [l. 11]) than about his changing works of literature and covering up America's past.

One of his black critics, denouncing Gribben's approach to avoiding racial discrimination, is an expert on the use of the N word, whose "troublesome career" (cf. l. 26) he has researched in a widely discussed social history book. Professor Randall L.

Kennedy's main objection is about pleasing public demand and changing works of literature for this purpose. He points out that even in Malcolm X's biography the N word is used and would have to be removed if one followed Gribben's logic. The fact that Malcolm X, in contrast to Mark Twain, was a black person does not make much difference to Kennedy.

At this stage, the author's own opinion comes into play. Seán O'Driscoll, a white, Irish journalist, wonders whether in fact a person's skin colour creates a different context altogether (l. 31). Furthermore, Driscoll speculates about whether the controversy at hand has not established "a certain power play" (l. 34) directed against Whites.

Kennedy does not reject this idea completely but claims that by removing offensive words and thus changing the meaning of original texts, opportunities for discussion might be lost in which teachers and students could express their own feelings – instead of simply looking at the N words as being hurtful and contemptuous (l. 32).

Driscoll finally decides to find out what other black people think about the N word, suspecting that its removal could stop Americans from confronting their own history and help to cover up a distressing past (ll. 42–44). By interviewing black subway passengers at random he finds a mixture of attitudes, some agreeing that being addressed as "nigger" by a white person would be regarded as being very offensive and would make them "mad as hell" (l. 60), whereas this would have been normal 100 years ago. Black teenagers even call each other "nigga" in a jocular way (ll. 45/46). That racial discrimination goes deeper than words is shown by another youth, who points out the irony of a slave owner talking about black people as African-Americans. Not covering up America's past and history of slavery seems to be more important to the interviewees than using words the way Mark Twain did.   *(551 words)*

Great Britain

Although there has been – and still is – racial discrimination in Great Britain as well, its history and origins are quite different from the American context. As the colony's motherland, Great Britain was instrumental in the slave trade between Europe, Africa and North America but never used slaves itself to any considerable extent. It was only after World War II that significant numbers of different ethnic communities, such as Caribbeans, Commonwealth citizens and East and South Europeans, arrived in Great Britain.

Jamaican people especially had already served in the British army during the war and it is their social history that the plot of Andrea Levy's novel *Small Island* is based on. Gilbert Joseph (the novel's protagonist) was one of several thousand Jamaican men who joined the RAF to fight against Hitler. After the war, his wife Hortense joins him to start a better life in England. In spite of her training as a fully qualified teacher, her applications to the British school system fail. Both she and her husband experience many instances of racial discrimination on the grounds of their skin colour and because their neighbours are afraid of the immigrants.

The same sentiment becomes apparent in Enoch Powell's famous speech on the "Rivers of Blood", in which the right-wing politician warns the public against too many immigrants "flooding" Great Britain and demands that their numbers be restricted. He was opposed to the government's policy of allowing people who were not white to come from other countries to live and work in Britain in the late 1960s, and he predicted street violence between different races.

The British government, however, promoted equal opportunities and helped make improvements in social conditions and employment. In this context, black people in Great Britain protested against continued discrimination and the lack of houses and job opportunities, in a campaign that resulted in the Brixton riots. More recently, attempts to encourage the integration of ethnic minorities have been successful. Social, economic and educational programmes have been put into place, so that different cultures can take pride in their traditional festivals and practices, and racial harmony remains part of official government policy.

As of today, Great Britain has emerged as a multicultural nation promoting integration rather than assimilation. Shared values and an active membership are supported at large, although particularly within the Muslim communities there appears to be a split between the older, integrated members and younger Muslims, some of whose aims seem to point to parallel societies.

All in all, racial discrimination still seems to be an unresolved problem in Great Britain but rather on the grounds of social and traditional values, compared to the situation in the USA, which has seen considerable progress since the arrival of the Civil Rights Movement but still suffers from inequality based on skin colour. This has also led to affirmative action, where members of particular ethnic groups, mostly Blacks and Hispanics, have enjoyed preferential treatment. However, this policy has also caused a lot of disagreement and members of the ethnic minorities concerned feel that this is just another form of discrimination.   *(512 words)*

Canada

Whereas the concept of a melting pot is now being replaced by the idea of a salad bowl or cultural quilt in the US, Canadian society has been trying to overcome the racial divide and discrimination since the 1970s by establishing an official policy of multiculturalism in their legislation, promoting the idea of a mosaic. Different cultures are encouraged to maintain their own qualities, languages and cultural practices. In this respect, Canada is regarded as a model for other immigration countries. This does not mean that ethnic minorities have never been disadvantaged or discriminated against. However, in contrast to the USA, Canadians never employed slaves but often provided a safe haven for African-Americans who were able to escape from their slave owners in the south. Ethnic tension in Canada has developed on two other historic lines: those of the French-Anglo relationships and the attitudes towards the First Nations – the so-called Canadian Indians.

In terms of easing the historical tensions between French and British settlers, the Canadian government has repeatedly tried to employ pro-active policies and introduced official bilingualism as a means to preserve cultural traditions, especially in the minority group of people with a French background.

In another contrast to the USA, the French and English cultures have always been considered the two founding cultures of Canada, and the issue here is not one of discrimination against each other but of political influence and economic resources.

In terms of social and political equality, the First Nations of Canada have had a much more difficult stance, and whereas Mark Twain's usage of the word "nigger" would not raise an eyebrow in Canada, the change of Twain's "injun" to "Indian" would. There is an ongoing debate in the country about whether the members of the First Nations can feel happy about being addressed as Indians, or whether this is just another sign of the cultural and social suppression they suffered in Canada's past.

Apart from being refused the right to vote in their own country of origin until 1960, the people of the First Nations were not considered part of Canadian society for a long time and even had special status under the Indian Act, according to which they were exempt from some taxes. In particular, their children were subject to government control and many of them were forcibly sent to what were known as residential schools, where they were not allowed to speak their native languages or follow their traditional customs.

This aspect of discrimination is part of Dawn Dumont's novel *Nobody Cries at Bingo*, which describes her experiences on an "Indian" reserve. Her parents had to attend residential schools themselves but never complain much about this. It is only after Dawn's parents discover that the Canadian government hands out "Common Experience payouts" that they remember any maltreatment at these schools. Such payouts were made to compensate former students of residential schools for their negative experiences. Similar compensation was given to the Stolen Generation of Australia. In her novel, Dumont argues that her parents deserved the money but criticises their hypocrisy at the same time.

A couple of months after Australia, Canada, through Prime Minister Stephen Harper, apologised in Parliament to the Aboriginal peoples of Canada for their forced assimilation in the Indian residential schools. In his speech he deplored the role of both government and the Church in using force and inflicting much harm on the children in their custody, in forbidding cultural practices and destroying family ties. This apology, although seen as a first step towards reconciliation, did not meet with unequivocal approval. Leaders of the First Nations have reacted by pointing out that Harper's apology was not specific enough and it was not clear what he was apologising for. The issues their communities are struggling with on the reserves, namely drug abuse and serious social problems, were not really addressed. There is little or no funding from the government to deal with these issues.

As a conclusion, it has to be said that there has been, for a long time, a certain condescension in the way the mainstream societies of Canada and the USA have been dealing with their Aboriginal and Native American population, respectively. In Canada, many problems have been resolved by official government policies regarding the First Nations as well as other ethnic minorities. In the USA the success of the Civil Rights Movement has brought about considerable changes and the election of the first black president, Obama, is a sign of hope. *(747 words)*

3. *In order to assess this quotation by Malcolm X you are required to put it in both its historical and autobiographical contexts.*
   Step 1 *The history of the African-American population is characterised by slavery, Reconstruction and the Civil Rights Movement. So first you need to delineate these developments and the current situation of the black community.*
   Step 2 *The role of Malcolm X within the Civil Rights Movement needs to be scrutinised in order to explain his pessimistic outlook as the leader of the Muslim Black Panthers.*
   Step 3 *Finally, you will have to take both contexts into account and come to your own conclusions as to whether you agree or disagree by following your line of argument.*

The quotation by Malcolm X shows a strong distrust in the role of the white man and his tendency to exploit rather than support black people in the USA.
Looking at the history of African-Americans, this distrust seems to be justified. Brought to the USA as slaves since the 17th century, they were bought and sold, treated as property and abused in the worst possible manner. They did not have a place in the American Constitution and were excluded from the pursuit of happiness promised in the Declaration of Independence of 1776.
As a result of the Civil War (1861–1865) slavery was officially abolished in the USA and, with the 14th Amendment to the Constitution, Blacks became US citizens by law and were subsequently granted the right to vote. However, segregation followed and discrimination against black people did not stop, and, especially in the south, continued well into the second half of the 20th century. In particular, what were known as the Jim Crow laws in the 1890s made sure that black people were hindered from voting, were not allowed to eat a meal in a white restaurant, even had to use different and inferior public toilets and could not sit in the front of a bus. The Jim Crow laws were meant as a mockery of the black man, based on the cliché of the Jumping Jim Crow figure, a caricature of a singing, dancing and uneducated black man.
Technically, all slaves were freed by the 13th Amendment to the Constitution (1865) and also allowed to rent land to farm on. However, they were still dependent on the Whites and often led poor lives as sharecroppers, agreeing to deliver a certain share of their crop every year to the landowner, trapped in a cycle of endless hard work and relentless poverty. This situation is best outlined in two novels by Toni Morrison.
A Mercy describes how Florens, a slave born in America, suffers a great deal of hardship from her owners but also enjoys human mercy later in a family. In *Beloved*, set just after the Civil War and focused on the psychological impact of slavery, the main character tries, in vain, to leave the memories of a horrific past behind her. Both novels show a certain victim mentality of African-Americans in the past and are very much in accordance with Malcolm X's statement and opinion about the white man.
It took a long time to change the living conditions of black people in the USA. Reconstruction after the Civil War had not brought the improvements hoped for by the African-Americans.
Rosa Parks, a member of the National Association for the Advancement of Colored People (NAAP), sparked off the fight against segregation and the start of the Civil

Rights Movement. In 1955, she refused to give up her seat to a white passenger in a Montgomery bus, was arrested, and in her support black citizens came together to fight for their rights. Led by Martin Luther King, boycotts of the public transportation system were organised and one year later the Supreme Court of the US declared segregation of public transportation unconstitutional.

Based on Mahatma Gandhi's principle of non-violent resistance, Martin Luther King organised national protests against the discrimination of Blacks with sit-ins and freedom rides. His activities culminated in his famous speech of 1963, "I have a dream", but he was assassinated in 1968.

Malcolm X's radical views made him an opponent of Martin Luther King. Instead of non-violent agitation he proposed a Black Revolution and criticised his black fellow-countrymen for an attitude where they would turn the other cheek. He was very popular at a time when poor housing, little education and no jobs for Blacks were the order of the day. This also explains his distrust of any promises of the white man, who from his point of view (expressed in this quotation) would do nothing to support the Civil Rights Movement but only acted according to his own advantage, meaning exploitation of the Blacks. Malcom X was shot by black gunmen in the same year.

As much as Malcolm X's statement seems to be supported by the history of Blacks in the USA, it also suffers from over-generalisation. Not every white person has been opposed to the emancipation of African-Americans and his opinion does not reflect the obvious advancements in the black cause and the success of the Civil Rights Movement, despite certain setbacks.

Since the 1960s, the federal government of the US has passed laws forbidding discrimination of ethnic minorities at work. The policy of affirmative action has played a major role in admitting black students to universities, although this has been criticised as another form of discrimination. Cultural diversity has been experienced by white people as a positive element of daily life, and as the numbers of people making up the traditional mainstream get smaller in the light of a growing Black and Hispanic population, attitudes toward minorities are changing and giving way to more tolerance and less pressure to assimilate.

In economic terms, there is a considerable black middle class in cities like Chicago, and from there the first black president, Obama, emerged. Although Malcom X's statement is true in a historic sense, it does not express the chances of a more optimistic future for a multicultural America. *(886 words)*

Fight Club

Palahniuk's cult novel Fight Club *depicts a sinister, nightmarish big-city-USA. The protagonist, a well-to-do young office worker, becomes the founder of 'fight club' which involves secret after-hours brutal (boxing) fights between upper-middle class males in the basement of bars.*

What you see at fight club is a generation of men raised by women. [...]

Last week, I tapped a guy and he and I got on the list for a fight. This guy must've had a bad week, got both my arms behind my head in a full nelson[1] and rammed my face into the concrete floor until my teeth bit open the inside of my cheek and my eye was
5 swollen shut and was bleeding, and after I said, stop, I could look down and there was a print of half my face in blood on the floor.

Tyler stood next to me, both of us looking down at the big O of my mouth with blood all around it and the little slit of my eye staring up at us from the floor, and Tyler says, "Cool."
10 I shake the guy's hand and say, good fight.

This guy, he says, "How about next week?"

I try to smile against all the swelling, and I say, look at me. How about next month?

You aren't alive anywhere like you're alive at fight club. When it's you and one other guy under that one light in the middle of all those watching. Fight club isn't about winning
15 or losing fights. Fight club isn't about words. You see a guy come to fight club for the first time, and his ass is a loaf of white bread. You see this same guy here six months later, and he looks carved out of wood. This guy trusts himself to handle anything. There's grunting and noise at fight club like at the gym, but fight club isn't about looking good. There's hysterical shouting in tongues[2] like at church, and when you wake up Sunday
20 afternoon you feel saved. [...]

When we invented fight club, Tyler and I, neither of us had ever been in a fight before. If you've never been in a fight, you wonder. About getting hurt, about what you're capable of doing against another man. I was the first guy Tyler ever felt safe enough to ask, and we were both drunk in a bar where no one would care so Tyler said, "I want you
25 to do me a favor. I want you to hit me as hard as you can."

I didn't want to, but Tyler explained it all, about not wanting to die without any scars, about being tired of watching only professionals fight, and wanting to know more about himself.

About self-destruction.
30 At the time, my life just seemed too complete, and maybe we have to break everything to make something better out of ourselves.

I looked around and said, okay. Okay, I say, but outside in the parking lot. So we went outside, and I asked if Tyler wanted it in the face or in the stomach.

Tyler said, "Surprise me."

³⁵ I said I had never hit anybody.

Tyler said, "So go crazy, man."

I said, close your eyes.

Tyler said, "No."

Like every guy on his first night in fight club, I breathed in and swung my fist in a
⁴⁰ roundhouse[3] at Tyler's jaw like in every cowboy movie we'd ever seen, and me, my fist connected with the side of Tyler's neck.

Shit, I said, that didn't count. I want to try it again.

Tyler said, "Yeah it counted," and hit me, straight on, *pow*, just like a cartoon boxing glove on a spring on Saturday morning cartoons, right in the middle of my chest and I fell
⁴⁵ back against a car. We both stood there, Tyler rubbing the side of his neck and me holding a hand on my chest, both of us knowing we'd gotten somewhere we'd never been and like the cat and mouse in cartoons, we were still alive and wanted to see how far we could take this thing and still be alive.

Tyler said, "Cool."

⁵⁰ I said, hit me again.

Tyler said, "No, you hit me."

So I hit him, a girl's wide roundhouse to right under his ear, and Tyler shoved me back and stomped the heel of his shoe in my stomach. What happened next and after that didn't happen in words, but the bar closed and people came out and shouted around us in
⁵⁵ the parking lot.

Instead of Tyler, I felt finally I could get my hands on everything in the world that didn't work, my cleaning that came back with the collar buttons broken, the bank that says I'm hundreds of dollars overdrawn. My job where my boss got on my computer and fiddled with my DOS[4] execute commands. […]
⁶⁰ Nothing was solved when the fight was over, but nothing mattered. […] There's nothing personal about who you fight in fight club. You fight to fight. *(795 words)*

From FIGHT CLUB: A Novel by Chuck Palahniuk. Copyright © 1996 by Chuck Palahniuk. Used by permission of W. W. Norton & Company, Inc.

1   a full nelson – a wrestling hold
2   shouting in tongues – shouting in foreign languages (biblical reference)
3   a roundhouse – weit ausholend angesetzter Boxhieb
4   DOS – veraltetes Computer-Betriebssystem

Assignments

1. Point out what you get to know about 'fight club' and its 'members'.
   (Material)   (25 BE)

2. Relate the text to the concept of the American Dream as discussed in
   class, taking into account the narrator's statement *"my life seemed too
   complete"*.   (40 BE)

3. You are a member of a project team on 'violence in modern society'.
   Write a comment on the surge of violence for the project report.   (35 BE)

Lösungsvorschläge

Teaching modules referred to:
The text and questions dealt with here relate to the major theme Ideals and reality *(Q3)*, focusing on structural problems (violence). *Other teaching modules are also covered, such as the module* USA *(Q1) with the major themes* American Dream and living together, *and the module* Extreme situations *(Q2), focusing on* initiation *and* the troubled mind.

1. **Step 1** *As with a summary, it is a good idea to start your own text with an umbrella sentence that refers to the name of the author and the title the extract comes from. You should also mention the main theme and details of the situation described.*

   Step 2 *In contrast to a formal summary, the assignment "point out" means both to identify and explain certain aspects, in this case the rules of fight club, its location and proceedings and the motivation of its members.*

   Step 3 *Make sure you understand certain hints, such as "generation of men raised by women" (l. 1), "a bad week" (l. 3), "how about next month" (l. 12), "carved out of wood" (l. 17) etc. After working out the meaning of these references you might want to underline the points you consider important and then structure them according to the assignment.*

   Step 4 *Describing the main points, you should only use your own words as much as possible. The main points should include a description of the particulars of this fight club, like secrecy, location, proceedings and its members, who become brutal and aggressive and enjoy extreme situations. What are also important are the aims and objectives of this informal institution.*

   In this excerpt from the novel *Fight Club*, the author Chuck Palahniuk portrays the practices of a secret fight club for middle-class men in a big city in the USA.
   Fights usually take place in the basement of bars and are characterised by utter brutality and the cheering support of spectators.
   The narrator and his friend Tyler started these informal meetings after they had got into their first fight with each other, in a parking lot (l. 32). They had wanted to learn how far they could take things (ll. 47/48) – without pleasantries and using extreme violence. After the fight no problems were solved but nothing mattered anymore. It was fighting for its own sake and not on personal grounds.
   After that they invented a fight club for "men raised by women" (l. 1), those members of their own middle class who were looking for adventure and extreme situations and wanted to end up as tough guys (ll. 16/17) roughened by unlimited fights following hardly any rules.
   The idea is not to win or lose but to hit your opponent as hard as you can (l. 25) and receive scars and survive experiences you do not get in normal life. In fight club you can test your limits and gain self-knowledge; it is also about self-destruction (l. 29). Additionally, breaking everything may help you to overcome your daily stress and after that you are able to handle any situation you may come across (ll. 56–59).

   (249 words)

LK 2012-14

2. *The assignment requires you to focus on three things: firstly, you need to have a
    closer look at the social and psychological background of the fight club members. After
    considering some of the aspects of the text at hand you should then establish a mean-
    ingful connection ("relate") to elements of the American Dream as discussed in class.
    Finally, the author's statement "too complete" could point you towards understand-
    ing similarities and differences between the fight club and the promises of the Ameri-
    can Dream.*

The American Dream and its reversal, often called the American Nightmare, has tended to consist of promises rather than being based on the "survival of the fittest" – as
the rules of the fight club seem to suggest.

Before considering relationships here, a closer look at the origins of the American
Dream will be helpful, as will following up on how this concept has changed over
time and, under certain social and political circumstances, might even have been perverted.

In the Declaration of Independence, the founding fathers had thought three elements
decisive for a better life in the New World: liberty, equality and the pursuit of happiness. When the historian James T. Adams coined the phrase "American Dream" much
later in 1931, he did not merely have "motor cars and high wages" on his mind, but a
social order where everyone could develop their social stature and be recognised by
others for what they were.

This dream has lured millions of immigrants to the American shores and is still based
on idealistic as well as materialistic views of the world. It includes the idea of equality, no matter what race, religion or political beliefs a person might have, and has
been connected to the "Manifest Destiny", which originally provided new settlers
with the justification to conquer land in the west of the continent – at the cost, however, of the Indian tribes who had to withdraw and suffered greatly from this expansion. The open frontier not only granted social and economic mobility, but also the
chance to rise from rags to riches and, supposedly, through hard work to successfully
engage in one's pursuit of happiness.

In the course of history, taking up opportunities has also led to fierce competition and
to exclusion. Older immigrants tended to close the doors after their arrival to protect
their jobs and lifestyle, so they argued, from new waves of immigration. This situation is shown in an exemplary way in T. C. Boyle's novel *The Tortilla Curtain*, where
an illegal Mexican couple is compared and contrasted with an American family who
seem to have fulfilled their American Dream.

The sequence of events in the novel shows that the American Dream means different
things to different people. The Mexicans fight for (physical) survival, have no health
insurance and finally lose their baby. The American family lives in affluence and is
more worried about fencing off their life to protect themselves from the illegal immigrants. Kyra, especially, a real estate agent and the breadwinner of the family, is successful at acquiring all the commodities she might wish for, and yet she is not happy
at all.

As in the narrator's case in the given text, Kyra's life is complete but not secure; she
imagines being in a fight for the survival of the fittest in her job and private life all the

time – in her case the illegal Mexican immigrants are enemies who take away the jobs, degrade housing areas and even steal food. This fight for survival is reflected in the often brutal and aggressive situations the Mexican couple find themselves in; but in contrast to the fight club, their fight is not about boredom but about carving out a decent livelihood, which they are denied by social pressures and political obstacles.

The Mexicans' experiences – ending with a catastrophic plight at the novel's climax – are a perversion of the American Dream, turning their fate into a nightmare. Compared to this, the narrator's statement "my life seemed too complete" has to be seen from a completely different perspective. These middle-class men he organises in his fight club are not fighting for their survival at all. Theirs is a quest for extreme experiences, self-confidence, testing their limits and overcoming their boredom. Like Kyra, they lead their lives in affluence, feel pampered by strong mothers ("men raised by women") and mistake liberty and equality for the promise of unfettered violence. By physically living out their stress and fantasies ("scars") they have perverted the American Dream in a cynical way, not to mention the physical abuse of others and over-indulging themselves due to their weariness of life. *(685 words)*

3. *Your comment should be based on facts collected by your project team and should evaluate possible reasons for the surge of violence in modern society.*
   Step 1 *Beyond the events mentioned in the text, you might want to refer to other manifestations of violence you have heard or read about (in your own country or in the world) and look out for reasons and consequences.*
   Step 2 *After following up and focusing on some events – e. g. the riots of 2011 in the UK or recent suicide bombers – you are supposed to assess possible reasons for the documented surge of violence as experienced by yourself and/or demonstrated in the media. Among those would be escaping from daily boredom, protest against regulations and alienation, a search for extreme experiences in an overregulated society, copying of celebrities and idols in the media, violence on TV and in computer games, disorientation in a fast-changing world, fighting for religious or ideological aims etc.*
   Step 3 *Your conclusion should include your own evaluation and possibly a perspective on further developments.*

A recent survey by the NSPCC (National Society for the Prevention of Cruelty against Children and Young Adults) documented a surge of violence, not only in Great Britain but all over the world. The findings were published in a report by our project team – the outcome of which I would like to comment on as follows:

With the fight against terrorism and the advent of suicide bombers since September 11, 2001 in New York, it is probably no surprise that there has been a general surge of violence in our societies.

Apart from the fact that most news in the media focuses on violent events, there is a widespread tendency towards presentations of violence on TV, including thrillers, crime stories and war reports. Beyond this close connection between news and violence, electronic media also base their success on violent animations, and first-person shooters are now at home in the families of teenagers. Whether this has increased shooting rampages at schools and in public places is open to debate and not as yet proven.

I assume, however, that the readiness to commit acts of violence is encouraged and reflected in these developments, as is a tendency to look out for extreme sports and experiences – from bungee jumping right to the spreading of fight clubs started in New York.

It would be an easy guess to connect this with the grind of everyday routine or the boredom in our overregulated society. The fact is, however, that the absence of real challenges – such as the older war generation had to face – and a surfeit of material gadgets has led to a weariness with life, where (self-)destruction seems to be a real and only way out.

A different kind of challenge became apparent in the UK riots of 2011, when cars were burned and shops looted in major English cities; there the government was quick to label the disorder as criminal pure and simple. Six months later, a report on this youth violence showed, nevertheless, that the disturbances could partly be blamed on the lack of opportunities for the young. Those that had to appear at the quickly in-stalled special courts in London and elsewhere were found to come mostly from de-prived circumstances, some from the poorest backgrounds. As a consequence, the British government promised to monitor the most troubled people in Britain – the so-called 500,000 forgotten families.

All in all, it would appear that there is no one reason for this surge of violence. Differ-ent elements, like poverty, deprivation, satiety and even overregulation need to be looked at and addressed in a combined manner; if this does not happen quickly, they are a certain recipe for disaster. *(444 words)*

Teil A: Aufgabe zur Sprachmittlung

Taschengeld

Interview mit Susanne Mattern, Diplom-Pädagogin und 2. Vorsitzende des Deutschen Kinderschutzbundes Rheinland-Pfalz (Dezember 2008)

Welche Bedeutung hat Taschengeld? Geht es einfach nur darum, Kindern eigenen „Konsum" zu ermöglichen?

Nein, es geht nicht nur um Konsum, sondern vor allem darum, Kindern und Jugendlichen ihrem Alter entsprechend Eigenverantwortung und Selbstbestimmung zu ermöglichen.
5 Darum geht es ja zunehmend in unserer Gesellschaft: Kinder auf dem Weg zu einem selbstbestimmten und autonomen Leben zu begleiten, in dem Selbstregulierung eine große Rolle spielt. Wir leben in einer Konsumgesellschaft und Kinder sind längst Zielgruppe der Wirtschaft geworden. Deswegen sollten sie frühzeitig Erfahrungen im Umgang mit Geld machen dürfen. Das ist wie mit Medien- oder Verkehrserziehung – das
10 fängt heute auch früh an, weil Kinder früh damit konfrontiert sind.

Ab wann sind Kinder im „Taschengeld-Alter"?

Das bestimmen vor allem die Kinder selbst, weil jedes Kind anders ist. Die meisten zeigen spätestens Interesse an Taschengeld mit dem Eintritt in die Grundschule. Das wird vor allem dadurch beeinflusst, wie wichtig das Thema Geld in der Familie ist. Für man-
15 che hat etwas einkaufen und bezahlen schon im Kindergartenalter eine große Bedeutung. Diese Kinder sind beispielsweise völlig fasziniert zu sehen, dass man etwas bezahlt und trotzdem Geld zurück erhält. Dann können Eltern das Interesse aufgreifen und ihnen auch schon im Alter von vier bis fünf Jahren einen spielerischen Umgang mit geringen Beträgen ermöglichen. Die meisten Kindergartenkinder interessieren sich aber noch nicht
20 für Taschengeld und sollten damit auch nicht belastet werden. Grundschulkinder, die sich für Taschengeld wenig oder gar nicht interessieren, sollten dennoch welches erhalten.
[...]

Wie viel Taschengeld sollten Kinder bekommen?

Die Summe sollte den Lebensumständen der Familie angepasst sein. Das bedeutet, wenn
25 Eltern viel Geld haben, sollten sie ihre Kinder nicht künstlich knapp halten – und andersrum. Auch im Vergleich zu dem, was Kinder im Umfeld bekommen, sollte der Betrag angemessen sein – sonst entsteht ein subjektives Gefühl von Mangel. Ich halte es für sehr sinnvoll, sich mit anderen Eltern über die Höhe des Taschengeldes auszutauschen – zum Beispiel auf Elternabenden oder mit den Eltern der Freunde. Grundsätzlich sollte der Be-
30 trag so hoch sein, dass sich das Kind seinem Alter entsprechende Wünsche ermöglichen kann: Für einen Erstklässler wären das dann wöchentlich etwa 50 Cent, mit denen er Schnuckelzeug am Kiosk kaufen kann. Bei Kindern, die großes Interesse am Umgang mit

Geld haben, kann der Betrag so sein, dass es reicht, um Schulmaterial und später Kleidung selbstständig einzukaufen.

35 **Sollten die Eltern die Höhe festlegen oder das mit ihren Kindern verhandeln?**
Alles, was Eltern mit Kindern gemeinsam und demokratisch aushandeln, wird in der Regel von Kindern akzeptiert. Das gilt auch für die Höhe des Taschengeldes. Da wird – je nach Verhandlungsgeschick und -lust der Kinder und Eltern – gefeilscht und argumentiert. Wenn die Eltern-Kind-Beziehung stimmt, wird es eine einvernehmliche Lösung
40 geben. Es sollte auch in die Verhandlung einbezogen werden, was davon gekauft werden soll. [...]
Das Ergebnis der Verhandlungen sollte man unbedingt schriftlich festlegen, damit nicht verloren geht, was im Taschengeld beinhaltet ist und was Eltern noch zusätzlich bezahlen müssen. *(478 Wörter)*

http://www.lokale-buendnisse-rlp.de/familienservice/familienkompetenz/taschengeld/taschengeld-das-interview.html [abgerufen: 02. 05. 2011]; Herausgeber: Viva Familia

Assignment

As part of a European-wide project on the living conditions of children and adolescents your class has been invited to contribute information on the issue of pocket money. You have already exchanged information about the personal experience of the participants and now you want to continue by adding short and precise reports concerning the ongoing public discussion in Germany. You have decided to inform your partners about the opinion of Susanne Mattern as presented in the December 2008 interview.
Summarize her thesis and her supporting arguments. (Material A)

Teil B: Verkürzte Textaufgabe

The Raid

This episode from Hanif Kureishi's novel The Black Album *is set in London's East End in the summer of 1989. Pakistani student Shahid and his friends Chad, Tahira, and Sadiq have decided to help a Bengali family that has been terrorized and attacked for months. They keep watch in the family's flat.*

[A]bout one hour before Shahid's shift was due to end, something happened.
    Chad was in the kitchen. Sadiq had gone. The other boy hadn't appeared yet. Shahid and Tahira were sitting down with their college books. Tahira offered Shahid a bag of sticky gulab jamans[1], which she knew he could eat all day. "Let's spoil ourselves," she
5 giggled. While they were together they had begun to take it for granted that the racists knew of their presence and didn't want a battle: either that or they were awaiting an opportunity. A bottle had been lobbed at Sadiq from a passing car but, living in the East End, he was accustomed to dancing around glass.
    Now there was a rattling of the letter-box followed by the sound of a brick being
10 hurled at the reinforced window beside the door.

Chad jumped to his feet, seizing his weapon. Shahid picked up a carving knife. For a moment, to instil courage, they clasped one another's free hand.

Chad unbarred the door. Tahira threw on her coat.

"Stay there," Chad warned, looking around the door.

15 He saw nothing. Cautiously, he and Shahid moved outside. Tahira followed. Some of the walkway lights had been smashed; the air was so cold it hung like a gauze. In the wan light it was difficult to make anything out.

"Better ring for reinforcements," Shahid whispered to Tahira.

The two men looked both ways. Shahid discerned a young woman standing along the
20 walkway with an object in her hand. She was accompanied by two kids, neither of whom could have been older than eight.

"Hey," Shahid called.

At this, the woman, who was wearing slippers, flung half a brick at them and tried to dash away. Chad and Shahid chased them. The smallest kid slipped at the top of the stairs
25 and Chad seized her by the collar. The mother, with a dingy raincoat thrown over her heavy shoulders, stopped and stared defiantly at them, clutching the other kid.

"Chad!" Shahid said. "No!"

Chad clenched his weapon over the child's head, and waved it about. He might have wanted restraining. [...] Around them lights went on. A door opened and a tattooed face
30 peered round. Dogs barked. No doubt the police were on their way.

In the hope that this might satisfy Chad, Shahid yelled at the woman: "Can't you leave these people alone? What have they ever done to hurt you? Have they come to your house and abused you or thrown stones? Did they make you live in these mildewed flats?"

35 The child escaped Chad's grasp, ran to her mother and turned screeching at them. The woman, who was unafraid, jerked her head forward and spat at Chad and Shahid. But her saliva blew back and spun through her daughter's hair.

"Paki! Paki! Paki!" she screamed. Her body had become an arched limb of hatred with a livid opening at the tip, spewing curses. "You stolen our jobs! Taken our housing!
40 Paki got everything! Give it back and go back home!"

She and the kids fled.

"You stay out here," Chad told Shahid. Both of them were trembling. "There might be more trouble. But don' worry, Hat, Sadiq and Tariq rushin' this way, reinforced up!"

Alone, Shahid paced the walkway, knowing the woman would return with rat-faced
45 brutes carrying bats. He wanted badly to go away, but his father had not been a coward, it wasn't in his family. Not that Chili[2], he reflected, could ever be described as an orthodox defender of his community. One of his black girlfriends did once persuade him to go on an anti-racist demonstration; and when the National Front yelled, "Get back, Pakis!" Chili, wearing a mink-coloured suit, had annoyed everyone by taking out his fat wallet,
50 waving it at the racists and shouting, "Get back to your council flats, paupers!" *(642 words)*

Hanif Kureishi, The Black Album, Faber and Faber, London 1995, p. 137–139

1   gulab jamans – a popular dessert in India
2   Chili – Shahid's older brother

Assignments

1. Summarize the text. (Material B). (25 BE)

2. Relate the experience of the Pakistani students to the African American experience in the USA.
    Include references to material discussed in class. (40 BE)

3. *"… if you want to live in AMERICA so badly, speak our language (English), salute our American Flag and accept being an American. Not African American, not Mexican American, not French American, just AMERICAN. Don't try to bring your country's ideals into ours. If you think your home country is so much better GO BACK!!"*
    (http://abcnews.go.com/WhatWouldYouDo/comments?type=story&id=6551048
    [retrieved: November 4, 2011])

    Comment on this statement and its implications. (35 BE)

Lösungsvorschläge

Teaching modules referred to:

The mediation text focuses on the topics social structures, social change *(Q2)*. The second text refers to the teaching module The United Kingdom *(Q2)*, with special emphasis on the topics social structure, social change. Another teaching module covered is that of the USA *(Q1)*, particularly with the topics living together *and* American Dream.

Teil A: Aufgabe zur Sprachmittlung

Your English summary will have to be much shorter than the German interview (95–125 words) and follows the rules of an ordinary summary (present tense, no direct speech, no quotations or comments). In the introductory sentence you would mention the institution, time, speaker, topic and source of the interview. Also try to find a title for your mediation.

Before writing your summary, follow the line of argument used in the interview and highlight the main points in the text.

In her interview in December 2008, Susanne Mattern, representative of the German Child-care Association, points out that pocket money is important even for younger children. Adolescents need to gain experience with handling money and learn to act independently and responsibly. As children are one of the target groups of the economy, they must be prepared to deal with money at an early age – either while they are attending kindergarten or when they start primary school at the latest. This depends on the child's interests, but encourages a playful approach towards money.

The amount of pocket money should be in accordance with a family's income and be the result of parent-child negotiations and fixed in writing. This will lead to a satisfactory agreement in intact families.

(125 words)

Teil B: Verkürzte Textaufgabe

1. Your summary should be no more than 180–210 words in length.

   Step 1 Before you start writing, make sure you comprehend the sequence of events, the protective intentions of the three students, the hatred and aggression of the English woman and the expectation that more trouble is to come.

   Step 2 Using the method of close reading (i. e. carefully studying the text in detail), highlight the most important aspects in this extract.

   Step 3 Your umbrella sentence at the beginning needs to contain a description of the time and place of action, the characters involved and the nature of the confrontation.

This excerpt from Hanif Kureishi's novel *The Black Album* describes a confrontation in an eastern suburb of London (in 1989), where a Bengali family has been subject to racist attacks for months and is now being defended by some Pakistani students.

Waiting in the family's flat one evening, the three students are aware of being watched by racists who have shown hostility towards the family. When a brick is thrown at a window, the students arm themselves and rush outside. There, they see a young woman with two small children flinging another brick at them and then trying to run away.

One of the children is caught by Chad, one of the students. His friend Shahid shouts at the woman to leave the family alone. However, she is full of hatred and accuses the Pakistanis of stealing jobs and housing and wants them to go back home. While she is able to escape with her children, the students expect her to return with reinforcement. Left alone while waiting for support, Chad summons his courage by remembering how his brother once even confronted the National Front. *(208 words)*

2. *You have to focus on experiences of racial discrimination and racist violence in two different countries and compare and contrast relevant aspects ("relate") to each other. This requires taking into account a number of facts that distinguish the historical developments in Great Britain and the USA and still influence the present situation.*

Step 1 Look for instances of violence in London's East End and identify them in the text at hand. You might also want to take into account the extent to which this situation influences the attitude and actions of the white woman.

Step 2 Briefly explain the background of racism in Great Britain. Often, xenophobia is used in the political agitation of right-wing politicians. Enoch Powell's attempt to undermine the official policy of the British government to support a multicultural society is a typical example. More recently, the development of parallel societies and the spread of sharia courts have not helped integration.

Step 3 The long history of slavery and segregation in the USA points at different sources of racial discrimination. In two of her novels, Toni Morrison has outlined the impact on the victims. Violent actions and lynchings carried out by the still existing Ku Klux Klan are another example. On the other hand, the success of the Civil Rights Movement needs to be considered and you should also mention recent steps in the emancipation of African-Americans in terms of political developments.

London's East End, where the extract from Kureishi's novel takes place, has traditionally been known for its poor housing, terrible living conditions and prevailing violence in the streets. The students who have decided to defend a Bengali family against racist attacks in these surroundings, with their mildewed flats (ll. 33/34), are used to violence and prepared for fights, having dodged flying bottles there before (ll. 7/8).

The confrontation the Pakistani students are faced with one evening (in this extract from the novel), however, comes as a surprise. It is not a gang of brutal racists who have come after the Bengali family but a young woman with her two small children, who throws bricks at their flat and abuses them, full of hatred. In her verbal attack she reiterates common prejudices against the Pakistani immigrants, stemming from popular opinion rather than relating to economic or social realities – namely that "Pakis" take away jobs or housing from the English.

The fact that this English woman draws her children into this violent confrontation is a sign of her deeply felt aggressions towards this visible minority, not so much because of their skin colour but because she assumes that they are responsible for her own poor living conditions. Her hatred, however, seems to come back at her when she spits at the students but the saliva flies back and hits her daughter's hair (ll. 36/37).

This sentiment of being socially and economically disadvantaged has been used by right-wing politicians before – a famous example was Enoch Powell in his "Rivers of Blood" speech, where he denounced the British government's policy of allowing immigrants, particularly from Commonwealth countries and the Caribbean, to live and work in Great Britain, creating a multicultural society. Powell claimed that in times of economic recession and cuts in employment figures the presence of too many immigrants would lead to street fights and recommended sending them home again.

This attitude is precisely picked up as the fear of families who live in poorer social conditions and serves as a ready explanation for their own economic plight. In this way social grievances are turned into racial discrimination with little resemblance to reality and no relevance to solving real problems in a globalised world.

Apart from this social background of racist agitation and intolerance, the development of parallel societies in Great Britain has also created concern and helped spread xenophobic actions. As outlined in Bali Rai's novel *(Un)arranged Marriage*, there is some resistance within the Sikh community to dropping traditional practices of their former home country, to the extent that in this example a teenage boy in the family is supposed to accept an arranged marriage according to Indian custom. Luckily, the boy is able to resist and successfully integrates in the mainstream society of Leicester.

Religious barriers can also lead to difficulties in the process of integration of ethnic minorities, as is shown by the spread of sharia courts in Great Britain, which deny female rights, practice rulings in open contradiction to British law and feed xenophobia once again.

Ethnic minorities are just as visible in the USA. The longest duration of racial discrimination had to be endured by the African-Americans, who did not immigrate by their own free will but were forcibly brought to the USA as slaves as early as the 17th century.

So, in contrast to the Pakistanis in Great Britain, for example, the slaves had never been immigrants in the true sense of the word and were treated as property rather than human beings from the beginning. Even after the abolition of slavery in the wake of the American Civil War (1861–1865), their situation did not improve much. Through the system of sharecropping they were kept dependent on their former masters; in compensation for renting land they had to pay the owners in shares of their crops and were even forced to buy their goods in overpriced shops owned by the same Whites. Toni Morrison has made their fate and suffering the subject of two of her novels. In *Beloved*, the main character, living just after the Civil War, tries in vain to leave her terrible past as a female slave behind and is haunted by traumatic psychological after-effects. In *A Mercy*, a slave born in America is only rescued from a similar fate by being accepted into a family that does not practise the mainstream discrimination against Blacks typical of the times.

Discrimination – regularly based on skin colour here, rather than on social difference – was not stopped by the abolition of slavery and similarly, the situation of African-Americans did not improve by the so-called Jim Crow laws. They resulted in complete segregation and widened the gap between Blacks and Whites. Violence had always been part of this relationship – and from its foundation in the second half of the 19th century to uphold white supremacy, the Ku Klux Klan had been instrumental in terrorising and even lynching black people for ridiculous reasons or no reasons at all. In some states this racist and violent organisation is active even today.

Only in the 1950s did the Civil Rights Movement successfully fight for the political and social rights of the black minority. Their leaders, foremost Martin Luther King and Malcolm X, were able to get to the bottom of the reasons for discrimination and paved the way for considerable changes. With the inauguration of the first black president, Barack Obama, discrimination on the grounds of skin colour is at least officially no longer acceptable. Thus, in both Great Britain and the USA pro-active policies of the respective governments were and still are necessary to fight against discrimination and encourage tolerance. *(942 words)*

3. *The implications of the quotation given come very close to the racist attitude expressed by the young woman in Kureishi's novel who wants the Pakistanis to go back home. So bear in mind that forced assimilation or even expulsion of ethnic minorities point towards a social situation of exclusion and little tolerance.*

   Step 1 Look at the harsh convictions of the speaker that immigrants have to abandon all of their cultural traditions and become part of the American melting pot. You might want to view this concept of "e pluribus unum" in contrast to ideas of a salad bowl or even cultural mosaic, as practised in countries like Canada and Australia.

   Step 2 Assess the social consequences of such demands and attitudes. They would lead to forced assimilation and little tolerance of minorities, who would lose their identity and cultural traditions. Even a rise in patriotism and nationalism might ensue. The pressure on minorities is in stark contrast to the promises of the American Dream, the reversal of which found its literary form in novels like T. C. Boyle's The Tortilla Curtain, *where the affluent members of society fence off their property as a protection against the poorer and often illegal immigrants.*

   Step 3 In your line of argument you need to consider problems and perspectives of an immigrant society like the USA.

The statement at hand reproaches newly arrived immigrants for failing to meet the demands of their new home country. If they want to live in America "so badly", they are supposed to speak English, accept American values and abandon their old ideas; the alternative for them is simply to go back to where they came from.

This concept stems from the traditional idea of a melting pot, the American motto "e pluribus unum", which was introduced as early as 1782 and is imprinted on the Great Seal of the USA. Originally referring to the union of individual states, it has developed into the concept of assimilation to American values and does not encourage the identity of diverse ethnic groups. In order to maintain their own cultural traditions and beliefs, the concept of a salad bowl or cultural quilt was introduced later and seems much more in accordance with the values of the American Dream.

Whether this is a realistic aim in present-day American society has been the subject of many controversial debates, where the reversal to an American Nightmare has often been described. This is particularly true for T. C. Boyle's novel *The Tortilla Curtain*, where both Dream and Nightmare are experienced by people from different walks of American society. Although immigrants themselves, a more affluent part of the community sees their success and wealth endangered by new waves of (illegal) immigrants and wants to see the door closed behind themselves. The Mossbachers, a typical, successful couple, have fulfilled their American Dream and are involved in pro-environmental activities. The female breadwinner of the family, an efficient real estate agent, fears the competition with low-paid immigrant labour and the downgrading of the housing estates she looks after. An illegal Mexican couple, on the other hand, is struggling on the poverty line and their American Dream is simply one of physical survival. They do not succeed in the end, because social prejudices are too strong and they are subject to ubiquitous discrimination and exploitation, helpless victims in a highly competitive society with zero tolerance.

The hatred of the woman in Kureishi's novel who yells at the Pakistanis to go back home expresses the same sentiments as those in the statement. Whereas in the situation in London's East End the fear of losing their jobs and housing leads to violent attacks and is due to economic competition and social envy, racial discrimination in the USA is more often based on skin colour and foreign cultures.

The proportion of mainstream Anglo-Americans is decreasing considerably with the rise of black and Hispanic minorities. In this light the chances of a peaceful development can no longer be seen in forced assimilation and the propagation of American core values. Countries like Canada have developed quite a different solution to these problems with their government-supported policy of a multicultural society.

In this concept of a mosaic, each and every culture has the right to preserve its identity and traditions under the umbrella of a unified community. That way the contribution of each ethnic group is valued for its own sake and encourages diversity and mutual respect. Xenophobia has never won a Canadian election and their cultural system is regarded as a model in a globalised world.

(537 words)

Elective Performance Enhancement Surgery[1] For Athletes: Should It Be Resisted?

Sport history reveals that athletes will use any means possible to get an edge[2]. [...]
Genetic engineering is advancing upon us and will create massive ethical complications in the performance enhancement debate. Meanwhile another performance enhancing practice, generally neglected as part of the discussion, has been around for over [a] decade
5 with new forms of it being rapidly advanced: elective performance enhancement surgery.
Surgical procedures are being employed to enhance general human performance in memory, concentration, vision, strength; it is naive to ignore these advances in sports competition. Ethical considerations of these procedures should be pursued.
The most common form of surgical performance enhancement is LASIK[3] eye surgery.
10 Its results have been very convenient for professional baseball players or golfers who no longer need to wear glasses or contacts; some have even claimed it has made them more effective players. The Tommy John[4] surgery on the arm [...] has been done on many professional baseball pitchers with over 90 % returning to pre-injury form. As this procedure has been refined it has also become common knowledge that some pitchers are actually
15 increasing their pitching speed after the surgery. [...]
The uncritical acceptance of this rather benign[5] [...] surgery, along with the advances in surgical techniques [...] and the lessening of recovery times opens the door to the possibility of athletes having elective surgeries to enhance their senses or to become bigger, stronger, or faster. Someone will soon choose to have advanced surgery to enhance per-
20 formance, such as electively having the Tommy John surgery with the hope of throwing a baseball harder afterwards. The possibilities of elective surgery seem endless. [...]
Picture this scenario: You are a twenty-seven-year-old professional minor league athlete or high-level amateur. You have been knocking on the door to become a true professional in your sport and to make a very substantial income. Your options are beginning
25 to run out and the end of your professional dreams is nearing.
You ask management for an explanation. They tell you they like your mental approach to your sport, it's just that you lack a little ability to really become successful. If you were a baseball pitcher and threw several miles an hour more there would be a place for you on a big league roster[6]. [...] You are shattered. You've already overachieved.
30 What options are left now? What about surgery on a tendon[7] or ligament[8] to increase driving distance or foot speed? What about optional Tommy John surgery to increase pitch speed?
These surgeries have little risk and there would actually be the chance of coming out of it in a year or two a faster runner or with a stronger than ever arm. [...] Knowing the
35 mentality of doing anything to "make it", athletes will obviously consider this type of surgery to enhance performance to achieve the highest levels possible. This is particularly true as the financial incentives skyrocket[9] [...].

It is self-evident that surgical practices which enhance the athlete beyond what is considered to be normal could certainly give the surgically enhanced athlete a competitive ad-
40 vantage.

Surgery has historically been seen as a means to correct or heal for therapeutic reasons. But as cosmetic operations have become acceptable as a non-therapeutic means of surgery, so it seems that what is now beginning among athletes is enhancement surgery for non-therapeutic means. And it has become an acceptable practice without much criti-
45 cal thought or established policy. The Professional Golfers' Association allows for enhanced eye surgery, but there could be great controversy if they allow a surgically enhanced swing where a golfer's drive is lengthened by fifty yards. The possibilities seem endless.

(588 words)

Mark Hamilton: Elective Performance Enhancement Surgery For Athletes: Should It Be Resisted?
In: Acta Univ. Palacki. Olomuc., Gymn. 2006, vol. 36, no. 2.

1   performance enhancement surgery – leistungssteigernde OP
2   to get an edge – sich einen Vorteil verschaffen
3   LASIK – eine Laser-Korrekturoperation am Auge
4   Tommy John – ein Werfer, an dessen Ellenbogen ein gerissenes Band durch eine Sehne ersetzt wurde
5   benign – gutartig, *hier:* harmlos
6   big league roster – Spielerliste eines Profiteams
7   tendon – Sehne
8   ligament – Band
9   to skyrocket – steil ansteigen

Assignments

1. Summarize the text. (Material)   (30 BE)

2. Relate the problem described in the text to developments in the field of science and technology discussed in class.   (35 BE)

3. In his book *Our Posthuman Future: Consequences of the Biotechnology Revolution*, Francis Fukuyama[1] raises the broader issue of performance enhancement:
   "The original purpose of medicine is to heal the sick, not turn healthy people into gods."
   Benedict Carey: Brain Enhancement Is Wrong, Right?
   In: The New York Times *from March 9, 2008*

   Discuss the statement and refer to dystopian models of society discussed in class.

or

One person who posted anonymously on the Chronicle of Higher Education[2] Web site said that a daily regimen of three 20-milligram doses of Adderall[3] transformed his career:

"I'm not talking about being able to work longer hours without sleep (although that helps)," the posting said. "I'm talking about being able to take on twice the responsibility, work twice as fast, write more effectively, manage better, be more attentive, devise better and more creative strategies."
Benedict Carey: Brain Enhancement Is Wrong, Right?
In: The New York Times from March 9, 2008

Discuss the statement and refer to dystopian models of society discussed in class.   (35 BE)

1   Francis Fukuyama – professor of political science at Johns Hopkins University
2   Chronicle of Higher Education – a newspaper/website on college education
3   Adderall – a frequently used amphetamine

Lösungsvorschläge

Teaching modules referred to:
The assignment centres on the teaching module Order, Vision, Change *(Q 3), with special focus on* models of the future (utopias, dystopias, progress in the natural sciences).
The material is also relevant to the core theme Science and Technology *(Q 1), with an emphasis on* Biotechnology.

1.   **Step 1** *Start with an umbrella sentence that contains information on the author, the title, the type of text, date and the topic of the text.*
     Step 2 *Then focus on the author's line of argument, avoiding unnecessary detail.*
     Step 3 *Your summary should have 170 to 200 words (about 1/4 to 1/3 of the original text). Use the present tense and do not quote from the text.*

The article by Mark Hamilton, retrieved from the Internet, is about unnecessary surgery which is thought to improve the efficiency of athletes and the ethical questions this development poses.
Within the context of genetic engineering, the author records that surgery serves other purposes than it used to do: in former times surgery was needed to treat injuries, whereas nowadays it helps to enhance athletes' performance. Several forms of enhancement surgery have emerged in this field: apart from memory and concentration these are LASIK surgery to improve eye sight by laser technology and the Tommy John surgery that replaces damaged elbow ligament to improve a baseballer's pitching speed.
Because of these new possibilities in surgery, athletes are faced with a new dilemma. Not only can they gain competitive advantage to achieve the highest level possible with the help of an operation but they might also be tempted by financial incentives. Many of them are put under pressure by their management to optimize their performance. The author points out that there is no public debate on the ethical aspects of this new technological opportunity and asks the question whether everything that is possible in theory should be put into effect.   *(198 words)*

GK 2013-3

2. **Step 1** *This task requires you to place the issue of enhancement surgery for athletes in the wider context of genetic engineering as made possible by technological innovations and the global demand for better farming and food supply. You may want to draw on e. g. genetically modified seeds or cloned animals or other examples of genetic engineering discussed in class.*

Step 2 *Before you start writing, take the following points into consideration: Scientific and technical progress are not necessarily met with unique approval and are related to issues of economic and social control as well as medical issues. Artificially acquired enhancement of performance can be taken as much to extremes as the unlimited pursuit of technological progress. In both cases questions of an ethical nature are raised, which should be discussed in your analysis.*

Performance surgery is not the only progress made in the field of science in recent years. Breakthroughs in medicine have made it possible for people to live longer and healthier. Developments in science and technology provided opportunities to fight starvation globally and brought about interesting findings in medical research, which shall be explained in detail using two cases of genetic engineering as examples. The positive and negative aspects of these two issues shall be stated below.

Technologically advanced nations like the US have embraced genetically modified (GM) foods on a broader level. In European countries GM technology is not met with the same public acceptance and its risks are widely believed to be uncontrollable. Apart from economic doubts, political measures were put into place by the European Union to ban GM products and stricter policies towards biotechnology were implemented. These strategies have also had repercussions on global trade and led to ongoing discussions within the World Trade Organization.

Another issue that attracted global attention was the cloning of Dolly the sheep by Scottish scientists near Edinburgh who successfully managed to create a genetically identical copy of the nucleus of an udder cell. In the ensuing controversy it was often pointed out that human identical twins are also a sort of clone. The experiment has allegedly led to new ways of producing medical supplies (e. g. stem cells) and has generally helped to understand genetics much better than before. Opponents raised doubts about the procedure on mainly religious grounds and discussions involving the use of stem cells have resulted in contradictory policies in different countries.

It cannot be doubted that the risk-benefit analysis concerning GM foods and the cloning of animals is highly controversial. The limits of technological progress therefore need to be defined by law. This seems to be true for genetic engineering as well as for enhancement surgery. The crucial question to be asked is whether progress should be facilitated at any cost. It is difficult to draw the line between the technical support and having an unfair advantage over your competitors. The case of Lance Armstrong's doping during the Tour de France is clear cut, whereas there have been debates on whether the South African athlete Oscar Pistorius should be allowed to participate in the Olympics 2012. His prosthetics gave him an edge over his competitors.

All in all, medical and technological progress are beneficial within legal limits, as long as they are able to meet the criteria laid down by an informed and objective public discussion. Taken to extremes, progress in the fields of genetic engineering and enhancement surgery cause dangerous developments far beyond human control, e. g. insects might become immune to pesticides due to GM food and the true spirit of sports might be lost as success depends on money rather than on capability.   *(469 words)*

3. *The two statements at hand clearly describe opposing attitudes, but refer to two sides of the same coin: the positive and negative aspects of medical progress.*
    Step 1 You only need to choose one of these quotations. It is expected that you start by focusing on the problem raised in the quotation chosen.
    Step 2 Think about novels, films or texts that best reflect the positive and negative outcomes of medical and technological progress in a future society.
    Step 3 At the end of your text, you need to assess your findings and take sides.
    Please note: *Both statements are part of the sample solution below. You are free to choose the one you feel better prepared to answer. Afterwards, there is a general part focusing on the dystopian societies of Orwell's* Nineteen Eighty-Four *and Huxley's* Brave New World *and the way progress is portrayed there.*

Statement 1

Francis Fukuyama issues a warning against the unreflecting support of modern medical research. Medical advances have helped to eradicate many diseases and increase life expectancy considerably. Even in severe cases new drugs have improved the quality of life and improved the chances of healing. This is commonly believed to be the main purpose of the work of doctors.
When it comes to enhancing the performance of athletes, ethical questions arise. The questions are when medical care crosses the line and becomes manipulation and who decides on this issue. The problem is not confined to medical improvements only but extends to what kind of society people would like to live in.   *(110 words)*

Statement 2

In sports the use of drugs has been a long-standing issue and is outlawed particularly in international competitions such as the Olympics and Paralympics. Temptation for sportsmen and -women is great. Fame and money are great incentives that come with the edge athletes hope to gain over their competitors. But beyond the area of sports, performance enhancement plays a major role in society as a general value. The capitalist society demands people to perform with constant efficiency and effort. Employees that work under pressure all the time develop stress-related symptoms and illnesses. The same goes for young people who study challenging subjects at university such as medicine and law, which require long hours of intensive preparation. It is evident that in those situations the offer of medical devices and even drugs is seen as an easy way out. It is this attitude that is displayed by the anonymous user the quotation is from.
But drugs will not improve performances in the long run and might cause mental disorders such as hallucinations or delusion or lead to dependency and the loss of self-control. Instead of becoming more creative individuals, people might fall victims of what seems like progress.   *(197 words)*

Models of a dystopian society

Especially those people that are over-optimistic concerning progress should have a look at some science fiction novels. Dystopian models of society highlight changes with regard to social relations and living conditions. Blind faith in the idea of social and technological progress requires further exploration, including the nature of social and political structures. I would like to refer to two dystopian societies pictured in famous works of literature.

A nightmare story of a totalitarian system is George Orwell's *Nineteen Eighty-Four*. In his dystopian society technological progress is driven to the extreme. A faceless individual named Big Brother is supposed to watch every citizen of Oceania and people are under control via interactive TV. The protagonist Winston Smith is trapped in a system where there is no privacy and where free thinking might be punished with death. The strategy of "Doublethink" helps people not to question the state propaganda they are exposed to constantly. The vocabulary of the common language "Newspeak" narrows the range of ideas and independent action. Although Smith is no hero he longs to know the truth about Oceania and is sick of the lie he is told all the time. In the end, he is declared a public enemy and has to undergo torture and brainwashing. In *Nineteen Eighty-Four* science and technology serve the purpose of controlling a starving population in a state where all important decisions in people's lives have already been made for them.

A similar situation is described in *Brave New World* by Aldous Huxley. Here, technological and medical progress is used to produce human beings hatched from test tubes who are brought up in state nurseries. Social stability is based on a caste system and the acceptance of social destiny. In fact, the babies' development is influenced heavily by drugs put into the test tubes. Thus, the future of the human beings can be planned and the exact number of people needed for a certain sort of work can be produced. Some embryos' cells are also divided so that identical people can be brought into existence. Individual freedom is unavailable in a trouble-free society. But there is a drug called "soma" that the citizens are free to take whenever they feel unhappy. For the sake of staying young for a seemingly endless period, never having to face death or suffering from pain of any kind, the society of *Brave New World* sacrificed true happiness.

These two examples show how the unlimited use of technology and scientific progress can transform communities into oppressive societies. Elaborate systems of machinery and ideological strategies are used to control and manipulate the population. There is no freedom of thought and will, instead strict conformity prevails. I believe that some of the patterns and trends are already common in contemporary society, e. g. the tendency to be available all of the time thanks to smart phones that connect us to the rest of the world. Therefore, people need to become aware of the inherent dangers of progress if technology is allowed to advance unfettered. *(504 words)*

The Neighbourhood

In this excerpt from Hanif Kureishi's novel Something to Tell You, *the narrator Dr. Jamal Khan, a successful psychoanalyst living and working in London, and his friend Henry take a walk around the area where they live.*

Carrying his own atmosphere with him, Henry swung around the neighbourhood like it was a village – he was brought up in a Suffolk hamlet[1] – continually calling out across the street to someone or other, and, frequently, joining them for talk about politics and art. His solution to the fact that few people in London appeared to speak understandable
5 English now, was to learn their language. "The only way to get by in this 'hood is to speak Polish," he announced recently. He also knew enough Bosnian, Czech and Portuguese to get by in the bars and shops without yelling, as well as enough of several other European languages to make his way without feeling marginalised[2] in his own city.
   I have lived on the same page of the A-to-Z[3] all of my adult life. At lunchtime I liked
10 to stroll twice around the tennis courts like the other workers. This area, between Hammersmith and Shepherd's Bush, I heard once described as "a roundabout surrounded by misery". Someone else suggested it might be twinned with Bogotá. Henry called it "a great Middle Eastern city". Certainly it had always been "cold" there: in the seventeenth century, after the hangings at Tyburn, near Marble Arch, the bodies were brought to
15 Shepherd's Bush Green to be displayed.
   Now the area was a mixture of the pretty rich and the poor, who were mostly recent immigrants from Poland and Muslim Africa. The prosperous lived in five-storey houses, narrower, it seemed to me, than North London's Georgian houses. The poor lived in the same houses divided up into single rooms, keeping their milk and trainers fresh on the
20 windowsill.
   The newly arrived immigrants, carrying their possessions in plastic bags, often slept in the park; at night, along with the foxes, they foraged through the dustbins for food. Alcoholics and nutters[4] begged and disputed in the street continuously. [...] New delis, estate agents and restaurants had begun to open, also beauty parlours, which I took as a
25 positive sign of rising house prices.
   When I had more time, I liked to walk up through Shepherd's Bush market, with its rows of chauffeur-driven cars parked alongside Goldhawk Road Station. Hijabed[5] Middle Eastern women shopped in the market, where you could buy massive bolts of vivid cloth, crocodile-skin shoes, scratchy underwear and jewellery, "snide"[6] CDs and DVDs,
30 parrots and luggage, as well as illuminated 3-D pictures of Mecca and Jesus. (One time, in the old city in Marrakech, I was asked if I'd seen anything like it before. I could only reply that I'd come all this way only to be reminded of Shepherd's Bush market.)
   While no one could be happy on the Goldhawk Road, the Uxbridge Road, ten minutes away, is different. At the top of the market I'd buy a falafel and step into that wide
35 West London street where the shops were Caribbean, Polish, Kashmiri, Somali. Along

from the police station was the mosque, where, through the open door, you could see rows of shoes and men praying. Behind it was the football ground, QPR[7], where Rafi and I went sometimes, to be disappointed. Recently one of the shops was sprayed with gunfire. Not long ago a boy cycled past Josephine and plucked her phone from her hand. But other-
40 wise the 'hood was remarkably calm though industrious, with most people busy with schemes and selling. I was surprised there wasn't more violence, considering how combustible[8] the parts were.

It was my desire, so far unfulfilled, to live in luxury in the poorest and most mixed part of town. It always cheered me to walk here. This wasn't the ghetto; the ghetto was Bel-
45 gravia, Knightsbridge and parts of Notting Hill[9]. This was London as a world city.

(610 words)

Hanif Kureishi, Something to Tell You, *Faber & Faber, London 2008, S. 13ff.*

1   hamlet – little village
2   marginalised – being made unimportant
3   A-to-Z – Geographer's A – Z Street Atlas: a series of street maps of cities in the UK; the first atlas, of London, was originally published in the 1930s.
4   nutter – *(Brit. slang)* foolish, eccentric or mad person
5   hijabed – wearing a headscarf (hijab) for religious reasons
6   snide – *hier:* schwarzgebrannt
7   QPR – Queens Park Rangers (a soccer team)
8   combustible *(adj.)* – catching fire and burning easily; explosive
9   Belgravia, Knightsbridge and Notting Hill – rather wealthy boroughs of London

Assignments

1. Outline what is special about the area from the narrator's point of view. (Material)
(30 BE)

2. Compare the narrator's experience of multicultural London to challenges the US society faces today referring to material discussed in class.
(35 BE)

3. "I was surprised there wasn't more violence, considering how combustible the parts were."
Discuss whether a functioning multicultural society is possible drawing on classroom discussions and/or your own experience. Refer to the statement from the text.
(35 BE)

Lösungsvorschläge

Teaching modules referred to:
The tasks relate to the teaching module The United Kingdom *(Q 2), with special focus on the topic* Social Structures, Social Change. *Task 2 also ties in with the module* USA *(Q 1) referring particularly to the topic* Living Together.

1. **Step 1** *Start with an umbrella sentence that contains information on the author, the title, the type of text, date and the topic of the text.*
    Step 2 *In your summary you are supposed to outline impressions from the narrator's neighbourhood in London that make it appear special to him. Omitting unnecessary detail and examples, your text should be written in the present tense, in your own words and without quotations. Including the umbrella sentence, the summary should have about 200 words (about 1/3 of the original text).*

    The text "The Neighbourhood" is taken from the novel *Something to Tell You* by Hanif Kureishi, published in 2008. It is about the narrator's multicultural neighbourhood and his impression of people from different nations.
    Many people speak languages other than English in this multicultural area, where various ethnic groups share the limited space. As English lost its function as a universal language, Jamal's friend Henry started to learn some Eastern European languages to make himself understood.
    This part of London is compared to Bogotá and Marrakech as many poor people live here. It seems that recently richer people have moved to the area so that the inhabitants live under very different social conditions now. Continuous changes are said to be typical of the area: new restaurants, delis, estate agents and beauty parlours have appeared, which is regarded as a good sign by the narrator.
    Although there is crime and violence, this neighbourhood seems remarkably quiet, which comes as a surprise due to the dense living conditions in the area. In his view the real ghetto is to be found in the wealthier boroughs of London, whereas he sees his own part of town as the reason why London can truly be called a world city.

    (205 words)

2. **Step 1** *You need to focus on the narrator's experience of multicultural London first and make sure to convey the view of the author who does not only focus on problems but also describes the new variety in lifestyles and positive changes.*
    Step 2 *Then compare the author's perception of the neighbourhood to the present US society concerning the situation of – illegal – immigrants and the strife of different ethnic groups for equal treatment.*
    Step 3 *Keep in mind that whereas multiculturalism is part of the official British policy on immigration, the current society in the United States is still based on the theory of "melting pot" and "salad bowl". To explore the similarities and differences, use the material discussed in class to make your comparison more plausible.*

The narrator has lived in this London neighbourhood all his adult life and notices the changes in its multiethnic, multilinguistic and multireligious set-up. In order not to be marginalized in their part of town, he and his friend had to become accustomed to a variety of languages particularly from the East of Europe and even had become familiar with some of them (cf. ll. 4–6). Of course, the area has manifold problems to cope with: overcrowding (cf. ll. 18–20), the constant influx of new – supposedly illegal – immigrants (cf. ll. 21/22), crime (cf. ll. 38/39) and the ever-widening gap between rich and poor due to gentrification (cf. ll. 17–20) are just a few named by the narrator. To the narrator these difficulties are outweighed by the positive changes: He is impressed by the variety found in markets and shops (cf. ll. 26, 34/35) and he particularly mentions rising house prices as a sign of a turn for the better (cf. ll. 24/25). The narrator seems biased and therefore unable to perceive the negative sides of change as a potential threat to his current lifestyle. Contrary to many other people in his position, he has no intention of leaving the neighbourhood although the reader gets the impression that he could afford it.

The relaxed attitude of Jamal Khan towards immigrants differs widely from the opinion of many US citizens who want the borders closed and oppose new waves of immigration especially of the Hispanic influx. This problem is depicted in T. C. Boyle's novel *The Tortilla Curtain*. The Mossbachers, a white couple, are able to live their dream in California but are confronted with illegal immigrants from Mexico. Delaney Mossbacher, a liberal humanist, changes his attitudes during the course of the story and ends up with xenophobic ideas as he feels threatened by Cándido, who, together with his wife América, struggles to make a living and is forced to take on the lowest jobs possible. The couple has come to the US illegally, hoping for a better life. But instead of finding acceptance, they experience a real nightmare and end up homeless, hungry and disillusioned back on their way to Mexico. The white community meanwhile has fences put up around their houses.

Another ethnic minority, the black Americans, had to wait a long time to be fully integrated in American society. In the 1960s the Civil Rights Movement brought about improvements but the blacks in the US are still far from equal to the white population. The re-election of Barack Obama as the first black American president is a sign of hope for many of them in their fight for equal rights.

Contrary to Great Britain, the US has always been a country of immigrants. Thus, the challenges the present US society faces are considerably larger and more diverse than the ones in Great Britain. The possibility of realising the American Dream has attracted millions of people from all over the world who sought religious and political freedom and wished to pursue their individual way to success. In both countries the ever-growing influx of migrants has led to restrictions and a quota system based on the needs of the labour market.

(535 words)

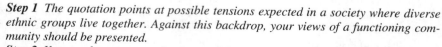

3. **Step 1** *The quotation points at possible tensions expected in a society where diverse ethnic groups live together. Against this backdrop, your views of a functioning community should be presented.*
   Step 2 *You need to use your background knowledge to weigh up the challenges of*

multiculturalism, but you could also include personal experiences. In the end, your conclusion has to be based on an assessment of the opportunities and limitations of such a community.

The quotation refers to challenges that people face when diverse ethnic minorities are crowded in limited space – nevertheless, in Jamal Khan's area this difficult situation does not result in an outbreak of violence. Immigrants leave their home country for various reasons and are confronted with a mainstream culture that might widely differ from their own values or traditions. The more serious this culture clash is, the less likely it is that immigrants can quickly integrate and adapt to their new home. On the other hand, a successful multicultural society also depends on the host country: the social structures, the labour market and previous experiences with ethnic minorities influence the readiness of the host society to accept new immigrants. If different expectations cannot be bridged, tensions will ensue, violent reactions will be the consequence and conflicts might not be reconciled. There is a big difference between expected assimilation and assisted integration and several concepts such as of the US melting pot or the Canadian cultural mosaic provide alternative models of a functioning society. As every society has its own values and traditions – and its specific mixture of ethnic groups, it depends on the make-up of the society itself which cultural concept predominates.

In the case of Great Britain, multiculturalism is necessary to integrate different sets of values. Here, the existence of at least 85 Sharia Courts has created a lot of problems because their rulings often contradict existing laws, for example when wives seek a divorce from their husbands due to domestic violence and are told to correct their lifestyle so that this treatment does not occur again. It is obvious that two contradicting laws cannot co-exist in the same country. In this case, the multicultural attitude has resulted in a divided society which cannot grant equal rights to every citizen. On the contrary, after the events of 9/11 and the London bus bombings on July 7, 2005, Muslim communities were very often regarded suspiciously in Western countries, and their members were subject to unwonted discrimination. It is not surprising that this unfair rush of judgement by a prejudiced and frightened host society would lead to counter-reactions and provide a hotbed for radical attitudes on both sides.

In Germany however, we have come to terms with the dominant ethnic minorities such as the Turks and the Russians. The younger generation is integrated quite well into our culture, which enriches the host society's attitudes as well and broadens our horizons. If misunderstandings occur, dialogue and mutual information have proved successful. Of course, young men's behaviour or the role of young women are a concern. Special courses for Muslim mothers and their children as well as many projects all over Germany that were founded by young Muslims should provide role models and thus enable young second or third generation immigrants to integrate better.

In conclusion, it is very important to overcome prejudices against immigrant cultures. Xenophobia very often is a result of social problems. Integration will work both for the immigrants and the host country, if both sides are willing to tolerate each other's values and beliefs. Of course, this cannot mean that basic human rights the whole European society is based on are neglected. *(533 words)*

Teil A: Aufgabe zur Sprachmittlung

Führerschein mit 16? Auf gar keinen Fall!

Es gibt Politiker und Jugendliche, die den Führerschein ab 16 Jahren fordern. Doch angesichts schrecklicher Unfälle gerade junger Fahranfänger muss man sich fragen: Sollte man ihn wirklich einführen? Jugendliche sind eben Jugendliche. Sie können Risiken noch nicht so gut einschätzen. Studien zeigen das. Junge Fahrer sind weitaus häufiger in Unfälle ver-
5 wickelt als andere Altersgruppen. Nun stellt sich die Frage, wenn schon 18-Jährige so viele Unfälle bauen, wie wäre es dann mit 16-Jährigen?

Wäre das nicht ein unkalkulierbares Risiko für die Gesellschaft? Außerdem steigt die Jugendkriminalität immer noch an. Könnte die Fahrerlaubnis nicht ein zusätzliches Werkzeug darstellen?

10 Freilich, es wird oft angeführt, Jugendliche würden immer früher erwachsen. Doch sie leben immer noch bei ihren Eltern und würden in aller Regel nicht genug Geld für ein eigenes Auto haben. Konflikte sind programmiert: Wer darf das Auto wann und wie lange nutzen? Was, wenn sich ein Unfall ereignet, was bei Jugendlichen schließlich häufiger vorkommt? Jugendliche könnten den Führerschein für eine Machtprobe mit den Eltern be-
15 nutzen, etwa einfach das Auto nehmen.

Befürworter des Führerscheins ab 16 Jahren führen oft an, Jugendliche bräuchten mehr Freiheit und Selbstbestimmung. Doch wo würden Jugendliche hinfahren? Zur Schule? Oder eher zur Kneipe oder einfach „zum Spaß" in die Stadt? Hätten sie kein Auto, könnten sie die Zeit in ihre Bildung investieren, was angesichts steigender Schulabbre-
20 cherzahlen umso wichtiger ist! Denn gerade Jugendliche, die die Schule abbrechen, würden vielleicht viel fahren, um der Realität zu entfliehen!

Jugendliche können schließlich auch noch nicht wählen und sind nicht strafmündig. Sie dürfen nicht rauchen und keinen Alkohol trinken. Warum sollten sie Auto fahren dürfen?

25 Es wäre doch sicher besser, wenn sie ihren Führerschein mit 18 machen würden, wenn sie auch die anderen Rechte erhalten. Es gibt ja bereits das begleitete Fahren für 17-Jährige. Das ist eine Möglichkeit. Jugendliche können es ausprobieren, werden aber kontrolliert. Aber der Führerschein ab 16? Nein!

Es lohnt sich ein Blick in die USA: Dort können Jugendliche mancherorts schon ab
30 15 Jahren den Führerschein machen. Und wozu führt das? Hohe Unfallzahlen und hohe Kriminalität. Wollen wir das wirklich in Deutschland?

(338 Wörter)

Matthias Aengenheyster, „Führerschein mit 16? Auf gar keinen Fall!", in: Hamburger Abendblatt,
26. 03. 2008; http://www.abendblatt.de/ratgeber/extra-journal/article526754/Fuehrerschein-mit-16-Auf-
gar-keinen-Fall.html

Assignment

Point out the arguments the text provides for and against driving at age sixteen. (Material A)

Hinweis: Die Rechtschreibung entspricht der Textvorlage.

Teil B: verkürzte Textaufgabe

Sorry Bill Gates: GMO Crops Proven to be Ineffective at Fighting World Hunger

Monsanto shareholder[1] Bill Gates has argued that GMOs[2] are the solution to world hunger, going as far as to say that they are actually needed to fight worldwide starvation. Unfortunately for Gates, who back in 2010 bought 500,000 shares of the company he is now promoting in mainstream media as the solution to the world's problems, a team of
5 900 scientists have found that GMO crops are actually not effective at fighting world hunger. In fact, the massive team found that Monsanto's seeds, which have led to thousands of farmer suicides due to excessive costs and failure to yield[3] crops, were outperformed[4] by traditional "agro-ecological"[5] farming practices.

Funded by the World Bank and United Nations, an organization was created known
10 as the International Assessment of Agricultural Knowledge, Science and Technology for Development (IAASTD). Consisting of 900 scientists and researchers, they set out to examine the complex issue of world hunger. While the issue of world hunger may be quite complex, their results were not. Quite plainly, the group found that genetically modified crops were not a meaningful solution to the problem. In other words, the expert team
15 showed through rigorous analysis and repeated study that the claims made by Bill Gates are completely inaccurate.

Perhaps what is most compelling, though, is the fact that Bill Gates was fully aware of these findings before going on air to inform the public that GMOs are the solution to world hunger. The same GMOs that have been linked to organ damage, mutated insects,
20 and a host of other issues.

[...]
The findings of the IAASTD regarding the ineffectiveness of GMO crops were published on April 15, 2008. That is long before Bill Gates' address to the public in late January of this year [2012]. Did Monsanto stockholder[6] Gates ignore this information, or
25 does he believe the 900 scientists to be incorrect? Perhaps the evidence generated from the expert team is not enough. In that case, then Gates should look no farther than the Union of Concerned Scientists.

Another massive research organization, the Union of Concerned Scientists also examined the true yield of GMO crops, only to find that the altered crops do not produce
30 increased yields over the long run – despite their excessive cost and extreme danger to health and environment. The lack of scientific support behind the GMO crops was so startling to the Union that they documented all the details in a 2009 report entitled "Failure to Yield."

GMO crops are not only ineffective at fighting world hunger, but are a genuine[7] threat
35 to public health. Even if they *were* effective at feeding more individuals than traditional

farming practices, would they really want to consume it? Bill Gates appears to have the interests of massive corporations in mind when perpetuating[8] the myth that GMOs are the answer to fighting starvation.

(455 words)

Anthony Gucciardi: Sorry Gates: GMO Crops Shown to be Ineffective at Fighting World Hunger.
In: Natural Society, *March 2nd, 2012.*
URL: *http://naturalsociety.com/gmo-crops-proven-to-be-ineffective-at-fighting-world-hunger/*

1 Monsanto shareholder – Aktionär von Monsanto, einem multinationalen Biotechnologiekonzern
2 GMO – genetically modified organism
3 to yield – *hier:* erbringen
4 outperformed – übertroffen
5 agro-ecological – *hier:* nachhaltig
6 stockholder *(AE)* – shareholder *(BE)*
7 genuine – echt
8 perpetuating – preserving sth. for a long time

Assignments

1. Summarize the text. (Material B)   (30 BE)

2. Relate the controversy over GMO crops to another debate in modern science as encountered in class.   (40 BE)

3. Write a letter to Bill Gates in which you develop your ideas concerning business ethics in today's world.   (30 BE)

In die Gesamtbewertung gehen die Ergebnisse der Teilaufgaben A und B im Verhältnis 1:3 ein.

Lösungsvorschläge

Teaching modules referred to:
The mediation text refers to the teaching module Work and Industrialization *(Q 2). The second text deals with the topic* Biotechnology *from the teaching module* Science and Technology *(Q 1). Another important point of reference is the module* Work and Industrialization *(Q 2) with the topic* Trade and Competition.

Teil A: Aufgabe zur Sprachmittlung

Step 1 Read the text carefully and focus on the topic and the pros and cons listed in the article.
Step 2 Remember to start with an umbrella sentence containing source and topic.
Step 3 Write a maximum of 110 words. Refer to relevant information only.

In the *Hamburger Abendblatt* from March 26, 2008 the author comments on driving at the age of 16. He accepts that teenagers mature more quickly nowadays and therefore want more freedom and responsibility. But the disadvantages for society seem to outweigh the benefits of this idea: according to US experiences, young people cause the most accidents. Possessing a driving license would distract teenagers from school work and result in conflicts with parents. The author cannot understand why young people should be allowed to drive but not to vote and to be treated as adults in court. He believes guided driving at 17 is a good alternative to the traditional way. *(110 words)*

Teil B: Verkürzte Textaufgabe

1. *In your summary you are supposed to outline the criticism directed against Bill Gates and his involvement with the biotechnology industry.*
   Step 1 Omitting unnecessary detail and examples, your text should include an umbrella sentence.
   Step 2 Remember to write the summary in the present tense and use your own words: Do not include quotations. The summary should be between 130–150 words (about 1/3 of the original text).

The text, retrieved from an Internet commentary on April 14, 2012, deals with Bill Gates' suggestion to use genetically modified organisms (GMOs) to ease global food shortage.
In his public speech in January 2012, Gates argued that GMO seeds from the biotechnological company Monsanto would be able to free the world from starvation. Gates is also one of the shareholders of Monsanto. Four years earlier, an organisation called IAASTD consisting of 900 scientists and researchers had already proven the inefficiency of GMO crops as compared to traditional methods. In 2009 these findings were confirmed by another research institute. Furthermore, the author claims that

GMO seeds are overpriced and dangerous to both health and the environment. Gates seems to ignore the fact that GMO crops cannot solve food shortages and only work in the interest of big companies and their shareholders. *(140 words)*

2. *The controversy over GMO crops is to be related to other issues in modern science also referring to examples and questions of a more ethical nature.*
Step 1 *Start with putting the issue of GMOs in the wider context of biotechnology and drawing on examples from discussions in your class (e. g. designer babies, reproductive and therapeutic cloning, designer food or cloned livestock).*
Step 2 *When you move on to a more principal level of ethical concerns, you will also focus on the question of who profits from the results of modern science.*

Bill Gates' high hopes in GMO have been unjustified as the commentary demonstrated. Despite excessive costs they were not productive and were the ruin of the farmers who believed in the new biotechnology (cf. ll. 6/7). In fact, the crops were a threat to health and the environment (cf. ll. 30/31).

Similar shortcomings can be experienced in other areas of biotechnology. A case in point is the cloning of animals and plants. Dolly the Scottish sheep, an artificial identical copy of an animal, triggered doubts concerning its scientific value, which questioned the sense of cloning altogether. Researchers claimed that it was a great step with regards to the development of new medicines and that useful protein could be produced by transferring genes. The understanding of genetics could also be improved by cloning. In the end, the opponents of cloning felt they had been proven right: Dolly was able to mate and have a normal offspring but had to be put down prematurely. Other attempts at cloning were rather short-lived so the benefits remain doubtful. An issue related to this topic is the heated discussion about designer babies. Those children are created artificially in order to help sick brothers or sisters as they have got the same genetic make-up. It is an ethical question whether the ill children should be helped by creating a clone that supplies the necessary cells.

In contrast, there is no doubt that the therapeutic value of cloning belongs to the positive aspects of medical research. In many countries, however, the implementation of stem cells does not meet with unequivocal public approval and politicians have to face the controversial question whether they wish to exclude their scientists from the global progress. This has led to a brain drain in the academic world and countries with strict legislation such as Germany seem to be left at a disadvantage.

Without a doubt, biotechnology has positive effects on the standard of living and life expectancy. On the other hand it is difficult to predict its long-time effects and the impact on the environment. Ethical concerns touch on the question whether biotechnology is a blessing or a curse. The case of Bill Gates tells us that the interests of big corporations, the profits from scientific research and progress are often closely related. This development might not be in the interest of the majority of the population as only a few people will benefit from it. *(404 words)*

3. *Writing a letter requires keeping important aspects of letter-writing in mind, such as using formal English, referring to the text in question, naming the date, address as well as the formal addressing of the addressee.*
    Step 1 *Begin with acknowledging the role Bill Gates plays in the IT world and the modern ideas he stands for. Also remember his commitment to charity.*
    Step 2 *By drawing attention to the contradictory research on GMO foods and the fact that Gates is a shareholder of a biotechnological company you might find a reason to raise questions of ethical responsibilities.*
    Step 3 *Then you will be able to refer to the social and political implications in everyday life, such as the decreasing privacy of individuals, the shaping of public opinion, increasing social obligations and the profit margins.*

Bill Gates
Main Office
500 Fifth Avenue North
Seattle, WA 98102
(206) 709-3100

April 15, 2013

Dear Mr Gates,

It was very interesting to read about your public speech on the advantages of GMO crops that you delivered in California. In Germany, you are well-known for the innovative role you have played in the world of IT. The Internet and digital resources in general have greatly increased access to information and are a great help in studying the phenomena of our globalised societies. I am also aware of your commitment to solving current problems and addressing the issues of food supply and starvation, which I have supported whole-heartedly up to now.

So it came as a surprise to me that you promote the activities of a biotechnological company claiming that GMO crops are the solution to the complex problems of world hunger. Research projects of a great number of scientists proved years ago that GMO seeds do not only refuse to yield crops but are absolutely harmful to human beings and nature. Your participation in this case seems very doubtful in a moral sense, even more so as a shareholder of Monsanto, the biotechnological company in question. I take it that you are aware of the research results. This also calls your ethical responsibility into question when it comes to corporate interests.

In Europe, Microsoft has come under close scrutiny for creating a monopoly for software applications. As beneficial as the digital innovations really are, we as consumers need to have a choice as to what system we would like to use and competition in this area is essential to find the best solutions. If Microsoft is only interested in defending their own monopoly and extending profit margins, social obligations are being ignored.

I would be very keen to know more about your attitude towards Corporate Social Responsibility (CSR), a concept that is nowadays taken on by many German companies. Although it is thought to belong to the soft skills of a corporation, people are very much aware of its social functions and companies embracing CSR find it helpful to sell their products.

It would be very kind of you if you could explain to me how you are able to reconcile your sense of social obligation with the pursuit of maximizing profits, which you apparently favour in the case of Monsanto.

I would find it very helpful, if you could explain some of these contradictions to me and let me know about your stance on CSR, as well.

Yours sincerely
Peter Schnell

(407 words)

A Clash of Values

Rick, the narrator, is a young man who has gone through difficult times and now joins his brother Philip, a successful doctor at an abortion clinic in Detroit. Rick wants to work there as an unskilled labourer. They are on the point of arriving at the clinic where they are confronted with anti-abortionist demonstrators. The story reflects a social problem in the U.S. where so-called "pro-life"-activists use non-violent and violent forms of protest against abortion clinics, i. e. protest marches and fire-bombings.

[…] there were people there, a whole shadowy mass of shoulders and hats and steaming faces that converged on us with a shout. At first I didn't know what was going on – I thought I was trapped in a bad movie, *Night of the Living Dead* or *Zombies on Parade*. The faces were barking at us, teeth bared, eyes sunk back in their heads, hot breath boil-
5 ing from their throats. "Murderers!" they were shouting. "Nazis!" "Baby-killers!"
We inched our way across the sidewalk and into the lot, working through the mass of them as if we were on a narrow lane in a dense forest, and Philip gave me a look that explained it all, from the lines in his face to […] the phone that rang in the middle of the night no matter how many times he changed the number. This was war. I climbed out of
10 the car with my heart hammering, and as the cold knife of the air cut into me I looked back to where they stood clustered at the gate, lumpish and solid, people you'd see anywhere. They were singing now. Some hymn, some self-righteous churchy Jesus-thump-ing[1] hymn that bludgeoned[2] the traffic noise and the deep-frozen air with the force of a weapon. I didn't have time to sort it out, but I could feel the slow burn of anger and hu-
15 miliation coming up in me. Philip's hand was on my arm. "Come on," he said. "We've got work to do, little brother."
That day, the first day, was a real trial. […] I had no illusions about the job – I knew it would be dull and diminishing, and I knew life with Philip and Denise[3] would be one long snooze – but I wasn't used to being called a baby-killer. Liar, thief, crackhead[4] –
20 those were names I'd answered to at one time or another. Murderer was something else.
My brother wouldn't talk about it. He was busy. Wired. Hurtling[5] around the clinic like a gymnast on the parallel bars. By nine I'd met his two associates (another doctor and a counsellor, both female, both unattractive); his receptionist; Nurses Tsing and Hemp-field; and Fred. Fred was a big rabbity-looking[6] guy in his early thirties with a pale red-
25 dish mustache and hair of the same color climbing up out of his head in all directions. He had the official title of "technician", though the most technical things I saw him do were drawing blood and divining[7] urine for signs of pregnancy, clap[8], or worse. None of them – not my brother, the nurses, the counsellor, or even Fred – wanted to discuss what was going on at the far end of the parking lot and on the sidewalk out front. The zombies with
30 the signs – yes, signs, I could see them out the window, ABORTION KILLS and SAVE THE PREBORNS and I WILL ADOPT YOUR BABY – were of no more concern to them than mosquitoes in June or a sniffle in December. Or at least that was how they acted.

I tried to draw Fred out on the subject as we sat together at lunch in the back room. We were surrounded by shadowy things in jars of formalin, gleaming stainless-steel sinks,
35 racks of test tubes, reference books, cardboard boxes full of drug samples and syringes and gauze pads and all the rest of the clinic's paraphernalia. "So what do you think of all this, Fred?" I said, gesturing toward the window with the ham-and-Swiss on rye Denise had made me in the dark hours of the morning.

Fred was hunched over a newspaper, doing the acrostic puzzle[9] and sucking on his
40 teeth. His lunch consisted of a microwave chili-and-cheese burrito and a quart of root beer[10]. He gave me a quizzical look.

"The protesters, I mean. The Jesus-thumpers out there. Is it like this all the time?" And then I added a little joke, so he wouldn't think I was intimidated: "Or did I just get lucky?"

45 "Who, them?" Fred did something with his nose and his upper teeth, something rabbity, as if he were tasting the air. "They're nobody. They're nothing."

"Yeah?" I said, hoping for more, hoping for some details, some explanation, something to assuage[11] the creeping sense of guilt and shame that had been building in me all morning. Those people had pigeonholed[12] me before I'd even set foot in the door, and
50 that hurt. They were wrong. I was no baby-killer – I was just the little brother of a big brother, trying to make a new start. And Philip was no baby-killer, either – he was a guy doing his job, that was all. Shit, somebody had to do it. Up to this point I guess I'd never really given the issue much thought – my girlfriends, when there were girlfriends, had taken care of the preventative end of things on their own, and we never really discussed
55 it – but my feeling was that there were too many babies in the world already, too many adults, too many suet-faced[13] Jesus-thumping jerks ready to point the finger, and didn't any of these people have better things to do? Like a job, for instance? But Fred wasn't much help. He just sighed, nibbled at the wilted stem of his burrito, and said, "You get used to it."

(871 words)

1   Jesus-thumping – christliche Ideale aggressiv vertretend
2   to bludgeon – *hier:* übertönen
3   Denise – Philip's wife
4   crackhead – *hier:* person with strange / crazy ideas or drug user
5   to hurtle – move at a great or dangerous speed
6   rabbity-looking – looking like a rabbit
7   to divine – *hier:* untersuchen
8   clap *(coll.)* – Geschlechtskrankheit (Tripper)
9   acrostic puzzle – *hier:* ein anspruchsvolles Kreuzworträtsel
10 root beer – a sweet drink that does not contain alcohol
11 to assuage – to lessen, to reduce
12 pigeonhole – give sb. a label (German: einordnen)
13 suet-faced – *hier:* fettig, aufgedunsen

Assignments

1. Point out the situation Rick finds himself confronted with at his brother's clinic. (Material)　(30 BE)

2. Analyse the image Rick creates of the demonstrators and his feelings towards them referring to the language he uses.　(35 BE)

3. *"Frequent violent protests against abortion clinics, in the form of arson, fire-bombing, and vandalism, started in the early 1970s in the U.S. after the U.S. Supreme Court's ruling [...] theoretically gave abortion access to all women [...]."*
   http://www.religioustolerance.org/abo_viol.htm (abgerufen am 03. 12. 2012)

   Discuss the legitimacy of different forms of fighting for one's most basic moral/ethical beliefs. Take the quotation as a starting point and refer to the text at hand and to material discussed in class.　(35 BE)

Teaching modules referred to:
The text at hand and the assignments refer to the teaching module Ideals and Reality *(Q 3)*
focusing in particular on the topic Structural Problems. *It also includes the teaching module* Extreme Situations *and the topic of* The Troubled Mind *(Q 2). One can also relate the text to other modules such as* Them and Us *and the topic* Values *(Q 1).*

1. **Step 1** *To start off, it would be a good idea to begin your text with an umbrella sentence giving the name of the author and the title of the book the extract is taken from. You should also generally refer to the content of the extract.*
   Step 2 *Then it is your task to find more information about the situation the character is in. Keep in mind that the story is narrated from the protagonist Rick's point of view. The following aspects should be focused on: Rick's first reaction to the protesters, what impact the demonstrators have on him and the other employees at the clinic and finally how Rick struggles to come to terms with the situation.*
   Step 3 *The task can be either completed by following the chronological order of the text or by concentrating on the reaction of the single groups involved: Rick's brother Philip, the other employees and most important of all, Rick himself.*

The extract of T. C. Boyle's "Killing Babies" published in *After the Plague* in 2001, provides an insight into the internal conflict of the protagonist and narrator Rick concerning the legitimacy of abortions which is caused by a group of abortion opponents gathering in front of the Detroit clinic where Rick is to start as an unskilled worker. Confronted with the religiously motivated protest of the loud demonstrators who accuse the employees of the clinic of murder, Rick is totally confused and unable to classify the event (cf. ll. 2/3). He does not really know how to deal with the situation, but soon realises that it is serious: (cf. l. 9). He feels overtaxed and humiliated (cf. ll. 14/15, 19). Trying to come to terms with the situation, he wants to talk to his brother Philip and the technician Fred. But Philip refuses to talk about the demonstration or the nightly calls even though he suffers from them (cf. ll. 7–9, 21). Rick soon realises that the other employees have got used to the demonstrators and don't seem to mind anymore. They refuse to discuss the matter and prefer to ignore the demonstration (cf. ll. 27–29, 57–59). Rick suspects the employees' behaviour to be mere pretence (cf. l. 32).
In the end, he is left alone with his growing confusion and shame. He suddenly feels forced to deal with the moral implication of an abortion – a matter he has only considered superficially before (cf. ll. 52–55) and thus avoided any responsibility. Now he strongly rejects the accusation of Philip or himself being murderers (cf. ll. 50/51), tries to defend their work (cf. l. 52) and even justifies the abortions (cf. l. 55). Thus, he gets angry at the demonstrators (cf. ll. 56/57) for disturbing his peace of mind.

(305 words)

2. *Dealing with such a task it is necessary to remember the stylistic devices learnt in class and apply them to the text at hand.*
   Step 1 First of all find text passages that contain references to the demonstrators and how they are described by Rick. Also analyse his feelings towards them.
   Step 2 Collect certain expressions that give an impression of the way the protesters look and behave in Rick's eyes. Identify and underline the stylistic devices. Make a list of all the examples and interpret their function in the text.
   Step 3 Then try to group your findings, make a plan and start writing.

The pro-life demonstration Rick witnesses on his arrival at the clinic provokes a series of mixed emotions that reveal his attitude towards the demonstrators. He is shocked, confused and irritated by the mass of people awaiting his brother. At first he questions his sense of perception and feels "trapped in a bad movie" (l. 3) The activists are depersonalised and metaphorically referred to as a "shadowy mass of shoulders and hats and steaming faces" (ll. 1/2), introduced as an instinct-driven animal that threatens the narrator: "The faces were barking at us, teeth bared, eyes sunk back [...], hot breath boiling from their throats" (ll. 4/5). The feeling of danger is once more evoked by the comparison "[we] inched our way across the sidewalk [...] through the mass of them as if we were on a narrow lane in a dense forest" (ll. 6/7) and underlines the protagonist's fear and feeling of helplessness caused by the faceless demonstration. The metaphorical exaggeration "This is war" (l. 9) reveals his upcoming anger towards them and their cold-hearted aggressiveness. He describes the protesters' songs as "self-righteous" (l. 12), used as weapons to drown every sound around them (cf. ll. 12–14). The alliteration "my heart hammering" (l. 10) shows Rick's rage and the humiliation that results from this confrontation with this unexpected danger. The gloomy atmosphere in the clinic only makes things worse, adding to Rick's "creeping sense of guilt" (l. 48). He feels more and more uncomfortable, morally insecure and ashamed of his ignorant attitude towards the abortion issue. He becomes aggressive and reveals his immaturity by insulting the protesters as "zombies with the signs" (ll. 29/30) and "Jesus-thumping jerks" (l. 56). The perception of the demonstrators as an uncontrollable, superior mass activated by some higher force once more shows Rick's helplessness. His feelings towards the demonstrators develop from confusion to anger and end up as sarcasm to ridicule the protesters: "[Didn't] any of these people have better things to do? Like a job, for instance?" (ll. 56/57). *(339 words)*

3. *Step 1 To be able to meet the requirements of this task it is necessary to fully understand the quote above. Translate it into your own words, express your personal interpretation of it and try to find out if it reflects the intention of the author.*
   Step 2 Examine the topics discussed in class to make sure they can be used as an input for your text.
   Step 3 Remember to structure the essay with useful linkers and connectors that help introduce a new argument.

The quotation reveals the writer's deep moral conflict about the legitimacy of abortion and informs the reader about the different attitudes to it in the US in the early 1970s. It shows that the intervention of the legislative authority was necessary to enforce the right for abortion and protect the women involved. But it also reveals that many people are ready to use violence in order to follow their moral beliefs; thereby ignoring legislation and the consequences of their actions. It is therefore necessary to ask oneself whether any form of fighting for one's ethical beliefs is legitimate.

In the text "A Clash of Values" by T. C. Boyle the narrator pictures the demonstrators in front of the abortion clinic as a bunch of fanatics with totalitarian attitudes and fundamentalist beliefs. They accuse the employees of the clinic of murder but do not become physically violent. Religiously motivated they seem to ignore secular legislation which they consider to be inferior. Consequently, their heavy protest causes the narrator to develop a more elaborate opinion on abortion than he had before. Using non-violent methods, the protesters reached their aims of drawing attention to their cause and getting people to think. Nevertheless, it cannot be approved of that some demonstrators obviously interfere in the private life of Rick's brother Philip and call him nightly on the phone just to wear him down.

Another example is the fighting for basic rights in the War of Independence. Originally wanting to achieve greater liberty in economic and political matters, the former British colonies demanded the right to enact legislations and impose taxes on goods. But as the British motherland, their only trading partner, refused to comply with their wish, the only alternative left to them was to break away. Basically, the settlers fought for a greater good in order to achieve the right to life, liberty, freedom and the pursuit of happiness for everybody. These values are now granted in the Declaration of Independence of 1776. Without the settlers' bravery, the US of today would not exist. Still, it has to be pointed out that a lot of innocent blood was spilt and many people did not live to witness the birth of the new independent nation.

Furthermore, Malcolm X and Martin Luther King used different strategies in fighting for civil rights for black Americans. M. L. King succeeded in achieving equal rights for Afro-Americans by organising sit-ins, boycotts or demonstrations. Malcolm X on the other hand adopted a different strategy that called for militancy and riots. He claimed that due to unequal treatment, exploitation and persecution, the Afro-Americans had the right to defend themselves and also to use violence. Malcolm X's protest increased public awareness and finally led to positive changes in American society that went beyond legally guaranteed equality. He helped the black community in America to gain more self-esteem. But he also caused many casualties and a lot of hatred. Malcolm X's legacy will always be overshadowed by his promotion of violence. Therefore he is viewed in a bad light whereas M. L. King still serves as an example of peaceful protest all over the world.

I believe that non-violent protests are the only legitimate way as they let activists maintain their integrity and avoid producing casualties and feelings of revenge. Thus, protesters respect other opinions but also show their determination and might even convince formerly neutral people. A non-violent exchange of words is an efficient and democratic way of finding solutions for any kind of conflict.   *(584 words)*

Multiculturalism is not the best way to welcome people to our country

[...]
I am the child of an immigrant myself, and I believe we should take more immigrants and refugees into Britain, not fewer. But it is increasingly clear that, forged with the best of intentions, multiculturalism has become a counter-productive way of welcoming peo-
5 ple to our country. It promotes not a melting pot where we all mix together but a segregated society of sealed-off cultures, each sticking to its own.
[...]
But there is another dysfunctional aspect to multiculturalism. In practice, it acts as though immigrant cultures are unchanging and should be preserved in aspic. This forces
10 multiculturalists into alliance with the most conservative and unpleasant parts of immigrant communities. For example, what would you do if, in your block of flats, there was a white family where the women of the house rarely left without the patriarch's permission, and – on the very rare occasions when they did – they covered their face so only their eyes were visible? What would you do if, in the same family, there was a gay son
15 who knew he could never tell his relatives, because he would be beaten and then ostracised[1] from everybody he has ever known?
The answer is easy (I hope): you would be disgusted, and you would try to help them. But there is a family just like this in the building where I live, and there is only one difference – they are Asian. So I do nothing, and nor do any of the other nice liberals
20 who live here, even though this family is as British as we are. Isn't there a word for treating people differently because of the colour of their skin?
Multiculturalism has caused British people to do this on a national scale. All this time, we could have been helping women and gay people from immigrant communities to enjoy the fruits of a free society. This would have created interesting and more pro-
25 gressive versions of Islam that would fight back against jihadism far more effectively than a thousand government initiatives or police raids. Instead, we have been inadvertently[2] helping the conservative men who want to keep these groups in a subordinate position.
We have been acting as though there is one thing called "Muslim culture", and elder-
30 ly imams or enraged, misogynistic[3] young men are its only voice. A few weeks ago, it was driven home to me how wrong this is. I wrote about how the best way to defeat jihadists was to empower Muslim women, and I was inundated with e-mails from Muslim women, many explaining how the logic of multiculturalism weakened their hand.
One, in particular, is worth quoting at length: "My younger sisters go to Denbigh
35 High School [in Luton] which was famous in the headlines last year because a girl pupil went to the High Court for her right to wear the jilbab[4]. Shabinah [the girl who took the case] saw it as a great victory for Muslim women ... but what happened next shows this is not a victory for us.

My sisters, and me when I was younger, could always tell our dad and uncles that we
40 weren't allowed to wear the jilbab. Once the rules were changed, that excuse was not possible any more so my sisters have now been terrified into wearing this cumbersome[5] and
dehumanising garment all day against their wishes. Now most girls in the school do the
same. They don't want to, but now they cannot resist community pressure … I am frightened somebody is going to fight for the right to wear a burqa[6] next and then my sisters
45 will not even be able to show their faces."

So to multiculturalists, we have to ask: which Muslim culture do you want to preserve? The jilbab-wearing culture of Shabinah and the mullahs, or the culture of the hundreds of Muslim girls who curse them? All immigrant communities are divided and diverse; it is a form of soft racism to assume they have One Culture that should be respect-
50 ed at all costs.

But multiculturalism binds the hands of those who want cultural change in immigrant
communities by demanding tolerance and respect for reactionary traditions. At a time
when there is a battle within British Islam whose outcome will affect us all, is it wise to
continue like this?
55 It is not too late to unpick the dysfunctional logic of multiculturalism. We can actively promote dialogue, meeting-places and inter-breeding. No more funding of divisive faith
schools. No more separate community centres.

Britain has the highest rate of mixed-race partnerships anywhere in the world, largely
due to sexual relationships between white and black people in London. This – not multi-
60 culturalism – is the British tradition to promote. No more bland "tolerance": let's have
rows and laughs and sex. Our future lies in this glorious mixing of races, not in separating them out and hermetically sealing them off in their own outdated "cultures".

Multiculturalism is dead; long live miscegenation[7].   *(813 words)*

*Johann Hari, "Multiculturalism is not the best way to welcome people to our country", The Independent,
05. 08. 2005; http://www.independent.co.uk/opinion/commentators/johann-hari/johann-hari-
multiculturalism-is-not-the-best-way-to- welcome-people-to-our-country-501506.html*

1   to ostracise – ausgrenzen
2   inadvertently – versehentlich
3   misogynistic – hostile towards women
4   jilbab – long and loose-fitting coat
5   cumbersome – hinderlich
6   burqa – full body cloak covering parts of the face
7   miscegenation – the mixing of races

Assignments

1. Summarize the article. (Material) (30 BE)

2. Relate the problems caused by multiculturalism in GB – according to the text – to those in either Canada or the USA. (40 BE)

3. Write a letter to Johann Hari defending the concepts of multiculturalism and diversity. (30 BE)

Lösungsvorschläge

Teaching modules referred to:
The task relates to the teaching module The United Kingdom *(Q 1) with particular refer-ence to the topics* Social Structure, Social Change. *The context then extends to the module* Them and Us *(Q 1) specifically on the topic* The One-track Mind *respectively the module* Promised Lands: Dreams and Realities *(Q 3) especially focussing on* Social Issues.

1. *Step 1 Create an introductory sentence that includes the following points: the name of the author, the date, source and topic of the newspaper commentary.*
   Step 2 Start writing. Your summary must not be longer than 1/4 to 1/3 of the original text, which is about 250 words. Use your own words, omit unnecessary details and avoid quotations.

The commentary by Johann Hari, "Multiculturalism is not the best way to welcome people to our country", published in the *Independent* on August 5, 2005, deals with multiculturalism and the impact it has on immigrants in Great Britain.
A son of an immigrant himself, the author has a particular perspective on immigra-tion and is especially critical of the outcomes of the concept of multiculturalism. Con-trary to the best of intentions, immigrants cannot fully benefit from multiculturalism in his opinion. So the author favours a melting pot, a concept that suggests that peo-ple can live together and cultures are not sealed off from each other resulting in a sepa-rated society.
Furthermore, the author believes that the multicultural perspective regards immigrant cultures as unchanging and homogenous rather than diverse, which emphasizes tradi-tional structures and beliefs. Thus, some members of the immigrant community such as women or gay people do not benefit from the blessings of a democratic society. The tolerant attitude of the majority of the British people only makes things worse as they tend to tolerate the behaviour of conservative religious leaders or sexist young men. Progressive and open-minded immigrants cannot rely on the support of main-stream society because the acceptance of multiculturalism weakens their position. Racism and discrimination are named as possible consequences. In order to over-come these negative effects, the author demands more opportunities to get in touch with other cultures and stresses the positive influence of mixed-race partnerships, which might provide a better future and understanding of immigrants. *(250 words)*

2. This task requires a closer look at the concept of multiculturalism as practised in Canada or the United States. Before you decide whether to focus on examples from either of these countries, take another look at the text at hand.

Step 1 The critical observations of the author will provide the terms of reference to discuss the impact of multiculturalism in Great Britain, before you turn to the country of your choice. So you need to examine some of the British attitudes and immigrant experiences first to assess if integration may be made easier or more difficult for (some groups of) immigrants in comparison to other countries.

Step 2 Independent of the country you decide to include in your analysis, it will be helpful to refer to novels, short stories or other material you have dealt with in class and which provide sufficient background for your argumentation.

Please note: The following essay will provide a solution for both Canada and the US.

There are a number of issues immigrants have to deal with when settling in their new host country. The attitude of the mainstream culture is therefore as important as the willingness of the immigrants to adapt to the new social and cultural conditions. At first sight, a tolerant attitude towards the immigrant cultures such as in Great Britain seems to be helpful, provided the new arrivals are able to acquire the necessary language skills and are willing to adapt to the rules of everyday life. Of course, integration is also a matter of practical elements like welcoming neighbourhoods and good conditions on the labour market.

The British model of separating immigrants from the host society concerning state-funded (faith) schools and community centres (cf. ll. 56/57) and maybe also housing and work places has so far contributed to widening the gap between the different cultures. This development proved helpful especially for conservative immigrants who value their own traditions highly and are opposed to change. With a host society that confuses tolerance with indifference (cf. ll. 19/20) and adherents of traditional values discriminating against more progressive forces within their immigrant community, the British need to make an effort to overcome these problems. *(202 words)*

Canada

In contrast to Great Britain and right from its beginnings, Canada has always been a country of immigration and it has been the policy of various governments to meet the needs of different groups of immigrants in the past and present. Thus, Canada's immigration policy is admired internationally. There are a number of factors for the success of this multicultural society, which shall be explained in detail below.

First of all, immigration to Canada is based on a qualifying quota requiring a job prospect. After a few years in Canada, the future citizen has to pass the citizenship test. Then the applicant will be granted Canadian citizenship. Therefore, there are highly motivated immigrants who identify with their host country.

Furthermore, the state supports the immigrant's efforts to integrate into the host society. A variety of organisations help the new arrivals and schools make sure that children learn the English language. This is a major task considering that two thirds of Ontario's total immigrants are living in Toronto.

This is all part of the concept of a multicultural mosaic that is officially supported by the Canadian government. This is a big difference to US policy, where the idea of the "melting pot" or "salad bowl" is still dominant. In Canada, each and every culture has the right to preserve its identity and traditions within a unified community. That way the contribution of each ethnic group is valued for its own sake and diversity and mutual respect is encouraged. Xenophobic parties have never won a Canadian election so discrimination and racism do not seem such big issues as they are in Great Britain.

Although Canadian society serves as an example to the globalized world, the mainstream society – an immigrant society itself – and the indigenous communities have not yet been reconciled entirely. Similar to experiences in Australia, the First Nations deplore a stolen generation as Aboriginal children were forcibly removed from their families and taken to Residential Schools, where they were abused and the native culture was suppressed severely. In 2008, Canadian Prime Minister Stephen Harper officially apologized for the harm done to these children and Aboriginals received so-called Common Experience payments. The apology was not met with unequivocal approval as the issues First Nation communities are struggling with on their reservations such as drug abuse and social problems were not really addressed. In this respect, the Aboriginals did not receive funding from government.

The complex relationship between Native Canadians and white Canadians plays an important role in Canadian literature. For example, Thomas King's novel *Green Grass, Running Water* is a satire on the ignorance of North American host societies as far as the genuine First Nation communities are concerned. *(447 words)*

United States

The promise of the American Dream has always attracted immigrants from all over the world. In contrast to Great Britain, the image of migration as a "melting pot" used to prevail in the US for a long time: The different immigrant cultures were supposed to disappear so that new identities could be established. Later the theory of a "salad bowl" or "cultural quilt" was introduced, as this seemed to be more politically correct. This cultural idea is based on the belief that there does not need to be a homogeneous society, but that the many different groups of immigrants keep their specific qualities. In short, this concept is more in accordance with the original values of the American Dream, for example, that everyone can achieve his or her aims regardless of social background.

Unfortunately, the black Americans could not benefit from the promises made in the American Constitution. In the 1960s the peaceful Civil Rights Movement under Dr. Martin Luther King drew public attention to the open discrimination against black people and organised boycotts and sit-ins. As a result, the Congress passed the Civil Rights Act in 1964 as well as the Voting Rights Act one year later. Finally, blacks were guaranteed the same rights as white people. King's speech "I have a dream" became a powerful manifestation of the integration of black people into white society. Still, Malcolm X's Black Power movement would not have gained so many followers in the late 1960s if the situation of black Americans had undergone a significant change after legislation had been passed. Nowadays, the (re-)election of Barack Obama as the first black US president shows that black people have many more possibilities than 30 years ago and that the attitude of mainstream society has changed considerably. Nevertheless, the living standard of the average black American family is far below that of a white family.

As far as ethnic minorities in the United States are concerned, the second largest group, the Hispanics, are in a comparable social and economic situation as the black Americans. T. C. Boyle describes this issue in his novel *The Tortilla Curtain*, where a couple from Mexico, Cándido and América, struggle for survival as illegal immigrants. This is in stark contrast to a typical white American family, the Mossbachers, who seem to be able to live their American dream. Meanwhile, Cándido and América find neither food nor a job in the US. Typically for illegal immigrants, the outcome of the story is rather pessimistic: América's new-born baby dies and the couple returns to Mexico. The plot of the novel serves as a warning that the American Dream may turn into a nightmare for the new arrivals.

All in all, as in Great Britain the situation of foreigners in the US is far from being resolved although the most pressing problems are different. In Britain traditional beliefs within the host society prevent certain groups of immigrants such as women and gay people from being fully integrated into society. The attitude of the British host society makes it worse as people prefer to ignore social evils claiming to act tolerantly. In the US, it is the discrepancy between the theoretical or legal situation of foreigners and the real state of affairs that result in poverty and a limited upward mobility for the new arrivals.

(552 words)

3. *In your letter to the author, you are asked to defend the concept of multiculturalism and diversity. Keep in mind that the author Johann Hari is an immigrant himself and that rather than reporting facts he wishes to draw attention to the negative aspects of multiculturalism.*

   Step 1 *First you need to explain the terms "melting pot", "salad bowl" and "ethnic diversity" and how these concepts might work for or against the attempts of immigrants to successfully integrate into the host society. This way you make sure that both writer and reader have a common ground to start from.*

   Step 2 *Then you need to elaborate on the advantages of multiculturalism and diversity by using examples and facts discussed in class. It is also important to refer to the doubts expressed in Hari's commentary and show that there is another way of interpreting his findings.*

Dear Sir,

It was very interesting to read your comment on the negative effects of multiculturalism. Although I can understand your reasons, I beg to disagree and would like to stress a few points in support of this concept which I still prefer to the cultural ideas of a "melting pot" and a "salad bowl".

Let me first explain my perception of melting pot and salad bowl, both of which you seem to be in favour of, and how they work against ethnic diversity. The idea behind the US concept of a melting pot was to blend all immigrant cultures into a mainstream culture and thus create a unified community. But in reality this meant that the immigrants had to abandon their own traditions and adapt to the mainstream Anglo-

Saxon values. Even the milder version of the salad bowl had the disadvantage that the mainstream society had no use for the new arrivals' traditions, which were lost eventually. As the immigrants' culture could not survive within the mainstream culture, especially older immigrants found it hard to integrate into their new host community. This shows that ethnic diversity can only exist in an open and liberal society that is able and willing to accept new ideas and values. To my mind, this can only be achieved in a multicultural society.

Rejecting a tolerant approach will make it much harder for immigrants to integrate. I agree with you that there should be a common ground such as meeting places or community centres where young people from different cultural backgrounds can meet and get to know each other. This will surely help to develop an intercultural competence. I do not believe that legislation and state regulation help to speed up this process. In France, for example, Muslim women are not allowed to wear a veil in school. Nevertheless, there have been riots in this country because the state failed to integrate the immigrants and merely concentrated on legislation while leaving everything else to fate. To my mind, what we need is to provide the opportunity for dialogue and an exchange of ideas.

In addition, it is wrong to assume that multiculturalism supports the conservative elements in society and helps to keep immigrant groups in a subordinate position. It is those groups that receive a lot of attention because they refuse to integrate into the host society, unlike many thousands of immigrants have done before and sometimes their behaviour causes damage and harm. I believe that you generalise the matter. As in every other society, there are conservative and more progressive people in immigrant communities. The same goes for members of the British Islam community. This is why I am not as alarmed as you are concerning the outcome of the battle.

Furthermore, I absolutely agree with you that people should not look the other way when a woman is beaten up by her husband in her own home. Unfortunately, I believe people would not have dared to interfere either had the couple been white and not Asian. This is human behaviour that you cannot attribute to a misunderstood concept of a multicultural society but to a general development of increasing indifference concerning one's fellow citizens.

To conclude, I am very much in favour of dialogue and meeting-places, but it will have to be a liberal space. I believe abandoning the concept of multiculturalism will make us lose more than we gain from returning to the idea of the melting pot. There is a lot we can learn from immigrant culture – why not give it a try? I would appreciate hearing from you and hope that you are now having second thoughts on the issue.

Yours sincerely,
Elias Becker

(613 words)

Teil A: Aufgabe zur Sprachmittlung

„Unsere Unternehmensspitzen müssen bunter werden"

Rita Pawelski, Sprecherin der Frauen in der Unions-Bundestagsfraktion, im Gespräch mit Tobias Armbrüster – vor einem Treffen von Vertretern der 30 DAX-Unternehmen mit mehreren Ministerinnen und Ministern der schwarz-gelben Koalition.

[...]

Armbrüster: Frau Pawelski, was erwarten Sie von diesem Treffen heute Mittag?

Pawelski: ..., dass ein Durchbruch sich entwickelt für Frauen in Führungspositionen, und wenn ich von Frauen in Führungspositionen rede, dann meine ich nicht nur die Frauen im
5 oberen Management, sondern ich meine ausdrücklich die Frauen in den Vorständen und in den Aufsichtsräten.

Armbrüster: Wie soll denn so ein Durchbruch aussehen?

Pawelski: Ich erwarte von den Unternehmen, dass sie heute ganz klar definieren, wie viele Frauen sie demnächst auch in Vorständen und Aufsichtsräten berücksichtigen wollen.

10 **Armbrüster:** Warum brauchen wir eine solche Quote, eine solche Voraussage für eine Quote?

Pawelski: Wir brauchen Unternehmen, die erfolgreich und wirklich mit einem festen Willen mehr Frauen in ihren Unternehmen entwickeln wollen, weil es bewiesen ist – es gibt da ja viele Wirtschaftsstudien –, dass geschlechtergemischte Unternehmensführungen
15 besser sind als rein männerdominierte, und darum ist es gut für die deutschen Unternehmen, wenn sie Frauen mehr berücksichtigen, auch vor dem Hinblick der demographischen Entwicklung, Fachkräftemangel. Wir müssen die Frauen fördern, wir müssen sie berücksichtigen und wir müssen zulassen, dass sie auch in den Vorständen und Aufsichtsräten sind.

20 **Armbrüster:** Reicht es denn dann aus, Frau Pawelski, wenn man da der Wirtschaft sozusagen freie Hand lässt, oder brauchen die vielleicht ein bisschen Druck?

Pawelski: Sie brauchen Druck, und was da Druck erzeugt, das haben wir in dem letzten Jahr gesehen. Die Gruppe der Frauen hat vor 14 Monaten einen Beschluss gefasst zu Frauen in Führungspositionen, sie haben einen Stufenplan bis hin zur Quote entwickelt, und
25 als wir diesen Plan aufgestellt haben, gab es zwei Frauen in den Vorständen, mittlerweile sind es sieben.

Armbrüster: Das heißt, Sie wollen konkrete Vorgaben machen für die Unternehmen, wie viele Frauen sie in Führungspositionen beschäftigen sollen?

Pawelski: Unser Endziel ist eine Quote von 30 Prozent, die 2018 erreicht sein sollte. Aber
30 wir sind mit einem ersten Schritt, mit einer Flexiquote für Vorstände, nicht für Aufsichtsräte, wären wir einverstanden, wenn es dann eine deutliche zweistellige Zahl ist.

Armbrüster: Das klingt jetzt alles nach Zwang, Frau Pawelski.

Pawelski: Druck!

Armbrüster: Druck.

35 **Pawelski:** Zwang ist es, wenn wir Gesetze erlassen, ist ja meist ein Zwang dahinter. Wer zahlt schon freiwillig Steuern? Auch das ist ja ein gewisser Zwang, oder?

Armbrüster: Aber meinen Sie, kann man mit Zwang wirklich wirtschaftlichen Erfolg erreichen?

Pawelski: Da in der Vergangenheit in dem Bereich wenig getan wurde, aber klar ist, dass
40 wir die Frauen in den Führungspositionen brauchen, denke ich, müssen wir einen gewissen Zwang ausüben. Aber noch mal: ich sage nicht Zwang, sondern ich sage Druck, und durch Druck entwickelt sich etwas.

Und allein, dass sich heute 30 DAX-Unternehmen treffen, um über das Thema zu reden, und zwar nicht das erste, sondern das zweite Mal, beweist, dass unser Papier schon Er-
45 folg hat, dass wir auf dem richtigen Wege sind, dass sie sehen, wenn sie von alleine nichts machen, kommt wirklich dann eine starre feste Quote. [...]   *(467 Wörter)*

Tobias Armbrüster/Rita Pawelski, in: Deutschlandfunk, 17. 10. 2011,
http://www.dradio.de/dlf/sendungen/interview_dlf/1580724/

Hinweis: Es handelt sich um das Transkript eines Radiointerviews.

Assignment

You are a participant in an EU schools project on women's rights and on the introduction of quotas concerning the representation of women at the top executive level in major companies. For your international partners you summarize German views on the topic, e. g. this interview, which was originally broadcast on Deutschlandfunk. (Material A)

Teil B: Verkürzte Textaufgabe

Airworld

In Walter Kirn's novel Up in the Air *the protagonist Ryan Bingham, 35, is an American business consultant who travels by plane so frequently that he reaches for the special goal of one million frequent flyer miles.*

Planes and airports are where I feel at home. Everything fellows like you dislike about them – the dry, recycled air alive with viruses; the salty food that seems drizzled with warm mineral oil; the aura-sapping[1] artificial lighting – has grown dear to me over the years, familiar, sweet. I love the Compass Club lounges in the terminals, especially the
5 flagship Denver club, with its digital juice dispenser and deep suede sofas and floor-to-ceiling views of taxiing aircraft. I love the restaurants and snack nooks near the gates, stacked to their heat lamps with whole wheat mini-pizzas and gourmet caramel rolls. I even enjoy the suite hotels built within sight of the runways on the ring roads, which are sometimes as close as I get to the cities that my job requires me to visit. I favor rooms

¹⁰ with kitchenettes and conference tables, and once I cooked a Christmas feast in one, serving glazed ham and sweet potato pie to a dozen janitors and maids. They ate with me in rotation, on their breaks one or two at a time, so I really got to know them, even though most spoke no English. I have a gift that way. If you and I hadn't hit it off like this, if the only words we'd passed were "That's my seat" or "Done with that Business Week?" or

¹⁵ just "Excuse me," I'd still regard us as close acquaintances and hope that if we met again up here we wouldn't be starting from zero, as just two suits. [...]

Fast friends aren't my only friends, but they're my best friends. Because they know the life – so much better than my own family does. We're a telephone family, strung out along the wires, sharing our news in loops and daisy chains. We don't meet face-to-face

²⁰ much, and when we do there's a dematerialized feeling, as though only half of our molecules are present. Sad? Not really. We're a busy bunch. And I'm not lonely. If I had to pick between knowing just a little about a lot of folks and knowing everything about a few, I'd opt for the long, wide-angle shot, I think.

I'm peaceful. I'm in my element up here. Flying isn't an inconvenience for me, as it

²⁵ is for my colleagues [...] I've never aspired to an office at world headquarters, close to hearth and home and skybox, with a desk overlooking the Front Range of the Rockies and access to the ninth-floor fitness center. I suppose I'm a sort of mutation, a new species, and though I keep an apartment for storage purposes – actually, I left the place two weeks ago and transferred the few things I own into a locker I've yet to pay the rent on, and may

³⁰ not – I live somewhere else, in the margins of my itineraries[2].

I call it Airworld; the scene, the place, the style. My hometown papers are *USA Today* and the *Wall Street Journal*. The big-screen Panasonics in the club rooms broadcast all the news I need, with an emphasis on the markets and the weather. My literature – yours, too, I see – is the bestseller or the near-bestseller, heavy on themes of espionage,

³⁵ high finance, and the goodness of common people in small towns. In Airworld, I've found, the passions and enthusiasms of the outlying society are concentrated and whisked to a stiff froth. When a new celebrity is minted in the movie theaters or ballparks, this is where the story breaks – on the vast magazine racks that form a sort of trading floor for public reputations and pretty faces. I find it possible here, as nowhere else, to think of myself as

⁴⁰ part of the collective that prices the long bond[3] and governs necktie widths. Airworld is a nation within a nation.

(623 words)

1   aura-sapping – *hier:* nivellierend
2   itinerary – Reiseplan
3   long bond – 30-jährige Staatsanleihe

Assignments

1. Describe the lifestyle the protagonist seems to be favouring. (Material B) (30 BE)

2. Examine the protagonist's vision of "Airworld" against the background of the American Dream. (40 BE)

3. Assess the lifestyle outlined by the protagonist and relate it to the lifestyle preferred by a protagonist referring to material discussed in class. (30 BE)

In die Gesamtbewertung gehen die Ergebnisse der Teilaufgaben A und B im Verhältnis 1:3 ein.

Lösungsvorschläge

Teaching modules referred to:
Both texts refer to the teaching module Ideals and Reality *(Q 3) focusing in particular on the topic* Structural Problems. *One can also relate them to the module* Them and Us *(Q 1), specifically to the topic* Values.

Teil A: Aufgabe zur Sprachmittlung

Do not try to translate the text literally. Identify the main topic of the interview. Mention this point in your "umbrella sentence" which provides the reader with the argumentative key to the article. Also include information on the author, the title, the type of text and the year in which the text was published. Do not hesitate to leave out insignificant details and illustrations. Remember not to use indirect speech or quotes from the text. Stick to the present tense. The text should be approximately 1/3 of the interview.

In her radio interview with Tobias Armbrüster from October 17, 2011, Rita Pawleski, the spokeswoman for female politicians in the Christian Democratic Party (CDU) in the German parliament, demands that a larger number of women should be members of the boards of major German companies. Pawleski hopes that with the help of a plan developed by her party about 30 % of the directors will be women in 2018. She is glad that her efforts seem to be paying off as at the day of the interview representatives of the leading German enterprises on the stock market will be meeting cabinet ministers in order to discuss the issue.

In her opinion a quota is absolutely necessary as scientific research has shown that mixed executive boards make companies more efficient and competitive. To her mind the demographic change and the predicted lack of qualified personnel call for immediate action. She believes that political pressure is necessary to encourage big enterprises to take action, but prefers companies to develop their own strategies so that there is no need for passing a law on fixed quotas. *(183 words)*

Teil B: Verkürzte Textaufgabe

1. **Step 1** Read the text several times. It is necessary to grasp the protagonist's point of view and avoid personal comments when asked to focus on the text only.
   Step 2 Mark representative text passages that help you to do the task so you find it easier to include the information found into a broader context afterwards.
   Step 3 Try to find meaningful criteria to structure your text. In this particular case it might prove helpful to concentrate on what makes the protagonist special, on the situation he is in as well as the special meaning "Airworld" has to him.

The 35-year-old business consultant Ryan Bingham is the main character of Walter Kirn's novel *Up in the Air*. His job requires constant traveling, which results in a restless lifestyle the character seems to appreciate very much.
He has completely adapted to the ways of a businessman who leads a life on the run. Bingham perceives himself as the representative of a new species that prefers the artificial scenery of airports, junk food and in superficial social interaction to having a home, healthy regular meals, close friendships and family ties.
The members of his substitute "family" are the cleaners and the people he accidentally meets on his journeys. Conversation is reduced to an absolute minimum and revolves around topics such as work, magazines or vacant seats. The protagonist nurses his intellect by reading either international newspapers focussing on the weather and the stock market or international bestsellers about espionage or high finance. He neither feels lonely nor sad at airports or on the way to a new destination – instead he is uncomfortable when he meets close family members "as though only half of [the] molecules are present" (ll. 20/21). The comparison reflects the process of alienation that the main character has undergone, but is unable to admit.   *(207 words)*

2. **Step 1** Before you start writing, list aspects that define the American Dream.
   Step 2 Then analyse the extract to find out in how far the protagonist wants to realise his own American Dream and whether he succeeds in doing so. Find relevant text passages that support your ideas.
   Step 3 Work out similarities and differences between the theoretical approach and the fictional text at hand. Think of criteria to structure your ideas and references to the text and then start writing.

The American Dream consists of a couple of ideas that make up the national concept of how success can be achieved in America. In the religious respect, America is considered a new paradise, where God's chosen people founded a new nation based on the general belief that everybody had the right to liberty and happiness which is guaranteed in the Declaration of Independence. Economic success is therefore the result of hard work and willpower regardless of one's social background, political beliefs, religious convictions or skin colour. This has encouraged people to strive for independence, autonomy, personal wealth and economic growth. The concept of the American Dream rejects a pessimistic attitude to the future.

In *Up in the Air* the protagonist Ryan Bingham pictures himself as a happy and successful businessman but is in fact the perfect example of the perversion of the ideals and promises of the American Dream.

Bingham seems to be completely satisfied with his job as a business consultant that requires him to lead an isolated life and claims that he would not desire "an office at world headquarters, close to hearth and home" (ll. 25/26). His whole existence has adapted to his new lifestyle: He has learnt to appreciate artificial emptiness and consequently rejects emotional depth: He has abandoned every kind of close relationship to friends and family and replaced them with a superficial life without commitments as he feels only understood by people with attitudes similar to his own (cf. ll. 17/18). He does not even own a flat anymore as it is only a burden to him (cf. ll. 28–30). In this respect, he serves as an example of somebody who has managed to live the American Dream in terms of economic success, mobility, autonomy, the ability to adapt well to circumstances and thus achieve true happiness.

Nevertheless, it has to be pointed out that Bingham's happiness seems to be artificial. This might be due to a false concept of the American Dream: He does not realise that there is a huge difference between liberty and independence on the one hand and absolute isolation on the other hand. Although he appears not to be aware of it, Bingham attempts to replace lost social contacts with surrogates: He cooks a Christmas dinner for the hotel staff (cf. ll. 10/11) and would like to be recognised by people he has met on a plane before so that they "wouldn't be starting from zero, as just two suits." (l. 16). To boot, he prefers hotel rooms with a kitchen – most likely to pretend that he is at home (cf. ll. 9/10). Claiming to be part of a group of Airworld inhabitants, Bingham uses the first person plural excessively (cf. ll. 16–23) thus pretending that his behaviour is normal in this particular circle of people and that he is not alone but in good company. Still, this only proves that he fails to understand the extent of his alienation because he is deadened emotionally. Tragically, he truly believes that he has achieved his aspirations while at the same time leaving the impression of a lonely, restless and homeless individual. Bingham's version of the American Dream is a surrogate of the original concept. It seems absurd and cannot result in true happiness.

(549 words)

3. **Step 1** *Preparing for this task it is necessary to assess the lifestyle described by Ryan Bingham first.*
Step 2 *Afterwards, you need to find a character that can be compared to Bingham in terms of lifestyle, profession, moral beliefs and definition of success etc. It might be helpful to concentrate on one book or film only and then analyse parallels and differences between the main characters (e. g.* Death of a Salesman *by Arthur Miller,* The Great Gatsby *by F. Scott Fitzgerald,* Of Mice and Men *by John Steinbeck).*

Ryan Bingham, the narrator and main protagonist of the novel *Up in the Air*, is a modern businessman, who lives a life on the run. He has got no place of residence or any particular aim in life. The airport has become his home and a springboard for new destinations at the same time. Bingham, the adherent of a new version of the

American Dream shies away from deeper moral or social commitments. He is the creation of an artificial environment and transcends all worldly limits but has not reached a final destination yet. But Bingham is not the only fictitious character who desires to realise the American Dream that does not really seem worth striving for. There are many characters in literature whose situation can be compared to Bingham's. For example, there is Willy Loman, the main character of Arthur Miller's play *Death of a Salesman*. He is married, has two grown-up sons, Biff and Happy, and struggles hard to make ends meet. Finally, he has to admit that he is not able to achieve his aims.

At the beginning of the play Loman's belief in success and hope for the future has already vanished and been replaced by physical and emotional exhaustion. Nevertheless he tries to keep up the illusion of a successful businessman which he is not. Unlike Bingham, he feels like a failure and needs his family to restore his confidence. The reverse is true for Bingham: He accepts the growing distance and alienation between himself and his family as a natural (cf. l. 21).

Additionally, it soon becomes evident that Willy Loman is unable to live in the present because it constantly reminds him that he is not able to meet his own expectations. Therefore he escapes into an imaginary past. His increasing inability to distinguish between present and past respectively shows his physical and moral decay. Loman's dream world finally prevents him from dealing with the challenges of the present. He is in conflict with himself, is unhappy with the development of his sons and has also lost his job. Ryan Bingham also escapes the real world because he only feels understood by his Airworld companions (cf. ll. 17/18). But unlike Loman, Bingham lives in the present and is full of energy and optimism (cf. l. 24).

Furthermore, both characters despise office work and idealise the autonomous businessman who is responsible only for himself. But in the end, Loman has to admit that only office work can help him overcome financial difficulties. The American Dream turns into a nightmare for Willy Loman as he realises that he has not reached anything at the end of the day. Out of desperation he commits suicide. Although Ryan Bingham seems to be satisfied with his life there are many signs that indicate that he might give up his attitude sooner or later because he cannot stand the anonymity and solitude of his existence.

In conclusion, both characters fall victim to their own high expectations. Their way of living the American Dream seems undesirable and ironic. Both characters' lifestyles can be interpreted as a warning not to take the theoretical promise of the American Dream too literally.

(529 words)

There's oil up there – Move ahead on pipeline from Canada

It's a boom time in the Canadian province of Alberta, where technological advances and sky-high commodity[1] prices have turned the region's oil sands into a sticky, tarry[2] gold mine.

Here's a safe prediction: The United States will share in this bounty[3], one way or
5 another. Canada will ship oil to its largest trading partner via rail, barge or truck, if need be. And the U.S., thirsty for energy, will soak up every drop from its reliable neighbor to the north.

That common interest leads to an obvious conclusion. The Obama administration should grant its approval without further delay for a proposed pipeline stretching 1,711
10 miles across the Plains from Canada's deposits to the U.S. refineries and terminals along the Gulf of Mexico. A pipeline is the safest and most efficient method for moving crude[4] by the millions of barrels.

Yes, the scale of the project is enormous. It could make Canada the world's second-largest producer of oil after Saudi Arabia. Americans should be celebrating a develop-
15 ment that will reduce the dependence on oil from less-congenial foreign sources. It will pump up job creation with private-sector investment and help keep prices in check when the economy starts growing in earnest again.

Yet the proposed Keystone XL pipeline has run into heated opposition. Some environmentalists are determined to stop it. Protests staged at the White House earlier this
20 month only hint at the passion it evokes – from actor Robert Redford to the Dalai Lama.

Opponents object for two main reasons: First, they want to discourage the mining of oil sands. No question, tearing up boreal forests[5] and ancient peat bogs[6] to get at the petroleum within can't help but degrade the land. The resulting semi-solid form of oil is dirtier than the smooth-flowing crude just below the Arabian desert. As with any fossil
25 fuel, burning it pumps carbon and other pollutants into the atmosphere, and emissions from processing this particular form of fuel pose a problem as well. On the plus side, the technology used to exploit oil sands is improving from the old strip-mining techniques, curbing the environmental costs.

The other big worry is more of a scare tactic than a valid concern. Pipelines can leak.
30 But to hear the anti-Keystone crowd tell it, you would think this one is about to be connected to kitchen sinks and lawn sprinklers from coast to coast. The fear-mongering about aquifers[7] being polluted and wildlife habitat destroyed has no basis in reality. On the contrary, plans call for a state-of-the-art system, subject to rigorous inspections. America already has oil and gas pipelines crisscrossing the country and the Canadian border. This
35 one, an expansion of a pipeline that already runs to downstate Illinois, will be built to a high safety standard.

Because it crosses the border, the Keystone plan has run into extra layers of red tape[8] and controversy.

Canada, justifiably frustrated by years of delay, has threatened to build a pipeline to
40 the Pacific and divert the bulk of its oil to China instead. The State Department recently
re-affirmed Keystone's minimal environmental impact, debunking claims about its supposed risks. After a public comment period closes in the weeks ahead, the Obama administration can seal the deal.

Since taking office, the president has slowed the issuance[9] of drilling leases and per-
45 mits, raised the cost of hydraulic fracturing[10] for natural gas production and sunk a fortune into clean-energy gambits[11] such as solar panels and ethanol fuel. Belatedly, he has
recognized that government interference puts a drag on growth. His decision earlier this
month to suspend tougher clean-air rules until unemployment abates[12] was a welcome
dose of realism from a White House in denial about U.S. reliance on gasoline – the econo-
50 my's much-maligned[13] lifeblood.

Maybe someday we'll all be driving solar-powered cars. Meantime, get that pipeline
built. We're going to need it.   *(634 words)*

There's oil up there: Move ahead on pipeline from Canada. From Chicago Tribune, 09/15/2011.
© *2011 Chicago Tribune. All rights reserved. Used by permission and protected by the Copyright Laws
of the United States. The printing, copying, redistribution, or retransmission of this Content without
express written permission is prohibited.*

Hinweis: Der Verfasser wird in der Textvorlage nicht genannt.

1   commodity – *hier:* Rohstoff (Güter)
2   tarry – full of tar
3   to share in this bounty – daran teilhaben
4   crude – *hier:* Rohöl
5   boreal forest – borealer Nadelwald/Taiga
6   peat bogs – Torfmoor
7   aquifer – Gesteinskörper mit Hohlräumen, der zur Leitung von Grundwasser geeignet ist
8   red tape – Bürokratie
9   issuance – the act of officially issuing something
10 hydraulic fracturing – fracking
11 gambit – erste Schritte
12 to abate – vermindern
13 much-maligned – viel geschmäht

Assignments

1. Delineate the author's argumentation. (Material)   (30 BE)

2. Relate the text to other ecological problems in material dealt with in class.   (35 BE)

3. Write a letter to the editor commenting on the problem of creating jobs at the
   cost of the environment.
                                                                                              (35 BE)

Lösungsvorschläge

Teaching modules referred to:
The assignment focuses on the main teaching module Science and Technology *(Q 1) with special emphasis on* ecology *and on the module* promised lands: dreams and realities *(Q 3, country of reference:* Canada*). Task 2 also requires references to texts dealt with in the module* Work and Industrialization *(Q 2) concerning the issues* business, industry *and the environment.*

1. **Step 1** *Before you deal with the assignment, read the text carefully. Then determine the author's opinion and underline the key arguments provided for and against his/her opinion that the pipeline is urgently needed.*
   Step 2 *Keep in mind that your delineation should only contain the central elements of the author's line of argument (e. g. stable oil prices, more jobs, independence from oil-producing countries, no significant dangers to the environment).*
   Step 3 *Use your own words as far as possible.*

   In the article the author argues that the US is dependent on Canadian oil. He/she hopes that President Obama will approve of the Keystone XL pipeline connecting the province of Alberta to the Gulf of Mexico since this is the safest way of transporting oil. Both countries are sure to profit from the deal. Whereas Canada will become the second major oil-exporting country in the world, the US could achieve relative independence from foreign imports.
   The author stresses that the construction of the pipeline will create jobs and keep oil prices stable. New mining technology helps reduce the environmental risks. Thus the author hopes that environmentalists' warnings of increasing carbon emissions and a transformation of the Canadian landscape might prove unfounded. The danger of leaks is dismissed as a tactical move to scare people. According to the author the pipeline does not pose any risks since there are strict controls and high safety standards, according to which many pipelines are already operating safely.
   Finally the construction of the pipeline is strongly recommended as Canada might otherwise decide to export its oil elsewhere. It is appreciated that Obama seems to give the economy priority over clean-air rules to make unemployment rates fall. However although the author clearly favours the Keystone pipeline, he/she enables the reader to see the controversial issue more discriminately.   *(225 words)*

2. **Step 1** *Remember that you are required to refer to one or more aspects of the text at hand and establish a connection to material dealt with in class. For example, you could focus on the main aspect of the text above (i. e. transporting oil from Canada in a pipeline is favoured for economic reasons while the hazards are played down) and compare this phenomenon to the ecological questions presented in texts you have dealt with in class (e. g. nuclear power stations vs. alternative sources of energy).*
   Step 2 *Establish links between the different issues and focus on both parallels and differences.*

In class we focused on the key problem of global warming and different approaches to tackling carbon emissions. Decisions on how to meet the twin challenges of climate change and energy security are highly controversial. Whereas the German government decided to reduce the number of nuclear power plants and encourages investments in sustainable projects such as wind farms, the former UK government declared that the best way to meet carbon-free energy needs was to construct new nuclear power stations in the UK. Government officials and industrialists argued that the replacement of older reactors with up to 12 new ones by 2030 would contribute to the reduction of greenhouse gases and at the same time help trigger economic growth. In 2013, the British government signed a contract with the French state-run electricity company EDF to build the first nuclear power station of this new generation in Somerset. Quite similar to the text, "There's oil up there" (cf. ll. 15–17), economic advantages play a pivotal role in the British line of argument: The new generation of power plants promises thousands of jobs and UK electricity could be marketed worldwide, thus providing unlimited opportunities for economic growth.

In the article at hand it is emphasised that new mining technologies and high safety standards will help to reduce the risks of possible negative impacts on the environment (cf. ll. 26–28, 32/33). British officials share this confidence in new technologies and point out that new reactors are safer and that nuclear energy is efficient and sustainable since it guarantees large quantities of electricity and emits relatively low amounts of carbon dioxide.

Local activists and environmental organisations such as Greenpeace or Friends of the Earth stress the disadvantages of nuclear technology with reference to the accidents in Chernobyl, Fukushima and the leaks in Sellafield. They also warn the public of unknown risks such as terrorist attacks or earthquakes that might damage the nuclear power stations with devastating effects. Furthermore the unsolved question of where and how to store the radioactive waste is frequently brought up. Similarly to the fears of the opponents of Keystone XL, proposals to invest in natural gas, wind or solar power are dismissed as curbs on economic growth (cf. ll. 44–47).   *(373 words)*

3. *Step 1 Consider the advantages and disadvantages of creating jobs at the cost of the environment and take a stand. Remember to boil the problem down to the question of priorities.*

   Step 2 Make a list of the arguments that come to mind (e. g. mostly only temporary jobs due to the construction of the pipeline, the toxic lakes in Alberta as a consequence of underestimating the harm done to the environment in the past, call for investment in renewable sources of energy as part of Obama's idea to create green jobs) and decide on the most convincing order in which to mention them.

   Step 3 Keep in mind that you are required to write your comment in the form of a letter to the editor and thus need to address the person who receives the letter adequately (e. g. "Dear Sir or Madam"). Also find a suitable expression to end your letter (e. g. "Yours faithfully") and use formal language only.

Dear Sir or Madam

I would like to comment on the rather uncritical attitude displayed in the article "There's oil up there" on the construction of the Keystone XL pipeline from Alberta to the Gulf of Mexico, published in your newspaper on September 15, 2011. Although the author admits that the burning of fossil fuels emits carbon and other pollutants, he or she seems to feel very confident that new technologies will minimise the risks this pipeline poses to the environment. Economic benefits and US independence from foreign energy markets are emphasised, which are of course vital factors in any national economy. Yet, I believe that the author underestimates the price we might all have to pay for our ignorance. It is precisely this materialistic logic which has given rise to the phenomenon of global warming and the depletion of the ozone layer.

First of all, the nature of the jobs promised by the supporters of the Keystone pipeline needs to be taken into consideration. I assume that most of them will be low-paid construction jobs that are most probably downsized after the pipeline is built. There is, of course, maintenance work and emergency supervision to be done, but I cannot imagine that there will be thousands of permanent jobs and infinite economic growth. Besides, fossil fuels are not endless resources.

Then, there are enormous environmental risks connected with the construction of the pipeline. Apart from the great amounts of carbon emissions into the earth's atmosphere, there is the danger that leaks in the pipeline might contaminate ground water, rivers and lakes. The mining of tar sands has already had devastating effects on both the landscape and the population of Alberta. Toxic lakes have been created and cancer rates have risen. Therefore, it is not appropriate to simply dismiss the serious concerns of environmentalists as fear-mongering. Against this backdrop, I simply cannot share your trust in strict controls and high security standards.

It is high time that we focussed on the question of how to save energy and at the same time invest more in research on sustainable sources. This might also provide jobs. Whereas the Keystone pipeline project is short-sighted, as it might only provide energy for the generations that are living today, renewable sources of energy guarantee our future. However developing a concept for sustainable living on earth requires individual effort and international cooperation. I regret that Canada has left the Kyoto Agreement and really hope that President Obama will not permanently give priority to the economy at the cost of the environment. In the interest of both future generations and the current world population, he should pursue his idea of the green jobs he promised to create. This might require further state investment, but I am convinced that it will pay off a thousand times over in health and future prospects. Our planet and its resources should have top priority over a short-sighted view of economic progress and temporary jobs.

Yours faithfully
Hannah Schwarz

(497 words)

Hassan: A Case Study

Jenni Fortune, a London Tube driver of the Circle Line, and the student Hassan al-Rash-id are two of seven characters portrayed in Sebastian Faulks' novel on modern urban life.

In the rear carriage of Jenni Fortune's Circle Line train Hassan al-Rashid sat staring straight ahead. Normally, without a book to read, he would move his head up and down so that the reflection of his face in the convex window opposite would develop panda eyes, elongate[1] like an image in a fairground mirror and then pop. But this was not the
5 day for such frivolity: he was on his way to buy the constituents of a bomb.

Two white-skinned teenagers opposite him were kissing, sticking their tongues out and laughing when they touched. Although they were absorbed by one another, there was a challenge in their public intimacy. A black-skinned youth with feet in padded white trainers the size of small boats was leaning forward. From his earplugs came a hissing,
10 thumping noise. Hassan could sense that this youth's eyes, though looking down, were ready to lock on to those of anyone who caught them, so he was careful to keep his own gaze somewhere to the left of the hunched shoulders.

To Hassan's left, in the standing area by the central doors, were Japanese and Euro-pean tourists. It was Sunday, Hassan thought; most of these people should have been in
15 church, but these days Christians viewed cathedrals as monuments or works of art to be admired for their architecture and paintings, not as the place where they could worship God. Their final loss of faith had happened in the last ten years or so, yet in the *kafir*[2] world it had passed with little comment. How very strange they were, he thought, these people, that they had let eternal life slip through their hands.

20 Where Hassan had grown up in Glasgow, the Christians (he hadn't by then adopted the word *'kafir'*) blasphemed and drank and fornicated, though most of them, he knew, still more or less believed. They were unfaithful in hotel rooms, but they got married in churches. They went on Christmas Day or when they buried a friend; they took their ba-bies to be named there, and when they were dying they still sent out for a priest. Now
25 you could read statistics in newspaper surveys which confirmed what anyone could see: that they'd given up God. And barely a *kafir* seemed to have noticed.

The conviction that the rest of the world lived in a dream was one that grew in Has-san each day. With the exception of those in his group and some of the more committed members of the Pudding Mill Lane Mosque, he viewed everyone he knew as deluded[3]. It
30 was perplexing to him that people paid so little heed[4] to their own salvation; he was puzzled by it in the way he might have been by the sight of a mother feeding whisky to a baby. There might have been some short-term benefit in the respite[5] from crying, but it wasn't something that a reasonable person would do. Yet the truth of life, and of life after death, was not exactly hidden.

35 Hassan licked his lips and swallowed. Although the individual parts that made up the bombs were easy enough to find and buy, he was aware that the grimiest corner shops these days had CCTV[6] cameras. The purchase of even three or four bottles of soft drinks at once might be remembered by the man at the counter, then recalled from the digital memory of the camera. He was therefore spreading his custom[7] right across London, one
40 bottle at a time. [...]

At Gloucester Road, Hassan stepped off the train and went up into the street. Batteries and disposable cameras were easy and cheap enough to find; the only thing he was having trouble with was hydrogen peroxide. But he had a plan for that. *(624 words)*

Sebastian Faulks, A Week in December, *Hutchinson 2009, pp. 20/21.*

1 to elongate – verlängern
2 kafir – an offensive word used by Muslims to refer to a person that is not a Muslim
3 deluded – misled
4 to pay heed – to pay attention to
5 respite – *hier:* (temporary) relief
6 CCTV cameras – Video-Überwachungssystem
7 spreading his custom – *hier:* an unterschiedlichen Standorten einkaufen

Assignments

1. Summarize the text. (Material)   (30 BE)

2. Explain Hassan's attitude towards modern British society and relate it to the attitude(s) of other British people with an ethnic background in material (fiction/non-fiction) discussed in class.   (40 BE)

3. Electronic/digital surveillance? Discuss the tension between the protection of individual rights and the discovery of extremist tendencies or activities.   (30 BE)

Lösungsvorschläge

Teaching modules referred to:
The task relates to the teaching module The United Kingdom *(Q 2), with particular reference to the topics* social structures, social change. *The assignments also extend to the thematic focus* Science and Technology *(Q 1) with the topic* electronic media.

1. *In your summary the essence of the given text should be presented briefly and precisely. Keep the general conventions of a summary in mind: present tense, no direct speech and quotations or comments.*
   Step 1 Begin your summary with an umbrella statement giving the author and title of the novel, the type of text and the year of publication. Briefly refer to the contents of the excerpt, concentrating on the author's observations, his feelings and convictions.
   Step 2 Only refer to the most relevant aspects and structure your summary well.
   Step 3 Your text should be one third of the length of the source text at a maximum.

   The excerpt from Sebastian Faulks' novel *A Week in December* is about a Muslim on his way to assemble parts of a bomb. Taking a ride on one of the London Underground trains, Hassan al-Rashid observes his fellow passengers from different ethnic backgrounds.
   As a devout Muslim, Hassan only feels contempt for the unbelievers, the *kafir*. He despises them for their blasphemous behaviour, their lack of values and morals and the fact that they have lost their belief but still tend to use churches for weddings, christenings and funerals out of tradition. He believes that Christians are no longer interested in their salvation and are misled in their egotistical lifestyle. Hassan cannot understand these people and feels alienated from them. He is determined to build a bomb and has already made a plan to overcome all obstacles in his path when acquiring the necessary constituents.
   (145 words)

2. *Step 1 You are asked to explain Hassan's negative attitude towards the modern Western society in which he grew up: Give evidence from the excerpt at hand by examining Hassan's thoughts and behaviour.*
   Step 2 Comparing Hassan's attitude and convictions to those of other British people from an ethnic background, either refer to fictitious characters from literary texts (e. g. Natalie Black in Zadie Smith's latest novel NW*) or real issues you learned about in class (e. g. the problem of the Sharia Courts). You can draw upon a variety of beliefs and convictions as well as an analysis of the current situation in Britain.*

   Hassan al-Rashid is described as a committed member of the Pudding Mill Lane Mosque who takes his Muslim beliefs very seriously and judges people's behaviour from a strictly religious point of view. During his ride on the London Tube, he witnesses his fellow passengers showing behaviour that he considers typical of the godless Western society. Two white teenagers make a show of kissing each other in public, which offends him and challenges his cultural convictions (cf. ll. 6–8). Similarly, the conduct of a black-skinned youth makes him feel uneasy due to the young man's body language. He is "leaning forward" (l. 9), listening to quite loud and aggressive music and seems ready to jump at anybody who does not take care to avoid eye contact (cf. ll. 9–12). Some European and Japanese tourists on the train make Hassan wonder why they do not fulfil their religious duties and go to church on a Sunday (cf. ll. 13–15). To Hassan, all these people are typical examples of a society that has long lost its faith and turned its back on religious principles both in public and private life. His attitude is based on generalisations and a subjective perception that makes him condemn all kinds of behaviour that deviate from his strong beliefs and sets of values. Hassan cannot tolerate these differences even though they are part of mainstream lifestyle in Britain. He is convinced that these blasphemous people are misled as they have sacrificed their chances of eternal life for the petty pleasures of life on earth (cf. ll. 18/19, 29/30).

The reasons for Hassan's deeply rooted dislike of Western lifestyle are to be found in Glasgow, where he grew up. He seems to have felt lost for a long time in the society of people and several times he refers to non-believers as "*kafir*" (ll. 17, 21, 26). Only the truly devoted members of the Pudding Mill Lane Mosque and his "group" (l. 28) of possibly fanatic Muslims are respectable to him (cf. ll. 28/29). Over the years, Hassan has developed a strong urge to punish *kafir* society. He is probably on a suicide mission, thus taking justice into his own hands.

Hassan's could be a typical story of a second-generation immigrant unable to understand his parents' attempts to assimilate into a society whose values he abhors. Looking for his roots, he might have got in touch with fanatics who managed to turn his feelings of alienation towards Western society into open hatred. Clashes between the host and immigrant societies as shown in Hassan's story are an issue in some areas in Britain. Typical examples of this are the Sharia Courts, whose decisions follow the laws of the Koran. Quite often, they contradict the British law system and might even violate human rights. There have been cases where a divorce was granted by a British judge due to domestic violence. Later, the decision was overturned by a Sharia Court. Problems are difficult to avoid, especially for conservative immigrants who insist that their children follow religious rules and would rather obey to the Sharia Court's decisions. From a legal point of view, two different kinds of law cannot exist in one country and national law needs to be obeyed by all citizens regardless of their ethnic background.

One of the most prominent contemporary British writers from an ethnic background is Zadie Smith, who frequently gives us an insight into the struggles of immigrants through her novels. In her most recent novel, *NW*, Smith depicts young second- and third-generation Jamaican immigrants, such as Natalie Black, a successful lawyer. Natalie has changed her name as Keisha sounded more middle-class to her. Natalie despises people from her own generation and ethnic background who blame the mainstream white culture for their own lack of success. Through imitating her host society perfectly, Natalie has made it from rags to riches and seems to have lost touch with her cultural roots entirely. Thus, she chose a completely different way from Hassan to deal with clashes between her family's Jamaican traditions and British mainstream society. *(683 words)*

3. ***Step 1*** *First of all, you need to explain briefly in which cases people are being watched or even spied upon through the use of electronic or digital media.*
Step 2 *Then focus on showing the tension between the need for public security and the protection of individual rights.*
Step 3 *Do not forget to state your own opinion on that matter. Give reasons for your opinion.*

Hassan's case has shown how the lives of innocent people might be endangered by the actions of political or religious fanatics, such as through a suicide bombing, for example. To protect their citizens, many European states feel the need to tighten security. However, many people have mixed feelings concerning these measures. There is a certain tension between the demand to respect individual rights and the state's duty to protect its citizens from extremists, which shall be discussed in detail in the following.

Since 9/11 protective measures have changed travelling, domestic policies and border controls considerably. One of these security measures is the use of Closed Circuit Television (CCTV) that has been installed in Britain to monitor public places and areas prone to criminal activity. According to statistics of the Metropolitan Police, CCTV helped to identify over 2,500 wanted people in 2010 and thus contributed to protecting the public. Of course, the individual rights to privacy are infringed in this case, but greater harm might have been prevented.

Recently, the activities of the US National Security Agency (NSA) have caused an international outcry and shown how meticulously individual data can be collected and abused at state level. In this case, individual rights are neither protected nor is there any intention to take action to make sure this never happens again. The US administration merely promised that citizens from friendly foreign countries will only be spied on if national security is at stake.

Both examples illustrate the dilemma in which many states currently find themselves: the citizens' right to privacy versus their need for protection against terrorist attacks, for example. However, whereas the first case shows that this balance can be kept within reasonable limits, the second incident serves as an example for failing to do so. If not even friendly foreign countries can trust one another and innocent people can be spied upon without any valid suspicion, democracy fails its citizens in the extreme. In this case, the measures taken to protect the citizens infringe their basic human rights. I cannot but doubt that the end justifies the means here.

As far as I am concerned, there are some surveillance measures which need to be taken and everybody should contribute his or her share to making the country safer. We are watched by CCTV in public places, but we can decide if and how long data is stored as we can vote for parties that share our opinion on the issue. We can use additional electronic gadgets to protect ourselves against the abuse of our personal data or simply be careful about how much personal information we reveal on social networks. However, we are helpless if our rights are infringed on an international basis. This is where we need protection from the state, such as through an international no-spy agreement, for example. Unfortunately, there still seems to be a long way to go.

(482 words)

Teil A: Aufgabe zur Sprachmittlung

Material 1: US-Schnüffelprogramm Prism – Setzt Google, Apple und Facebook endlich Grenzen!

Datensammlungen, Steuerprivilegien und Vermarktungsmonopole: Amerikanische Internetkonzerne haben unsere Wirtschaft revolutioniert. Doch ohne Schranken gefährden sie den Wettbewerb

Es ist ein heikles Thema – nicht erst seit Prism. Das Schnüffelprogramm des amerikanischen Geheimdienstes NSA hat leichten Zugriff auf Server und Datenleitungen weltweit tätiger US-Internetkonzerne wie Google, Facebook, Skype oder Apple. Die Konzerne müssen in den USA auch die Daten ihrer deutschen Kunden den Geheimdiensten zugäng-
5 lich machen. US-Bürger dürfen diesen Zugriff vor Gericht überprüfen lassen. Wir Deutsche können das praktisch nicht. Damit sind wir so rechtlos wie in einer Militärdiktatur. [...]
    Die marktbeherrschende Stellung der US-Konzerne in unserem Privat- und Wirtschaftsleben macht es fast unmöglich, der unheimlichen wie unkontrollierten Überwa-
10 chung zu entgehen. [...]
    [Google und Co.] diktieren die Bedingungen, unter denen auch andere Anbieter am Markt agieren können. Das ist gefährlich: Denn Marktwirtschaft basiert auf Freiheit und Wettbewerb, der [...] aber unter fairen Rahmenbedingungen für alle Teilnehmer garantiert sein muss. Deshalb darf eine Diskussion über gefährliche Monopole gerade für An-
15 hänger einer freien marktwirtschaftlichen Ordnung kein Tabu sein. Sie ist längst überfällig. [...]
    Es kann dabei nicht darum gehen, etwa den genialen Erfolg von Apple mit zunächst fast konkurrenzlos einfachen Produkten wie dem iPhone zu verteufeln. Die Politik darf keine Konzerne zerschlagen oder in die unternehmerische Freiheit eingreifen. [...]
20 Kontraproduktiv oder gar schwachsinnig wären Scheinrezepte mit den Zutaten Nationalismus, Anti-Amerikanismus oder Sozialismus. [...] Auch innere Einsicht wäre wichtig – bei Politikern wie Konzernlenkern. Denn ein kurzfristiger Vorteil kann sich langfristig in einen Nachteil verkehren: Arroganz und Ignoranz führen zu Erstarrung.

(240 Wörter)

Frank Thewes, "US-Schnüffelprogramm Prism: Setzt Google, Apple und Facebook endlich Grenzen!",
FOCUS Online, 20. 06. 2013; http://www.focus.de/finanzen/steuern/thewes/us-schnueffelprogramm-
prism-setzt-google-apple-und-facebook-endlich- grenzen_aid_1020003.html (abgerufen am 23. 06. 2013).

Assignment

Your Spanish exchange partner is going to take part in an international discussion forum on the NSA Prism spying scandal. He has asked you for help in trying to find information on the subject.
Outline Thewes' view on the topic. (Material 1)

Teil B: Verkürzte Textaufgabe

Material 2: Is Google Making Us Stupid? – What the Internet is doing to our brains

Over the past few years I've had an uncomfortable sense that someone, or something, has been tinkering with my brain, remapping the neural circuitry[1], reprogramming the memory. My mind isn't going – so far as I can tell – but it's changing. I'm not thinking the way I used to think. I can feel it most strongly when I'm reading. Immersing myself
5 in a book or a lengthy article used to be easy. My mind would get caught up in the narrative or the turns of the argument, and I'd spend hours strolling through long stretches of prose. That's rarely the case anymore. Now my concentration often starts to drift after two or three pages. I get fidgety, lose the thread, begin looking for something else to do. I feel as if I'm always dragging my wayward[2] brain back to the text. The deep reading
10 that used to come naturally has become a struggle. [...]

[M]edia are not just passive channels of information. They supply the stuff of thought, but they also shape the process of thought. And what the Net seems to be doing is chipping away my capacity for concentration and contemplation. My mind now expects to take in information the way the Net distributes it: in a swiftly moving stream of particles.
15 Once I was a scuba diver in the sea of words. Now I zip along the surface like a guy on a Jet Ski. [...]

[A] recently published study of online research habits, conducted by scholars from University College London, suggests that we may well be in the midst of a sea change[3] in the way we read and think. As part of the five-year research program, the scholars ex-
20 amined computer logs documenting the behavior of visitors to two popular research sites [...] that provide access to journal articles, e-books, and other sources of written information. They found that people using the sites exhibited "a form of skimming activity", hopping from one source to another and rarely returning to any source they'd already visited. They typically read no more than one or two pages of an article or book before
25 they would "bounce" out to another site. Sometimes they'd save a long article, but there's no evidence that they ever went back and actually read it. [...]

Thanks to the ubiquity[4] of text on the Internet, not to mention the popularity of text-messaging on cell phones, we may well be reading more today than we did in the 1970s or 1980s, when television was our medium of choice. But it's a different kind of reading,
30 and behind it lies a different kind of thinking – perhaps even a new sense of the self. "We are not only *what* we read," says Maryanne Wolf, a developmental psychologist at Tufts

University. [...] "We are *how* we read." Wolf worries that the style of reading promoted by the Net [...] may be weakening our capacity for the kind of deep reading that emerged when an earlier technology, the printing press, made long and complex works of prose
35 commonplace.   *(502 words)*

1   neural circuitry – Vernetzung des Gehirns
2   wayward – eigensinnig
3   sea change – radikaler Wandel
4   ubiquity – Allgegenwärtigkeit, ständige Verfügbarkeit

Assignments

1. Summarize the text. (Material 2)   (30 BE)

2. Explain the role of reading and/or of the media in models of the future (utopian/dystopian societies) dealt with in class.   (35 BE)

3. *"The faster we surf across the Web – the more links we click and pages we view – the more opportunities Google and other companies gain to collect information about us and to feed us advertisements. Most of the proprietors of the commercial Internet have a financial stake in collecting the crumbs of data we leave behind [...]"*
    (N. Carr, in the same article)
    Comment on this statement and its implications.   (35 BE)

In die Gesamtbewertung gehen die Ergebnisse der Teilaufgaben A und B im Verhältnis 1:3 ein.

Lösungsvorschläge

Teaching modules referred to:

The texts at hand refer to the teaching module Science and Technology *(Q 1), focusing in particular on the topic* electronic media. *Another important point of reference is the teaching module* Order, Vision, Change *(Q 3) with the topic* models of the future (utopias, dystopias).

Teil A: Aufgabe zur Sprachmittlung

Step 1 Read the text carefully and highlight all aspects that hint at the author's view on the topic.

Step 2 Identify the main topic of the interview. Make this point your "umbrella sentence" which provides the reader with the argumentative key to the article.

Step 3 Write a maximum of 110 words. Do not forget to present your information in form of a letter to your Spanish friend. Refer to relevant information only. The text should be about 1/3 of the original article.

Dear Pedro,

I have found an article on the "US-Schnüffelprogramm Prism", published in *Focus Online* on June 20th, 2013 to help you prepare for the discussion on the NSA scandal. The author points out the consequences of increasing data processing from global players like Google and Facebook to the NSA.

Unlike US citizens, Germans cannot legally stop the monitoring of their data. The monopoly position of US companies provides no escape from constant observation and limits the free market economy. Thewes demands an open discussion on monopolies focusing on the moral insight instead of political interventions.

Hopefully, this was helpful.

Best wishes,

Yannik

(103 words)

Teil B: Verkürzte Textaufgabe

1. *Step 1* The first thing you should do when dealing with a non-fictional text is to go through it thoroughly. It is necessary to grasp the main thesis, i. e. the negative influence of the Internet on the human brain. Then make a list of the arguments provided by the author (i. e. the Internet as a source of information, its impact on data processing in the mind and the capability of deep reading). Try to put the single aspects in a logical order to structure your ideas.

Step 2 Begin your text with an umbrella sentence. Avoid personal comments and quotations in the summary. Remember to write in the present tense and use your own words. The length of your summary should be about 1/3 of the original.

The article "Is Google Making Us Stupid? – What the Internet is doing to our brains" published in *The Atlantic Magazine* in 2008, deals with the negative impacts both surfing the Internet and text messaging have on the human brain.

According to the author, both activities reduce our ability to concentrate and capacity for deep reading. He blames modern media for this phenomenon. On the one hand, the Internet provides the reader with innumerable sources of information; on the other hand it transforms the human mind by creating the expectation that information must be absorbed swiftly. Thus, people nowadays fail to concentrate on longer text passages anymore, as a research project at the University College London revealed lately. Instead of deep reading, people tend to hop from site to site reading no more than a few pages and rarely read the information they have saved.

Psychologists like Maryanne Wolf from Tufts University express their concern about the threatened intellectual capacities of the contemporary human being. *(164 words)*

2. *Now the role of reading and the media as portrayed in materials dealt with in class should be explained. The task already suggests works focusing on utopian or dystopian societies.*

Step 1 *Choose suitable novels from your coursework. Make a list of the aspects that are related to the role of reading and the media in dystopian societies.*

Step 2 *Structure your ideas, think of criteria to organize your paragraphs and then start writing.*

Please note: *The following essay focuses on the dystopian novels* Brave New World *by Aldous Huxley and* Fahrenheit 451 *by Ray Bradbury. Another possible example would be* Nineteen Eighty-Four *by George Orwell.*

Reading and the media are important topics in many works of literature. Reading is mostly considered an intellectual activity and a cultural achievement. Consequently, texts are not only seen as a source of information, knowledge and wisdom, but also as an important instrument of education. Free and self-determined individuals and autonomous political citizens can only exist in a liberal-minded society with uncensored information tolerating various points of view. Thus, the media in general and texts in particular might be said to contribute to scientific progress, political equality and social stability.

On the contrary, in the fictitious totalitarian states shown in dystopian novels, reading is rather considered a threat. It is either banned completely or reduced to a mindless free-time activity, while non-print media, e. g. television, is used as a tool of political propaganda.

In the novel *Fahrenheit 451* by R. Bradbury, it is considered a major crime to own books as they are supposed to trigger anti-social behaviour and thinking. Since they are considered to be the root of all political evil, it is the task of the fire brigade to track down people in possession of books. While the books are burned, their owners are killed. Television as a compulsory form of mass entertainment has replaced reading and any other form of intellectual activity completely. The power of the authoritarian government ruling the country is based on its citizens' ignorance and the artificial feeling of happiness created by the dull TV programmes. The protagonist Guy Montag's wife, Mildred, is a good example of this phenomenon: She spends hours in front of the TV performing role plays either alone or with friends and has become an indifferent couch potato. It seems as if the incapacitation of Montag's fellow citizens is not the work of a totalitarian government entirely, but has been brought about by humanity itself: According to Captain Beatty, Montag's fire chief, it has been a slow process caused by the increasing neglect of literature, culture and independent thinking. Apparently, people preferred an artificial concept of equality as they believed it to guarantee stability.

In his novel *Brave New World*, Aldous Huxley explores the same idea as Bradbury did. The ideology of the government is based on a perverted idea of stability, identity and community. It relies on the immediate satisfaction of wishes as well as cheap forms of entertainment, consumerism and promiscuity. In order to guarantee a conflict-free life and a smooth, unobstructed functioning of society, the government uses genetic engineering and conditioning as basic means of education. In the view of the World Controllers, who run the state, all kinds of books and art disturb people's minds; they create emotional disorder and thus cause social instability. Consequently, works on history and literature have been banned from society. Children are conditioned to hate books at a very early age and to prefer erotic games instead. Art and literature have been replaced by the so-called "feelies" (a special kind of movie, in which the audience can literally feel the substances the hero touches) and propaganda slogans are created to encourage people's desire for the consumption of mass-produced goods, free-time activities and promiscuous behaviour. In contrast to books, the mass media is used to shape people's taste, thinking and feelings and to create the expected form of sameness. In general, the citizens have accepted this new life due to conditioning and show withdrawal symptoms when hindered from the consumption of the intellectual fast food.

Both dystopian societies are totalitarian and redefine education as a means to create a society that keeps its citizens uninformed and disinterested in all matters of the state. Mass media like the cinema, the radio and television are used for dull entertainment to create demands which can easily be satisfied and make people superficially happy. Books on the other hand are considered dangerous as they encourage independent thinking and are therefore banned.

(647 words)

3. **Step 1** *First read the statement your task is based on and make sure you understand its meaning. Sum up the quote in your own words.*
   Step 2 *Keep in mind that you need to express your own opinion when commenting on the quote. Collect arguments that support or speak against the author's position. To make your own line of argument more plausible, you need to give reasons for your opinion and find convincing examples. If you can think of recent examples of public interest, do not hesitate to include them. Try to avoid stereotypes and prejudiced ideas.*
   Step 3 *Structure your ideas in paragraphs and then start writing.*

The author's statement is a warning of using the Internet too thoughtlessly. According to Carr, global digital players like Google deliberately take advantage of their technological know-how to create consumer profiles and to offer new shopping opportunities. The traces we leave on the Web are used by the digital companies to pro-vide individual advertisement campaigns out of huge financial interests.

I only partly agree with Carr's statement. I would like to point out that the Internet surely has its positive sides: It helps people overcome geographical and physical limits and provides an infinite source of information. It cannot be doubted that the Internet has made us more independent and keeps us up-to-date all around the world. Unfortunately, these positive examples of technological progress are overshadowed by the negative aspects such as economic exploitation, political paternalism or the incapacitation of the mind, if the Internet is used thoughtlessly.

First of all, the easy access to information can create a feeling of security and easily deceive people about their true intellectual abilities. As described in the text "Is Google Making Us Stupid?" many people hop from site to site without actually questioning the information provided. This way they might slowly but surely lose their capacity to concentrate and process difficult information in everyday life. This can also have deep political and economic implications. Especially people who do not interact a lot personally outside the digital world might easily be manipulated by one-sided information or even propaganda.

Furthermore, there is the fact that the Internet has a perfect memory. Messages and comments once sent are stored forever and can be reactivated. In many cases, there is not even need of special software as links to deleted information might still exist, e. g. on social networking sites or friends' profiles. Thus, future employers can easily find out about compromising details of one's personal life.

Finally, there is no way of knowing whether personal data is processed and towards which sources. For example, recent events have shown that the Internet has been successfully undermined not only by Internet giants with economic interests, but also by secret services from all over the world which randomly access our data without any evidence of wrongdoing as has been proved by Edward Snowden. Apart from the intelligence services, criminals use all kinds of tricks, such as creating misleading e-mails from friends allegedly in need to make us perform financial transactions. They might even hack our online banking accounts. Many people feel manipulated and demand that new measures to control the way personal data is processed need to be found and applied internationally to better protect users against the infringement of their privacy.

All in all, those negative implications should not be underestimated. Still, it depends on every single person whether those potential threats will also have a negative impact on the individual. Simply being aware of mass surveillance, the need for critical thinking or the dangers in sharing information on social media sites can do a lot of good. Knowing how to protect oneself and one's data might go a long way. Personal contact and a legislative framework may provide additional support.   *(523 words)*

Whitegirl

I was not always a white girl. I used to be just Charlotte. A person named Charlotte Halsey. But when I met Milo, when I fell in love with him, I became White, like a lit lightbulb is white. In the mirror there is my skin the color of sand, hair the color of butter, eyes blue as seawater. Just so bleachy white I am practically clear. In a heavy snowfall
5 you'd have trouble picking me out. Even in the photographs from my so-called glamour-puss[1] career it's hard to tell which blond is me. There I am, with what they called my "trademark smile", square teeth like Chiclets[2], my "fresh" look; there's my "peaches-and-cream" complexion, more cream than peach, all of them talking about me as if I were food.
10 Milo is black, what they call "Black," only not to me. Brown skin, a shade the newer catalogues would call cinnamon stick or cocoa. The palms of his hands are pink as the lining of seashells, and his eyes are green like beer-bottle glass. You in your sunny kitchen, or your office cubicle, or your local shopping mall may not mind that the word black means "soiled and dirty," means "characterized by the absence of light" or "evil or
15 wicked or gloomy". God knows, I could have cared less myself, before.

Look it up, Milo says, it's what you hear of black: blackmail, black magic, black sheep, black mark, black-hearted, et cetera. You see what I'm saying? When I argue about this, somebody white always says: "Get over it. It's a word. It describes a group. Why be technical about it?" It's not a word, I think now. It's sticks and stones[3]. [...]
20 Names will never hurt you. Ha. Names like Black, like White, will break your heart, crack it open like a melon dropped on the pavement.

Milo is always preceded by Black, and trailed by it. He wakes up in the morning to "the first black Olympic skier", "the black athlete who ..." and goes to bed at night with it, "the blond wife of black Olympian Milo Robicheaux". His skin, my hair. Our little
25 piano key relationship.

To me he has mostly been just Milo. I stopped seeing skin a long time ago with him. They say lovers can find each other just by using the sense of smell; that we are all really animals in that way, no different from dogs or deer. I know it's true. I could find Milo blind in a room of men, would know him by the keloid[4] lump of a vaccination scar on his
30 left upper arm, would know by touch the large knees knotted from surgery, the smell of him like pine trees in a snowy wind. I could pick him out just by the slow rising of his breath while he slept. So no, until this happened, up to the time of the assault, he was not black, not to me. He was Milo. He was my husband; a man – famous, okay – who liked parties and dancing, fast music, high speed of any kind. We had fights that made me cry.
35 And him, too, he cried, too. We had long weeks without talking. We had days of just fucking, all day in bed, eating and drinking and never getting dressed. He made me smile.

He cut a smile, they said, in my neck.

Tried to kill me with broken glass, a smashed wine bottle, one of a couple I emptied
40 that night. But he botched it, mostly hitting the silver necklace, missing the important
arteries and veins, which saved my life, but not my voice. Left me mute and bleeding on
the marble tiles of our kitchen floor.

Or maybe he didn't. I don't know. Jesus, I just really don't know if he did, so get
away from me please. Leave me alone with your questions.

45 Milo loves me, I believe this. He loved me, he always said, more than he loved himself, more than he loved screwing, or skiing deep powder, or drinking dark cognac. Loved
me. Despite her. I believe that. In his jail cell where he is now he writes to me: "Charlotte, please, please." He wants me to come see him, says if I'll only come, he knows I'll
see the truth. Will see, goddammit. But if I go – if I could go, if I would – would I find
50 out anything new? Who would my eyes discover? Milo of my dreams, of my whole early
life and up till now? My Milo? Or the man who cut me up? [...]

They say. It's certainly possible. It's certainly something he might have resorted to,
what with all those green algae blooms of jealousy between us, the he-said, she-said of it,
not to mention living through all our fucked-up, zebra-stripe, history-book history played
55 out right here in the spotlight of our breakneck lives.

The police say: no question. They run down the evidence: My blood on his hands.
Cuts on his hands. Glass on his shoes. The fact that he resisted arrest. Punched a cop.
They found him leaning over me where I lay bleeding.

He says: He was trying to save me, breathe some air back into my lungs, kiss of life,
60 mouth to mouth. So did he try to kill me? I don't know. Maybe. If he didn't, though, who
did? It was dark when it happened, and I was out of it, messed up, messed up.

(915 words)

1   glamour-puss – a person (especially a woman) who is very attractive but not talented, smart, serious, etc.
2   Chiclets – chewing gum brand
3   sticks and stones – from the nursery rhyme: "Sticks and stones will break my bones, but names will never hurt me."
4   keloid – scar tissue

Assignments

1. Delineate the facts of the case narrated by Charlotte Halsey. (Material)   (25 BE)

2. Compare the narrator's relationship to Milo to that of Othello and Desdemona.   (45 BE)

3. *"The familiar space between 'white' and 'girl' has gone missing in this novel's title, leaving not the smallest space in which to maneuver, as if a girl and her color are one circumstance, one fact, not two – a condition as much as a life. The word's construction, tight and claustrophobic, speaks to the color boxes that function, still, as a fact of American life."*

   (Lynna Williams: Exploring the possibility of racial colorblindness. From *Chicago Tribune* 02/24/2002. © 2002 Chicago Tribune. All rights reserved. Used by permission and protected by the Copyright Laws of the United States. The printing, copying, redistribution, or retransmission of this Content without express written permission is prohibited.)

   Comment on the "color boxes" that apparently still function in American society.   (30 BE)

Lösungsvorschläge

Teaching modules referred to:
The task relates to the teaching module Them and Us *(Q 1), with particular reference to the topic* the one-track mind *(e. g. prejudice, intolerance). The context also refers to the module* Extreme Situations *(Q 2) with the topic* love and happiness *and asks for comparisons to William Shakespeare's play* Othello.

1. *The first assignment asks you to present the central elements of the line of action in the given text to create a vivid image of the situation described.*

   Step 1 *Begin your text with an umbrella sentence: Give the author, the title of the novel and the year of publication. You should also refer to the central event described in the excerpt.*

   Step 2 *You can structure your essay chronologically or by following the way the first-person narrator gives evidence of the attack she suffered. If you choose the second possibility, bear in mind that the incident is narrated in retrospect and as part of the narrator's emotional flashback.*

In this excerpt from *Whitegirl* by Kate Manning, published in 2001, the first-person narrator Charlotte Halsey describes her relationship to her husband Milo and his alleged attack on her. Charlotte points out that she only became aware of her white skin colour when she fell in love with black athlete Milo. Up to then it had not mattered to her but rather furthered her career as a model. She describes in detail how Milo seemed haunted by his skin colour and took offence at the media coverage of his athletic successes that frequently referred to the different colour of the couple's skins.

The narrator herself seems to remember nothing of the night of the attack. While the police suspect Milo of cutting Charlotte's neck with a broken bottle, she was too drunk to recall details of what really happened. Evidence suggests that Milo was found next to his wife with his hands full of blood and cuts and that he had glass splinters on his shoes. He injured the policeman who came to arrest him and claimed to have been trying to reanimate her. Luckily, a silver necklace saved Charlotte from a lethal wound in the end, but her voice seems to be gone forever.

Charlotte herself is in doubt now as to whether she should follow Milo's pleas to visit him in his prison cell, believe in his love for her again and let him show her the truth. She recalls the instances of jealousy and betrayal in their restless relationship and can neither believe Milo nor trust her own blurred recollections.   *(263 words)*

2. **Step 1** *Before drawing any comparisons to Othello and Desdemona, a detailed analysis of Milo and Charlotte's relationship is needed. You should especially focus on the nature of their partnership and the impact of the different colour of their skins.*
Step 2 *Then find similarities and differences by comparing Milo and Charlotte to Othello and Desdemona concerning the development of the relationship, the role of public opinion and the way both stories end.*

In retrospect, the protagonist, Charlotte, recalls instances of violence and jealousy that seem to have dominated her relationship with Milo in the end (cf. ll. 52–55), but also remembers that they once had a deep love for each other (cf. ll. 35–37). Milo's skin colour did not matter to Charlotte, and it was only after the assault that she became aware that the press labelling Milo as a black sports person might have caused a feeling of inferiority in him. Charlotte remembers Milo referring frequently to the negative meanings of the word "black" (cf. ll. 13–15). After the assault, she feels haunted by the public interest in the case and is unsure what to make of Milo's motives and the role he played in the attack.

There are several parallels to the protagonists in Shakespeare's play *Othello*, who also lead a "piano key relationship" (cf. l. 25) under the wary eyes of the Venetian public: Just like Milo, Othello is a victim of prejudice and clichés, though at first he does not seem to be aware of the stereotypes used frequently and in public in connection with black people in general and himself in particular. Desdemona's father, for example, accuses Othello openly of having used black magic to seduce his daughter and Othello even has to defend his rightful marriage in front of the Duke. On the other hand, both Milo and Othello are in a distinguished position in their respective societies and their achievements are held in high public esteem: Milo is a famous skier (cf. l. 23), Othello a foreign general whose services are indispensable to Venetian society.

Neither Desdemona nor Charlotte minds her partner's skin colour, though. Desdemona even strongly defends her decision to marry 'the Moor' before her father at the Duke's court, although she is well aware of the scandal she is causing: Othello is highly respected and his service essential to Venetian society in the struggle against the Turks, but as a foreigner with dark skin he is an outsider and the subject of gossip and prejudice. However, like Charlotte, Desdemona is determined to put her own happiness before the conventions of her close-knit community, thereby displaying a rather modern attitude.

As far as the differences between the relationships of the two couples are concerned, the reasons for the misunderstandings in both relationships and their outcome vary a great deal. In *Othello*, it is clearly Iago's evil influence on Othello – and Othello's willingness to be manipulated – that causes a chain reaction: Othello, blinded by jealousy and an increasing feeling of inferiority violently attacks Desdemona and kills her, in spite of her pleading her innocence. Milo also takes offence at references to his and his wife's skin colour in the media (cf. ll. 22–25). Though his motive for attacking Charlotte – if he was the assailant at all – does not become clear in the given text, Charlotte hints at jealousy being an issue between them (cf. l. 53). Whereas Othello kills Desdemona and himself, Milo and Charlotte survive and are able to reflect on the assault. Although Milo claims to love her still, from that moment onwards, Charlotte is no longer able to ignore the differences between black and white people (cf. l. 15).

The role the two women play in the course of the action is different as well. Whereas Charlotte apparently contributed to the miserable state of her marriage due to her drinking habits (cf. ll. 39 /40) and frequent arguments with her husband (cf. ll. 53/ 54), Desdemona's role is less active and is disputed even amongst scholars. Some critics have claimed that Desdemona – as emancipated and modern as she would have appeared in her time – failed to see how much she must have infuriated Othello by insisting that he should re-install his former lieutenant Cassio to his old position. When Othello demanded an explanation for the lost handkerchief (a token of his love for Desdemona), his wife underestimates the importance of the issue and puts Othello further under pressure to help her friend Cassio.

All in all, it has to be said that all comparisons are only based on a short excerpt in Milo and Charlotte's case, whereas a great deal more is known about Othello and Desdemona. *(708 words)*

3. **Step 1** *Paraphrase the meaning of the quote using your own words.*
   Step 2 *Then decide to what extent the "colour boxes", i. e. prejudices and discrimination based on racial differences, are still apparent in American society.*
   Step 3 *Before you start writing, think of materials and literature you have encountered in class and use them to support your argument (e. g. the abolition of slavery, the achievements of the Civil Rights Movement and Barack Obama as the first black US president). It would also be possible to refer to novels read in class, such as* Beloved *or* A Mercy *by Toni Morrison, to illustrate the situation of the blacks before and after the abolition of slavery, although this is not part of the solution here.*

In the novel's title *Whitegirl* the usual space between the adjective and the noun is left out, which seems to indicate that the protagonist and her experiences are closely connected to her being a white person. To Charlotte, her skin colour has only become important after being allegedly assaulted by her black husband Milo. She assumes that Milo's aggressive behaviour might have been triggered by his feeling of inferiority due to the colour differences between them. Thus, Milo might have become a victim of "colour boxes" that still exist in their society, as he could not separate the personality of his wife from the colour of her skin, just as the media could not see beyond his skin colour no matter how successful he was as an athlete.

In fact, the discrimination against people with a different skin colour has had a long history in the US and Lynna Williams' quote indicates that this is still an issue nowadays. The long struggle of black Americans to be given the same rights as their white fellow citizens seems to prove Williams right. Although slavery was abolished throughout the US in the wake of the American Civil War in the 1860s and blacks were granted civil rights by the Constitution in 1868, the social conditions of the former slaves did not improve greatly. As sharecroppers they quite often had to work for their previous white masters and did not gain real freedom. Additionally, "black codes" were introduced, which infringed the rights of black people at state level. It took another one hundred years for the Civil Rights Movement to finally put an end to the political and social discrimination of blacks both in the workplace and in private life. The first "legal" layer of the colour boxes blacks were caught in was finally broken.

Still, besides the boxes imposed upon blacks from the outside, colour boxes also existed within the black community depending on the political views of the single community member. This is best explained by taking a look at the development of the Civil Rights Movement: Initially sparked off by Rosa Parks, who refused to give her seat to a white passenger on the bus, the fight for civil rights for blacks was soon led by Baptist preacher Martin Luther King and activist Malcolm X. Only in hindsight, however, did this process seem to work smoothly: There were heated discussions in the leadership and open hostility when Malcolm X's Black Panther Movement resorted to acts of open violence. The discussion about the right "black" strategy in the fight for civil rights divided the black community from within; Williams' colour boxes continued to exist in people's minds.

As Lynna Williams has pointed out, the racial divide in the US is still quite obvious even today. Chicago, the third-largest city in the US, for example, is divided into a black South Side and a North Side, which is more affluent and predominantly white. On the other hand, it is from this city that the first black US president Barack Obama emerged, who used to work as a lawyer for a partnership specialising in civil rights issues. Whether Obama's success indicates the beginning of a new era without colour boxes remains to be seen, but it can be taken as a sign of hope for the future of the US and its citizens. *(560 words)*

Material 1: The failed promise of multiculturalism –
Policy has not served Canada or immigrants well

Forty years ago, then prime minister Pierre Trudeau created a policy – multiculturalism – that allowed immigrants to become Canadians by integrating into our culture without abandoning their own. He was trying to differentiate between Canadian integration and American assimilation (the melting pot). Without question, integration is more appealing
5 to newcomers than assimilation. But is it working for everyone?

In reality, the origin of multiculturalism predates the 1970s. It all started when the first Canadian prime minister, John A. Macdonald, said: "A British subject I was born and a British subject I will die." While Thomas Jefferson[1] decided to create America and Americans, Macdonald decided to create Canada but not Canadians.

10 A geographic compromise between the French and English people was found (by creating Quebec), while later they tried to assimilate the aboriginal population with cruel policies. When they failed, they showered the native peoples with money and accords that were never respected, creating the results we see today.

Within this shaky balance, Canada was built with the help of immigrants who created
15 important infrastructure like railroads, and there is no doubt that Canada is a success story.

However, in the second part of the last century, these immigrants were becoming restless because they couldn't be anglophone, francophone or native and they became a social problem because they had no national identity in a country they now considered theirs.

20 The multiculturalism of Pierre Trudeau filled that gap by creating a social container for the "ethnics," but what about integration?

It was impossible to integrate with the natives and very difficult with the francophones [...], so the only real chance multiculturalism had to work was within English Canada.

Did it work? In my opinion, no. In fact, I would argue that the current system penal-
25 izes new and old immigrants. But multiculturalism became a mantra for the Liberals to secure votes from the "ethnics" and is now wielded by multicultural prophets who muzzle debate in order to protect their own interests.

They have erected a media and political firewall around the concept of multiculturalism (and immigration) that blocks any criticism of international criminals, dishonest con-
30 sultants and sneaky individuals who take advantage of our generosity at the expense of those in real need of help or who are willing to come into our country to work and prosper with us.

This intransigence[2] is forcing Canadians, who in general have supported the policies of multiculturalism and immigration, to take a second look at them because they want to
35 make sure that our country remains a destination for people in need of help, not a cow to milk.

I read in the *Globe and Mail*[3] a few weeks ago that "the positive link between multi-culturalism and citizenship is further supported by comparing Canadian policy with that of the United States."

40 The article reported that while in the '70s, both in Canada and the U.S., almost 60 per cent of foreign-born residents acquired citizenship, by 2006 in the States that number was down to 42 per cent while in Canada it was up to 73 per cent, "one of the highest rates in the world."

Numbers don't lie but they can mislead. In fact, having a Canadian passport, doesn't 45 mean one lives in Canada. For example, more than a million Canadians live in California and Florida and almost 2 million live in other continents. In 2003 (the numbers are higher now), there were 250,000 people with a Canadian passport living in Hong Kong. For most of these people, Canada is not their country, it's a life insurance policy, a place to rush to when in need of medical services or secure shelter.

50 Two summers ago, Ottawa had to spend $ 114 million ($ 94 million just for transpor-tation) to repatriate 14,000 "Canadians" living in Lebanon. We sent planes and boats to bring them "home" – and most of them are now back there.

The numbers seem to imply Canadian multiculturalism is a better system than the American melting pot. However, the reality is that in the States, people like Cuomo, 55 Dukakis, Ferraro and Pelosi[4] can go right to the top, up to the White House of Barack Obama, while I'm wondering when multicultural Canada can have at least a black mayor in Toronto.

At times I wonder whether multiculturalism is a policy to invite "ethnics" in or to keep them out. In the meantime, we keep writing cheques for people who are not even liv-60 ing in Canada. *(735 words)*

Angelo Persichilli, "The failed promise of multiculturalism: Policy has not served Canada or immigrants well", The Star, 07. 11. 2010.

1   Thomas Jefferson – U.S. American President, 1801–1809
2   intransigence – Kompromisslosigkeit
3   *Globe and Mail* – Canadian newspaper
4   Andrew Cuomo, Michael Dukakis, Geraldine Ferraro and Nancy Pelosi – successful U.S. politicians with an ethnic background

Material 2

© 2005 Cox & Forkum

Assignments

1. Summarize the article. (Material 1) (20 BE)

2. Explain how Persichilli's intention is reflected in the cartoon. (Material 2) (45 BE)

3. *"The numbers seem to imply that Canadian multiculturalism is a better system than the American melting pot."* (Material 1)
   Compare the two concepts and comment on the author's statement. (35 BE)

Lösungsvorschläge

Teaching modules referred to:
The task is based on the teaching module Promised Lands: Dreams and Realities *(Q 3)* with Canada as the country of reference, focusing on the topics political *and* social issues. *The assignments also extend to the module* USA *(Q 1) with the topics* living together *and* political life, political issues.

1. **Step 1** *In the summary, the contents of the newspaper article at hand should be presented briefly. Remember to create an introductory sentence that informs the reader of the author, the title of the article, the year it was published as well as the topic.*
   Step 2 *Keep in mind that a summary requires the present tense. Avoid direct speech, quotations or comments. Your text should be one third of the length of the original.*
   Step 3 *Sum up the main reasons for the author's negative opinion on the way multiculturalism is practised in Canada (i. e. the lack of national identity, the abuse of Canadian social services, no chance of upward mobility for immigrants as well as the Liberals' failure to accept the truth) and present them in a structured form.*

The article "The failed promise of multiculturalism" by Angelo Persichilli, published in *The Star* in 2010, harshly criticises Canadian immigration policy. The author mainly focuses on Canadian attitudes towards immigrants and the political concept of multiculturalism, which is in contrast to the American idea of assimilation, also referred to as "the melting pot". Although integration seems more attractive to newcomers than assimilation, the author questions whether the Canadian approach does in fact work for everyone.
It is pointed out that Canada owes its present stance to immigrants but struggles to develop a national identity as the concept of multiculturalism requires everyone to remain as they are. As the Liberals especially reject any criticism of immigration policy, the situation is not likely to change in the near future, although Canadian generosity towards immigrants has been abused in the past. As far as the francophone and indigenous population is concerned, the author mentions that there are no such positive results as multiculturalism has achieved in the English-speaking part. He continues to argue that statistics allegedly proving the success of multiculturalism are in reality misleading as many Canadian passport holders do not even live in Canada anymore but exploit the advantages of Canadian citizenship. Furthermore, the author shows the two-faced nature of Canadian immigration policy: US politicians with an ethnic background hold influential positions to a much larger degree than in Canada. *(229 words)*

2. **Step 1** *Before you concentrate on the cartoon, the author's critical position regarding multiculturalism needs to be explained. It is necessary for you to quote from the text to give evidence of the author's line of argument.*
   Step 2 *Then describe the cartoon in detail and interpret it. Do not forget to relate the message of the cartoon to the concept of multiculturalism in general and the central ideas of Persichilli's article in particular.*

In the article at hand, the author questions the success of Canadian immigration policy throughout the text (cf. ll. 5, 20/21, 24, 58/59). He calls multiculturalism a "failed promise" (headline) and points out that the concept might actually prevent integration instead of encouraging it. Several reasons are given for the author's critical attitude. According to the author, attempts to reconcile francophone and anglophone interests remain futile, with special rights being given to the province of Quebec (cf. ll. 10/ 11), whereas the indigenous peoples of Canada were forced to assimilate at first and were then bribed into integration (cf. ll. 11–13). This concept is regarded as two-faced and is seen as a failure in retrospect: Persichilli diagnoses a "shaky balance" (l. 14) in the integration policies. Although immigrants have always played an important part in Canada's success story, they tend to become a social problem as they cannot find an identity of their own, do not participate in the political process and thus make integration impossible. Canadian liberals make things worse because of their unwillingness to differentiate. They continue to defend multiculturalism and turn a blind eye to the flaws of the concept as this serves their own political interests (cf. ll. 25–29). Statistics are also shown to be misleading as Canadian citizenship seems to be in high demand only due to the advantages it provides for citizens living abroad – such as protection and state-funded medical treatment (cf. ll. 46–49). On top of all that, the author claims that people with an ethnic background are more successful at aiming at top jobs in the US than in Canada. This leads to the conclusion that Canada has failed to make a success of the multicultural idea because the concept was put into practice with too much naïveté.

This scepticism is reflected in the cartoon, which depicts multiculturalism as an open threat to society. The concept is embodied by a scary-looking Arab who has a beard and is stereotypically wearing traditional headgear and a long coat, underneath which a suicide bomb is hidden. The man already has his thumb placed on the trigger to activate the bomb. To the left of the terrorist, there are three men of different ethnic backgrounds – supposedly of African-American, Caucasian and Southern European origin, whose reactions to the Arab's appearance vary greatly. Whereas the dark-skinned man to the left expresses his fear that the stranger might be an Islamist, the other two indifferently plead for tolerance and demand political correctness. On the right-hand side there is a couple with their son, who is asked not to stare at the Arab because he might cause offence. His mother reminds him that "it's bigoted to criticize [...] religion" but at the same time she seems terribly afraid. All in all, most people in the cartoon are so concerned with being politically correct that they fail to realise the danger they are in. The cartoon displays just another version of the "firewall" (l. 28) mentioned in Persichilli's article, which, perhaps not as strongly as the cartoon, criticizes the naïveté of the public concerning immigration. The multicultural attitude permits for abuse and exploitation instead of speeding integration up.   *(533 words)*

3. **Step 1** *First interpret the quote against the backdrop of the whole article.*

   Step 2 *Then introduce the American concept of a melting pot to trigger an expected assimilation process. Give examples from texts dealt with in class to support your argument. It is advisable to collect appropriate materials before you start writing as a logical order makes it easier to follow your argument.*

   Step 3 *Finally you need to compare both concepts of integration, the Canadian multicultural approach as well as the idea of the US melting pot. Support your views with evidence and remember to state your opinion. In the sample solution, the novel* Tortilla Curtain *by T. C. Boyle is referred to as well.*

According to statistics, Canadian multiculturalism seems a more adequate integration concept than the American melting pot (cf. ll. 53/54). Throughout the article, the author provides arguments to shake this belief. In his opinion, the fact that the US system has created far more successful people with an ethnic background than Canada proves the superiority of the American melting pot (cf. ll. 54–57). Multiculturalism on the other hand is blamed for keeping "ethnics" out of the country (cf. ll. 58/59).

The motto 'e pluribus unum' appeared in the Great Seal of the United States as early as 1782. The Founding Fathers had defined three core values for a better life in the New World: liberty, equality and the pursuit of happiness. Over the years, the promise of being able to realise those aims in the US has become known as the 'American Dream'. The phrase was coined by the historian James T. Adams and refers to a society that recognises people for what they are – and not where they came from.

The concept of a melting pot, where all immigrant cultures blend into one core culture, is an important element of this dream. Still, there are as many flaws in the concept as there have been found in the Canadian multicultural approach.

Especially for those immigrants who are not wanted for a variety of reasons, the American Dream quite often turns into a nightmare, as described in T. C. Boyle's novel *Tortilla Curtain*, which depicts the lives of two entirely different couples: the Mossbachers, affluent Americans, already live the American Dream, whereas the Rincóns are illegal immigrants from Mexico who hope to improve their poor living conditions in the US. At the beginning of the novel, Delaney Mossbacher, grandson of immigrants from Ireland and Germany, is a liberal humanist who wishes his fellow immigrants and the environment well. He strongly contradicts his neighbour Jack Jardine, who wants to fence their whole estate, Arroyo Blanco, to keep allegedly criminal immigrants out. The frequent and unfortunate encounters with the Mexican couple América and Cándido, who have no choice but to steal in order to survive, turn Delaney and his wife Kyra into ardent xenophobes who eventually succeed in forcing the illegal Mexicans out of their community. The Rincóns, who have been betrayed, assaulted and robbed, are left with less than they had come to the US with.

Despite the fact that Hispanics are the second-largest group of ethnic minorities in the US, they are not the only targets of xenophobia in US society. African-Americans have been discriminated against for centuries and only in the aftermath of the Civil Rights Movement in the 1960s did their situation improve in economic and social terms. In their case, disadvantages in the education sector are the most urgent problem that needs to be dealt with nowadays.

However, the idea of establishing a core culture through the concept of the melting pot is doomed anyway due to demographic developments. In California, for example, Hispanics are quickly losing their minority status: according to the 2010 census, 30 % of California's population is of Mexican origin, which makes the state the one with the highest percentage of Mexican Americans.

In general, many ethnic minorities have experienced that the melting pot neither worked for them as far as the creation of identity is concerned nor did it help to fulfil the promises of the American Dream. Moreover, the host society responded rather negatively to the immigrants' attempts to assimilate. Comparing the problems concerning immigration in the US with those in Canada shows that every concept has its flaws. Still, unlike in the US, the diverse ethnic groups in Canada find it less difficult to stick to their cultural roots and are even encouraged to do so by the state. It may be true that multiculturalism is prone to being abused by some and threatened by others, but it seems that the ideas of the American Founding Fathers are more genuinely reflected in a liberal and open community such as Canada that lives its diversity rather than insisting on people being part of a so-called core culture.   *(689 words)*

Teil A: Aufgabe zur Sprachmittlung

Material 1: Fast jeder fünfte Deutsche hat ausländische Wurzeln

Immer mehr Menschen in Deutschland haben ausländische Wurzeln – schon fast jeder Fünfte hat einen Migrationshintergrund. Annähernd 16,0 Millionen Menschen aus Zuwandererfamilien lebten 2011 in der Bundesrepublik.

Das waren rund 216 000 mehr als im Vorjahr. Die Mehrheit von ihnen hat einen deut-
5 schen Pass (8,8 Millionen). Wie das Statistische Bundesamt in Wiesbaden am Mittwoch mitteilte, steigt die Zahl seit Beginn der Statistik im Jahr 2005 Jahr für Jahr leicht.

Die meisten Menschen mit Migrationshintergrund stammen 2011 aus der Türkei (3,0 Millionen) gefolgt von Polen (1,5) und der Russischen Föderation (1,2). An vierter Stelle steht Kasachstan (900 000), knapp gefolgt von Italien (800 000).
10 Vor allem die zweite und dritte Generation der Zuwanderer sowie Ausländer – insbesondere aus Ost- und Südeuropa – haben zu dem Plus beigetragen. Die Zahl der in der Bundesrepublik geborenen Deutschen mit Migrationshintergrund ist innerhalb eines Jahres um 4,8 Prozent auf rund 3,8 Millionen gestiegen. Dazu kommt ein leichtes Plus bei den ausländischen Zuwanderern von 1,7 Prozent auf etwa 5,7 Millionen. Die Zahl der
15 Ausländer, die in Deutschland geboren wurden, hat dagegen weiter abgenommen, um 3,4 Prozent auf rund 1,5 Millionen.

Der Anteil der Menschen mit Migrationshintergrund an der gesamten Bevölkerung ist binnen eines Jahres um 0,2 Punkte auf 19,5 Prozent gestiegen. Gegenüber dem ersten Jahr der Statistik (2005) beträgt der Zuwachs 1,2 Prozentpunkte. Damals hatten 15,1 Millionen
20 Einwohner einen Migrationshintergrund. Dazu zählen die Statistiker alle Einwanderer seit 1950, alle Ausländer sowie in der Bundesrepublik geborene Deutsche mit mindestens einem Elternteil, der zugewandert oder als Ausländer in Deutschland geboren ist.

(260 Wörter)

DPA, *"Fast jeder fünfte Deutsche hat ausländische Wurzeln"*, FOCUS Online, *19. 09. 2012.*
http://www.focus.de/panorama/welt/bevoelkerung-mit-migrationshintergrund-fast-jeder-fuenfte-deutsche-
hat-auslaendische- wurzeln_aid_822502.html.

Hinweis: Der Verfasser wird in der Textvorlage nicht genannt.

Assignment

As an intern for an English news magazine you are asked to contribute the statistical background for an editorial about migration in Europe. Summarize the information about Germany given in the article. (Material 1)

Teil B: Verkürzte Textaufgabe

Material 2: Immigrants

In Marina Lewycka's novel A Short History of Tractors in Ukrainian, *the long estranged sisters Nadia and Vera bond again over their father's announcement that he will marry a much younger Ukrainian immigrant. One recurring topic of discussion between them is their past as immigrants in England. Nadia remembers her telephone conversation with her older sister Vera.*

Once, not so long ago, Big Sis's attitudes would send me into a rage of righteousness, but now I see them in their historical context, and I smile to myself in a superior way.

"When we first came here, Vera, people could have said the same things about us – that we were ripping off the country, gorging ourselves on free orange juice, growing fat
5 on NHS[1] cod-liver oil. But they didn't. Everyone was kind to us."

"But that was different. *We* were different". (We were white, of course, for one thing, I could say, but I hold my tongue.) "We worked hard and kept our heads down. We learned the language and integrated. We never claimed benefits. We never broke the law."

"*I* broke the law. I smoked dope. I was arrested at Greenham Common[2]. Pappa got so
10 upset that he tried to catch the train back to Russia."

"But that's exactly my point, Nadia. You and your leftish friends – you never really appreciated what England had to offer – stability, order, the rule of law. If you and your kind prevailed, this country would be just like Russia – bread queues everywhere, and people getting their hands chopped off."
15 "That's Afghanistan. Chopping hands off *is* the rule of law."

Both of us have raised our voices. This is turning into an old-style argument.

"Whatever. You see my point," she says dismissively.

"What I appreciated about growing up in England was the tolerance, liberalism, everyday kindness." (I drive home my point by wagging my finger in the air, even though
20 she can't see me.) "The way the English always stick up for the underdog."

"You are confusing the underdog with the scrounger[3], Nadia. We were poor, but we were never scroungers. The English people believe in fairness. Fair play. Like cricket." (What does *she* know about cricket?) "They play by the rules. They have a natural sense of discipline and order."
25 "No no. They're quite anarchic. They like to see the little man stick two fingers up to the world. They like to see the big shot get his come-uppance."

"On the contrary, they have a perfectly preserved class system, in which everyone knows where they belong."

See how we grew up in the same house but lived in different countries?
30 "They make fun of their rulers."

"But they like strong rulers."

If Vera mentions Mrs Thatcher, I shall put the phone down. There is a short pause, in which we both consider our options. I try an appeal to our shared past.

"Remember the woman on the bus, Vera? The woman in the fur coat?"
35 "What woman? What bus? What are you talking about?"

Of course she remembers. She hasn't forgotten the smell of diesel, the swish of the windscreen wipers, the unsteady sway of the bus as it churned newly fallen snow into slush; coloured lights outside the windows; Christmas Eve 1952. Vera and I, muffled against the cold, snuggling up against Mother on the backseat. And a kind woman in a
40 fur coat who leaned across the aisle and pressed sixpence into Mother's hand: "For the kiddies at Christmas."

"The woman who gave mother sixpence."

Mother, our mother, did not dash the coin in her face; she mumbled, "Thank you, lady," and slipped it into her pocket. The shame of it!
45 "Oh, that. I think she was a bit drunk. You mentioned it once before. I don't know why you go on about it."

"It was that moment – more than anything that happened to me afterwards – that turned me into a lifelong socialist."

There is silence on the other end of the telephone and for a moment I think she has
50 hung up on me. Then: "Maybe it was what turned me into the woman in the fur coat."

(630 words)

Marina Lewycka, A Short History of Tractors in Ukrainian, *Penguin Books USA, pp. 240–242.*

1   NHS – National Health Service
2   Greenham Common – former Royal Airforce station, used in the 1980s for women's peace camps protesting against the use of cruise missiles
3   scrounger – ugs.: Schnorrer

Assignments

1. Describe the different attitudes of the sisters regarding Britain and the British. (Material 2)

   (20 BE)

2. Analyse Vera's and Nadia's attitudes towards immigrants in Britain and compare them to attitudes towards immigrants in the USA as encountered in material dealt with in class.

   (45 BE)

3. *"One [n]ation doesn't mean one identity. People can be proudly, patriotically British without abandoning their cultural roots."*
   (Ed Miliband, Leader of the Labour Party, The Labour Party 2012)

   Comment on the quote by referring to British society.

   (35 BE)

In die Gesamtbewertung gehen die Ergebnisse der Teilaufgaben A und B im Verhältnis 1:3 ein.

Lösungsvorschläge

Teaching modules referred to:
The task is based on the teaching module The United Kingdom *(Q 2) with particular ref-*
erence to the topics political life, political issues. *Further aspects of the assignments re-*
fer to the teaching module USA *(Q 1) with the topics* living together *and* political life,
political issues.

Teil A: Aufgabe zur Sprachmittlung

In your mediation you are asked to only state the main aspects of the article in your own
words. Start with an umbrella sentence that provides information on the title of the text,
the type of text and the source and the year of publication. You should also briefly refer
to the contents in this first sentence. When you sum up the German text, keep in mind that
you should use the present tense. Do not use direct speech, quotations or comments.
Your mediation should be about one third of the length of the source text.

The Focus Online article "Fast jeder fünfte Deutsche hat ausländische Wurzeln" from
2012 contains statistical data about the number of Germans with an ethnic background.
In 2011, there were 16 million of these altogether, more than half of them owning a German passport. Since 2005 these numbers have been increasing due to more second- and
third-generation immigrants being born in Germany and a steady influx of immigrants
from eastern and southern Europe. The number of foreign babies born in Germany has
decreased. Migrants mainly come from Turkey, Poland, Russia, Kazakhstan or Italy.

(92 words)

Teil B: Verkürzte Textaufgabe

1. *This assignment asks you to portray the different attitudes of the two sisters regard-*
   ing Britain and the British. Go through the text and highlight the important points.
   Then structure your findings, leave aside unnecessary details and use connectives
   and other strategies to shorten the text.

In a telephone conversation with her older sister Vera, Nadia disagrees with most of
Vera's attitudes towards Britain and the British, although both sisters are immigrants.
Vera seems to believe that immigrants nowadays are lazy and abuse the British welfare state, whereas she and her family made it their priority to fully integrate into British society by working hard, obeying the law and learning the English language (cf.
ll. 7/8). She claims that Nadia never appreciated the stability and order of the British
system, while she is impressed with the prevailing fairness, discipline and order she
found in England (cf. ll. 12, 22–24). Vera even admires the class system, where
everyone knows their place (cf. ll. 27/28). She despises the people she calls "scroungers" (l. 22) who abuse the system.

Unlike Vera, Nadia believes that her family's successful integration into the British system was due to their simply being white (cf. l. 6) rather than through their adapting to British customs. In contrast to her sister, Nadia can see an anarchic trait in the English character, for example that they love making fun of their rulers (cf. l. 30) and that celebrities get what is coming to them (cf. l. 26), but also that they care about underdogs (cf. l. 20). All in all, it is their "tolerance, liberalism, everyday kindness" (cf. ll. 18/19) that Nadia appreciates most about the British.   *(237 words)*

2. **Step 1** *First, you need to go through the text again and collect the distinct opinions the two sisters express about immigrants living in Great Britain. Analyse which attitudes they share and where they differ.*

Step 2 *Then focus on US American attitudes towards immigrants. You can use the sisters' opinions as a benchmark for comparisons. Draw from examples from literature discussed in class, such as the novel* Tortilla Curtain *by T. C. Boyle, and from current developments under Obama's presidency.*

While both sisters show different attitudes towards the British people and their social system, they agree that immigrants have to deal with prejudice and stereotypes and are not particularly welcomed by their host society. Vera implicitly blames the immigrants' behaviour: she believes that many of them abuse the British welfare state, do not try hard enough to integrate, refuse to learn the language or even break the law (cf. ll. 7–9). Nadia, on the other hand, cannot find fault with immigrants in general but believes that it is the English arrogance towards the newcomers that prevents their successful integration. To prove her point, she names the condescending behaviour of a woman in a fur coat towards her own mother at Christmas time when Nadia was still a little girl (cf. ll. 36–44). She also suspects that the immigrants' skin colour plays a crucial role as the British seem prejudiced in this respect, too (cf. ll. 6/7).

An attitude similar to the one Nadia detects in British society is described in T. C. Boyle's novel *The Tortilla Curtain*, where the protagonist Delaney Mossbacher, a liberal humanist, gradually turns into a xenophobe, although he states that America has always been a country of immigrants. Put under pressure by his affluent neighbours and his own wife, Delaney agrees to fence the immigrants out of Arroyo Blanco, the luxurious estate where he and his family live. Delaney also has some unfortunate encounters with a poor illegal immigrant, Cándido Rincón from Mexico, and the shady "white" Mexican José Navidad. Furthermore, several houses in Arroyo Blanco are broken into and an elderly lady is even raped by the intruders. After he hits Cándido with his car by accident, gets another car badly damaged and discovers the Mexican close to a spot where parts of the canyon have been set on fire, nature-loving Delaney sets out on a crusade to track down Cándido, who he meanwhile regards as his archenemy. He does not even change his mind when it becomes clear that Cándido cannot be blamed for the theft of Delaney's car, the break-ins, rapes or the graffiti on the walls around the Arroyo Blanco estate. Through Delaney's change in character, T. C. Boyle shows his readers how quickly people turn against their liberal convictions and in Delaney's case develop xenophobic ideas and attitudes against immigrants.

However, the problem of illegal immigration does not only concern the Mexican-American border (hence named "Tortilla Curtain"), but also reaches a demographic dimension. In a number of federal states such as California, the rapidly growing ethnic communities exist outside the legal, health and educational system. The Obama administration has already come up with a number of strategies to alleviate the situation: by enabling the illegals to apply for citizenship, including them in social programmes, and providing health care and educational services so that the immigrants can at least learn the language of their host country. In particular, children of illegal immigrants can now apply for jobs and work in the US for a limited amount of time.

Whether the attempts of the Obama administration to ease the situation of both legal and illegal immigrants will be successful in the long run and help create more tolerance towards different ethnic communities remains to be seen. In the past, Democratic efforts were often curtailed by the Republican opposition. However, in January 2014, Republican leaders signalled their willingness to support laws that provide legal status – though not citizenship – to about 11 million illegal immigrants. With the upcoming elections for the US Senate in November 2014, where 33 of the 100 Senators will stand for election, the Republicans are afraid of losing the support of the Latino communities if they refuse to tackle the issue of illegal immigrants. This political climate makes an agreement between Democrats and Republicans quite likely, though modifications to the Democratic concept will surely be an issue.   *(648 words)*

3. **Step 1** *First of all, you are expected to paraphrase the quotation.*
   Step 2 *Then put the message of Labour politician Ed Miliband into the context of the current situation in Great Britain.*
   Step 3 *Finally, evaluate the opportunities and problems Miliband's proposal brings with it and state your personal opinion.*

Labour politician Ed Miliband combines the concept of national identity, British patriotism and different cultural roots in a new way. He claims that they are not mutually exclusive but can result in a diverse British culture to which each ethnic group contributes its share and keeps its traditions and values at the same time.

Britain has always been an attractive country to immigrate to, not only within the EU but especially for people from Commonwealth countries. To cut the huge influx of immigrants, new passport regulations for Commonwealth citizens were introduced in 1972 that no longer permitted automatic entry. As a result of social problems and a declining labour market, the right-wing National Front (NF) gained massive support in the mid-1970s. The lack of job opportunities and deteriorating housing conditions led to the Brixton Riots in South London in 1981. Whereas Conservative Prime Minister Margaret Thatcher refused to tackle the problem immediately, Labour favoured a multiculturalist approach and believed that different sets of values could enrich the communities, as long as new arrivals showed an appreciation of existing and diverse values and had a good command of the host language.

As a consequence of the EU expansion in 2004, the ruling Labour Party guaranteed free movement to Polish citizens. One of the biggest waves of mass migration followed, with about 500,000 Poles migrating to the UK. Due to the financial crisis in 2008, many British people were afraid of unemployment. Many are frightened of the implications as Romanians and Bulgarians are granted freedom of movement from January 1, 2014 onwards as their home countries become full members of the EU.

Moreover, the rise of Sharia courts following Islamic legislation has received a great deal of attention lately. Currently, about 85 Sharia Courts exist in Britain and their rulings sometimes contradict British law. An undercover documentary revealed that women were discriminated against in different ways. There have been a number of examples where a British court allowed a divorce, while a Sharia court ruled against it and forbade the wife to leave her husband. This development only adds to the negative reputation of Islamic communities, which has already suffered massively since 9/11.

All these examples show that multiculturalism depends on the good will of both new and host cultures. It seems to be a successful model in the context of British history in general, but a further development of national identity is surely necessary. Fears within the white British society should not be underestimated. In May 2013, the right-wing populist United Kingdom Independent Party (UKIP) won 23 % of all votes in the county council elections by calling for a five-year freeze on immigration, the removal of illegal immigrants and a points system for issuing work permits. To prevent the UKIP from gaining more ground, positive experiences could be gained by representatives of both host and new culture working together on programmes at the local level. Old and new citizens might find it easier to develop an interest in shared goals and feel proud of mutual achievements. This way, prejudices and stereotypes could be done away with and fears might quickly disappear. In the end, such cooperation might eventually lead to the feeling of patriotism Ed Miliband hopes for, a feeling that comes from within the community. *(547 words)*

Ihre Meinung ist uns wichtig!

Ihre Anregungen sind uns immer willkommen. Bitte informieren Sie uns mit diesem Schein über Ihre Verbesserungsvorschläge!

Titel-Nr.	Seite	Vorschlag

Bitte hier abtrennen

24-V_Abi

Bitte ausfüllen und im frankierten Umschlag
an uns einsenden. Für Fensterkuverts geeignet.

Zutreffendes bitte ankreuzen!

Die Absenderin/der Absender ist:

☐ Lehrer/in in den Klassenstufen:

☐ Fachbetreuer/in
Fächer:

☐ Seminarlehrer/in
Fächer:

☐ Regierungsfachberater/in
Fächer:

☐ Oberstufenbetreuer/in

☐ Schulleiter/in

☐ Referendar/in, Termin 2. Staats-
examen:

☐ Leiter/in Lehrerbibliothek

☐ Leiter/in Schülerbibliothek

☐ Sekretariat

☐ Eltern

☐ Schüler/in, Klasse:

☐ Sonstiges:

Unterrichtsfächer: (Bei Lehrkräften!)

STARK Verlag
Postfach 1852
85318 Freising

Kennen Sie Ihre Kundennummer?
Bitte hier eintragen.

Absender (Bitte in Druckbuchstaben!)

Name/Vorname

Straße/Nr.

PLZ/Ort/Ortsteil

Telefon privat   Geburtsjahr

E-Mail

Schule/Schulstempel (Bitte immer angeben!)

Bitte hier abtrennen ✂

Erfolgreich durchs Abitur mit den STARK-Reihen

Abitur-Prüfungsaufgaben

Anhand von Original-Aufgaben die Prüfungssituation trainieren. Schülergerechte Lösungen helfen bei der Leistungskontrolle.

Abitur-Training

Prüfungsrelevantes Wissen schülergerecht präsentiert. Übungsaufgaben mit Lösungen sichern den Lernerfolg.

Klausuren

Durch gezieltes Klausurentraining die Grundlagen schaffen für eine gute Abinote.

Kompakt-Wissen

Kompakte Darstellung des prüfungsrelevanten Wissens zum schnellen Nachschlagen und Wiederholen.

Interpretationen

Perfekte Hilfe beim Verständnis literarischer Werke.

Und vieles mehr auf www.stark-verlag.de

(Bitte blättern Sie um)

Abi in der Tasche – und dann?

In den STARK-Ratgebern finden Abiturientinnen und Abiturienten alle Informationen für einen erfolgreichen Start in die berufliche Zukunft.

Alle Titel zu Beruf & Karriere www.berufundkarriere.de

Bestellungen bitte direkt an:

STARK Verlagsgesellschaft mbH & Co. KG · Postfach 1852 · 85318 Freising
Tel. 0180 3 179000* · Fax 0180 3 179001* · www.stark-verlag.de · info@stark-verlag.de
*9 Cent pro Min. aus dem deutschen Festnetz, Mobilfunk bis 42 Cent pro Min.
Aus dem Mobilfunknetz wählen Sie die Festnetznummer: 08167 9573-0

24-V_Abi

Lernen · Wissen · Zukunft
STARK